Maoism, Democracy and Globalisation

Maoism, Democracy and Globalisation

Cross-currents in Indian Politics

Ajay Gudavarthy

SAGE www.sagepublications.com
Los Angeles • London • New Delhi • Singapore • Washington DC

First published in 2014 by

 SAGE Publications India Pvt Ltd
B1/I-1 Mohan Cooperative Industrial Area
Mathura Road, New Delhi 110 044, India
www.sagepub.in

SAGE Publications Inc
2455 Teller Road
Thousand Oaks, California 91320, USA

SAGE Publications Ltd
1 Oliver's Yard, 55 City Road
London EC1Y 1SP, United Kingdom

SAGE Publications Asia-Pacific Pte Ltd
3 Church Street
#10-04 Samsung Hub
Singapore 049483

Published by Vivek Mehra for SAGE Publications India Pvt Ltd, typeset in 10/13 pts Berkeley by Diligent Typesetter, Delhi and printed at Chaman Enterprises, New Delhi.

Library of Congress Cataloging-in-Publication Data

Gudavarthy, Ajay.
  Maoism, democracy and globalisation : cross-currents in Indian politics / Ajay Gudavarthy.
    pages cm
  Includes bibliographical references and index.
    1. Communism—India. 2. Democracy—India. 3. Globalisation—India. 4. India—Politics and government—1977– I. Title.
    HX393.5.G83   320.954—dc23   2014   2014017762

ISBN: 978-81-321-1847-3 (HB)

The SAGE Team: Rudra Narayan, Isha Sachdeva, Anju Saxena and
                    Rajinder Kaur

Dedicated to

Kushi, Krishna and Vijay

Thank you for choosing a SAGE product! If you have any comment, observation or feedback, I would like to personally hear from you. Please write to me at contactceo@sagepub.in

—Vivek Mehra, Managing Director and CEO,
SAGE Publications India Pvt. Ltd, New Delhi

Bulk Sales

SAGE India offers special discounts for purchase of books in bulk. We also make available special imprints and excerpts from our books on demand.

For orders and enquiries, write to us at

Marketing Department
SAGE Publications India Pvt. Ltd
B1/I-1, Mohan Cooperative Industrial Area
Mathura Road, Post Bag 7
New Delhi 110044, India
E-mail us at marketing@sagepub.in

Get to know more about SAGE, be invited to SAGE events, get on our mailing list. Write today to marketing@sagepub.in

This book is also available as an e-book.

Contents

Preface and Acknowledgements

This book is a result of my continued engagement with political and economic developments in Indian politics over the last couple of decades or so. Political scientists have engaged with democracy, globalisation, and less so with Maoist politics in India, separately, and as independent political phenomenon. Here, I however have attempted to look at the interface between these three disparate looking phenomena that coexist, and pulling the political dynamics in different directions. What then is the direction, and what then is in hold for democracy in India, in the near and not so near future? I will consider this a worthwhile academic exercise, even if we are able to throw partial light on the problem that is complex and manifold.

In the making of this book, over the last few years I have undoubtedly benefitted from many friends, colleagues and activists. I am thankful to all my colleagues at the Centre for Political Studies for providing a very enabling atmosphere. Both positive and negative liberty have been working in organising the life in the centre, sometimes through active and rich debates and at other by letting you be.

All the chapters have been presented at many seminars, workshops and conferences in India and abroad. The first chapter on Maoism was presented at Jawaharlal Nehru University; Observatory Research Foundation; Centre for Peace and Conflict Resolution, Jamia Millia Islamia; University of Delhi (I am thankful to Rajesh Dev for extending the invitation); and Tribhuvan University, Kathmandu (I am glad that this provided me with an opportunity to know Professor Om Gurung and get to spend time with my friend Mukta Lama). The second chapter on middle classes was presented at Osmania University, Hyderabad; Gujarat Central University, Ahmedabad; GNDU, Amritsar (I am thankful to Paramjit Judge for the many academic discussions that we have been having over the years); University of Chile, Santiago; and Brown University, Providence, RI, which was made possible with the support of Jeffrey Alexander. I especially thank him for his indulgence and friendship. I have benefitted immensely from his erudite scholarship and insightful exchanges, and fondly look forward to continuing the dialogue. The survey presented in this chapter was possible with the support of a Hyderabad based research centre, People's Pulse. It was due to Ravichand's initiative that the survey was taken up, and the credit should go to him.

The third chapter on backward classes was presented at Council for Social Development, Delhi; Ambedkar University, Lucknow; Jawaharlal Nehru University; Centre for Human Rights, Hyderabad; Anveshi Research Centre, Hyderabad; Allahabad University, Allahabad; Jamia Millia Islamia, Delhi; Centre for Study of Social Exclusion and Inclusive Policy, Hyderabad; NMML, Delhi, for which I wish to thank Mahesh Rangarajan. His support and encouragement has been very reassuring. Finally, this chapter came out of a joint project with Tribhuvan University and Goldsmiths College, University of London. I thank my colleagues Alpa Shah and Sara Shniederman for their support in the project. I also wish tó thank Sajjan for his help all through the project, and many a time going beyond the call of his duty. The fourth chapter on subaltern classes was presented at University of Calcutta; I thank Sanjeebda for it and his invite to come as a visiting faculty to the Department of Political Science. I am grateful to Srirupa Roy (Göttingen University) for the keen interest she has shown in my work on 'political society'. I remain thankful to Trevor at CISRUL, University of Aberdeen; he has been a constant source of support and encouragement. I also benefitted from his deep insights into issues related to citizenship and civil society. I also wish to thank Partha Chatterjee for the dialogue on 'political society', including the rejoinder he wrote for an earlier volume I edited on that theme. This chapter is in part a response to his rejoinder. The fifth chapter on the human rights was presented at an event jointly organised by LASSNET and CPR; South Asian University, Delhi; and Department of Political Science, Jamia Millia Islamia. The sixth chapter on regionalism was presented at ISA, Florence, Italy. I thank Martin Aranguren for many riveting discussions on Latin America. I hope there is more to come. Finally, the epilogue was presented at an international seminar at the University of Goa. I thank Rahul Tripathi for the invite.

Many friends and well-wishers have been a great source of support, academically and also on personal front. I especially thank my colleague

Rajarshi Dasgupta for taking interest in my earlier writings and also for the ongoing dialogue on many of the issues that are taken up in this book for discussion. I thank Bhangya Bhukiya, whose scholarship and friendship have been enriching and I stand to benefit. I thank Ashutosh Kumar, Nissim Mannathukaren, Swagato Sarkar and Divyaraj Amiya for continuing academic interactions. Sethu, who I missed thanking in my first book, I make it up here. His rather loud and abrasive self has provided immense joy all through. I hope he is around for long to continue entertaining! I especially thank Gopal Guru for his personal warmth and silent support. I thank Zoya for many interesting discussions and her continued concern for 'Indian politics'; I hope this book will at least partially placate her! I am especially thankful to Sudha Pai for sharing her unpublished work on the OBCs. I thank Manoranjan Mohanty; he has remained a pillar of strength to me and my family all along. I extend my thanks to Anand Teltumbde, whose critical insights and radical postures have helped not losing one's way in these disorienting times. It has always been a pleasure conversing with him and sharing many experiences. I also extend my thanks to Satish Jha, who is a mine of information and diligent analyst of Delhi's changing academic discourse; I continue to enjoy our conversations and affection. I also wish to thank Rakesh Kumar, whose honesty and indomitable reputation in Uttarakhand have been inspiring and also unusually helpful! I am immensely grateful to Mr Varavara Rao who readily agreed to share the photos of Kishenji. His support means a lot for this book.

My family undoubtedly has been so indulgent that I cannot possibly think of throwing myself into academic work without their reassuring presence. My parents, I remain indebted, as ever. I remain grateful to family in Almora, my in-laws, Dhiraj and Kanchan. It has been a great source of joy spending time with Divya and Lakshay during sunny vacations in the abode of the Himalayas. I especially thank Sekharda for his immense positive and public spiritedness. Many a political solution lies in this gentle demeanour. I am grateful to Poonam for her quiet confidence and unquiet compassion and care. They have gone a long way in the making of this book. Finally, I thank my brother Vijay, whose spirit continues to excite and haunt! I benefitted from his rich collection of books, from where I liberally borrowed some of the stuff referred to here. I thank Krishna for her silent but assured support and the new and the most sought-after member of our family, Kushi, who has stood by her name, and hopefully this book will remain of some relevance by the time she begins to read and write! It is to the three of them that I dedicate this book.

I am grateful to Rudra Narayan, Commissioning Editor, and Isha Sachdeva, Associate Production Editor, SAGE Publications for their enthusiasm, insight and perseverance to get this book published. I wish to acknowledge that some of the chapters in this book have been published earlier, though they have been substantially rewritten, in tune with the focus here. The chapter titled 'Democracy against Maoism, Maoism against Itself' was published in the *Economic and Political Weekly*, Vol. 48, No. 7, 16 February 2013. The chapter titled 'Backward Classes: Reservations, Recognition and the Republic' was published earlier with the title 'Can We De-stigmatize Reservations in India?' in the *Economic and Political Weekly*, 11 February 2012. The chapter titled 'Subaltern Classes: Governmentality, Resistance and "Political Society"' was published earlier with the title 'Why Interrogate Political Society?' in the volume *Reframing Democracy and Agency: Interrogating Political Society*, edited by Ajay Gudavarthy (Anthem Press, London, 2012). The chapter titled 'Politics of Global Human Rights in India' was earlier published as 'Human Rights' in the volume *International Relations: Perspectives for Global South*, edited by B.S. Chimni and S. Mallavarpu (Pearson, Delhi, 2012). The chapter titled 'Globalisation and Regionalisation: Mapping the New Continental Drift' was published in the *Economic and Political Weekly*, 19 June 2009.

Introduction
India Disconnected: Joining the Dots

Maoism, democracy and globalisation are three distinct but inseparable currents marking Indian politics today. They are distinct in terms of their goals, direction and modalities of forging social, political, economic and even cultural change, while mutually influencing each other in the emergent political process. The moot question remains whether this mutual influence is moderating the excesses and inadequacies in bringing about radical democratisation understood as expansion of substantive participatory ethos and egalitarian concerns or it is emptying them of any identifiable radical democratic agenda. This book is an attempt to precisely map processes that are internal to each of these currents, while exploring and identifying the moments of mutual influence and possible areas of conflict and mutually exclusive pulls they bring to the contemporary politics in India. It is an exercise to grasp the double-edged character of politics, where each of the currents, while contributing in its own way to the expansion of processes of democratisation, is also arresting them, making it extremely difficult to trace the direction and shape it is assuming.[1] It is witnessing robust bottom-up mobilisation that is quickly countered by top-down counter-mobilisation, actively aided by insular public institutional structures that have been put in place, in the name of global governance in the last two decades after the introduction of processes of globalisation and neoliberal reforms. On the one hand, in the last two decades, we have witnessed the processes of 'deepening democracy' and the 'second democratic upsurge', neo-welfarism, with far-reaching policies such as the Mahatma Gandhi National Rural Employment Guarantee Act (MGNREGA) or the Right to Work, the Right to Information (RTI), the Right to Education (RTE) and the proposed Food Security Bill, apart from a range of imaginative policies in each state, while, on the other hand, we have also witnessed a very obscene debate initiated by Planning Commission fixing the below poverty line figures at rupees 23 for rural and rupees 32 for urban areas, massive agrarian crisis leading to a spate of farmers' suicides, rise in unemployment, growing rural–urban divide marked by distress migration, land acquisition and land grab, violence and displacement of tribals, to name a few. In essence, it is around this contrast that contemporary political currents are pulling Indian politics in varied directions.

While Maoist politics have essentially raised structural issues that are leading to the phenomenon of growing impoverishment and dispossession, blaming both (formal) democracy and neoliberal globalisation for this, votaries of globalisation have all along claimed that after the collapse of developmental state and the balance of payments (BOP) crisis there was little option left and it is the new growth rates that have made expansive welfare policies possible,[2] and the accompanying inequalities have and can be moderated by processes of representative democracy.[3] Democracy, in a sense, emerges as a mediating modality between militant armed mobilisation at one end of the spectrum and globalisation marked by private and global capital flows at the other end. Democracy itself seems to be fraught with double-edged processes of increasing representation but with decreasing responsiveness of the state. The hiatus between representation and responsiveness has added further complexity as to how effective is parliamentary democracy, and the need to shift to the local in search of alternatives, including growing decentralisation, social activism and heightened sectoral mobilisation. These processes have promised to bring positive and inclusive change without resort to militant mobilisation and violence. One way to get a handle on this labyrinthine terrain is to examine each of these currents in itself and in relation to each other. In focusing on the concrete processes of democratisation that each of these currents have initiated, we may get an opening into what could be the kind of processes, institutions and policies that need to be put in place, and above all what kind of alliteration is at all possible between these three dominant politico-economic currents in India that is increasingly looking disconnected.

Maoism

Communist Party of India (Maoist) came into existence after the merger of the Communist Party Unity and Maoist Communist Centre (MCC) in September 2004. The contemporary Maoist party in India aims at continuing the legacy of the peasant rebellion that was initiated in Naxalbari in 1967, under the leadership of Charu Majumdar. He was the first to articulate Maoist philosophy and strategy in building a revolution in Indian conditions and emerged as a breakaway group from the Communist Party of India (Marxist). 'In 1969, on Lenin's birth anniversary, Charu Majumdar announced the formation of a new Communist party—the CPI (Marxist–Leninist) or the CPI (ML)' (Pandita 2011: 23; also refer to Banerjee 2011). The party since then has had a long journey in the history of Communist politics in India. Though the Naxalbari insurrection was quelled in just 72 days, it has remained unflinchingly inspirational for many an experiment in revolutionary political mobilisation. Marxist–Leninist or the later day Maoist politics have since shunned the strategy of 'annihilation of class' enemies and individual annihilation as a mode of waging a class war, and instead laid emphasis on the 'mass line' as propounded by Mao, including forging open and legal 'mass organisations', with a strict focus on his strategy of guerrilla warfare and area-wise seizure of power declaring 'liberated zones', where the Maoist party claims 'sovereign' rule of the people. In some such zones in central India, the Maoist party claims to literally run a parallel government; it is a different matter that there is in fact no presence of the Government of India in those areas. These areas had always remained beyond the developmental plans of the state, until the government realised that these areas not only were inhabited by tribals but also were repositories to wealth of minerals and other natural re-sources. That is when the battle assumed current proportions of a 'civil war', which led Prime Minister Manmohan Singh to declare Maoists as the 'single largest internal security threat'.[4]

Officially, the Ministry of Home Affairs (MHA) has identified 400 police stations that are 'worst affected' by the 'Left-wing Extremism' (LWE).

> Subsequently, the MHA identified [police] stations in 83 worst Naxal-hit districts spread across nine-states—Andhra Pradesh, Bihar, Chattisgarh, Jharkhand, Madhya Pradesh, Maharashtra, Odisha, Uttar Pradesh and West Bengal. ... Of the stations chosen, 85 are in Bihar, while 70 each are in Chattisgarh and Jharkhand and another 70 in Odisha. In Andhra Pradesh 40 stations have been identified, while 18 are in West Bengal, 15 in Uttar Pradesh, 12 in Madhya Pradesh and 10 in Maharashtra. (Joshi 2012)[5]

In order to 'control' the spread of the Maoist movement, Union Government, along with the state governments, has primarily used extremely repressive methods, including extra-judicial killings that are referred to in popular parlance as 'fake encounter' killings; torture and other third-degree methods; illegal arrests that were/are actively supported by draconian legislations such as the Terrorist and Disruptive Activities (Prevention) (TADA) Act, the Prevention of Terrorist Activities (POTA) Act and Armed Forces (Special Powers) (AFSPA) Act; cases of disappearance in areas often declared as disturbed areas; using surrendered naxalites as private mercenaries and for covert operations; and floating government-sponsored organisations of tribals and equipping them with arms, such as the Salwa Judum in Chhattisgarh. The emphasis on 'security' strategies/operations has sometimes been pronounced along with rhetorical announcements of development-oriented programmes in 'Maoist infested' areas. Advancing this two-pronged strategy of 'security and development' in containing the influence of the Maoist party, the MHA in its 'Status Paper on the Naxal Problem' in 2006 identified various security measures, including modernisation of state police; revision of Security Related Expenditure (SRE) Scheme, under which a sum of ₹170.55 crores was disbursed and its period extended to the current date; supply of mine protected vehicles; long-term deployment of central paramilitary forces, under which 'the central government has also exempted the states from the payment of cost of deployment of these forces' involving funds to the tune of 1,200 crores; and sanctioning naxal-affected states India Reserve (IR) battalions, under which the central government promised to provide ₹20.75 crores for each battalion as against the earlier amount of ₹13 crores per battalion (MHA 2006). The draconian part of this status paper, in terms of violation of constitutional practices, was the support to arm tribals directly, instead of just deploying the paramilitary forces to fight the naxalites. This state-sponsored organisation was projected through a conscious state policy as a 'spontaneous movement'. The status paper declared that

> keeping in view the importance of Salva Judum movement as a major bulwark in sustained campaign against naxals and in view of the naxalite attacks on innocent Salva Judum activists, the State Government has been advised to enhance the deployment of security forces to provide effective area domination, ensure safety of Salva Judum activists and strengthen security of relief camps. (MHA 2006: 10)

Contrary to the official reports and media reports about the nature of the Salwa Judum being a 'spontaneous movement' of the tribals, a combined report released by various civil rights organisations stated that

> the fact is that the Salwa Judum is being led by sections of local elites, contractors and traders, that is officially part of anti-naxal initiatives, and that it is being actively supported by the state agencies to an unprecedented degree. It's far from being a 'spontaneous' response to Maoist 'tyranny' by the local populace at large, as the government is making it out to be. (PUDR et al. 2006: 14)

The Salwa Judum was part of the counter-insurgency strategy of the state that mobilised those social groups and classes that were affected in course of the political mobilisation by the Maoists as part of a larger strategy of the state that was referred to as the 'Operation Green Hunt'. It was, in other words, counter-class mobilisation by the state, which included headmen, *sarpanches*, who were losing their 'traditional' forms of hierarchical power, along with non-tribal immigrants who had economic interests in the tribal areas. It is these sections that were recruited as part of the Salwa Judum campaign/policy of the state as formation of Village Defence Committees (VDCs) and training of Special Police Officers (SPOs), where the tribals and non-tribal immigrants were being supplied arms and asked to fight the naxalites and carry out offences against the tribals who sympathise with them.

> Security forces are deployed in these, with each sector having a VDC (as well). Each VDC in a cluster will have between 40–50 members. The VDCs comprise village headperson, sarpanch, panch as well as young men. Surrendered sangham members [Maoist organisations] and young men and women from villages get trained to become SPOs. (PUDR et al. 2006: 31)[6]

This spiral of violence has many other undeclared effects on the tribal populations, such as escalating sexual violence and prostitution including those women who had been recruited as SPOs. One of the reports carried out by All India Women's Team reported that 'many of the young girls working as SPOs had unwanted pregnancies and about 50 women SPOs had had illegal abortions done by a health worker in Bijapur' (CAVOW [Committee against Violence on Women] 2006: 15).[7]

What explains such violence and extra-judicial mechanisms adopted by the state that proclaims itself as a constitutional and representative democracy? What does it then tell us about the nature of democracy itself? The answer that is often offered in the self-understanding of those representing the state's viewpoint has been that Maoist movement is not merely a struggle of the poor but it is also a 'war' to overthrow existing state and take over state power, and its use of violence challenging state sovereignty does not qualify such movements for the legal protection guaranteed in the Constitution. The moot question remains whether it is violence or politics of the Maoists that the state perceives as a real threat to its legitimacy.[8] Maoist movement is a protracted war to overthrow the state not through merely military means but around a strong and an alternative political mobilisation of the workers, peasants and the adivasis. 'Maoists want to construct a socialist state through a people's revolution where tribals have rights to "jal, jungle, jameen" (water, forests and land), and land to the tiller' (Chenoy and Chenoy 2010: 58).[9] The Maoist party characterises India as a semi-feudal semi-colonial economy with feudalism as the 'primary contradiction'; post-1990s it came to understand the struggle against imperialism as the primary goal. For about four decades now, Maoist politics have been struggling to get land reforms implemented along with mobilising workers for better work condition and a share in ownership. More recently they have addressed the issue of displacement of farmers and adivasis through a sustained policy of land acquisition by the state that is either forced or has inadequate compensation and formation of Special Economic Zones (SEZs) with tax rebates to the corporate sector and withdrawal of social security measures for the workers working in such zones. Against the recent agrarian crisis, they have highlighted the plight of farmers including the growing number of farmer's suicides; they have also highlighted the Memoranda of Understanding (MoUs) signed by many state governments especially that of Chhattisgarh with business houses such as ESSAR, TATAs and Vedanta, whose terms of conditions have not been made public. It is due to the sustained mobilisation of the tribals by the Maoists that none of these MoUs could be realised and no mining was allowed in tribal belts (Venugopal 2012). Maoists have been arguing for long that since the Indian state has only initiated policies that are patently anti-poor, it has very little legitimacy, and in order to realise this they have been giving an open call to boycott elections. In its place,

Maoists aim to run a parallel government known as the 'Janatana Sarkar' (Revolutionary People's Council) and a 'Nyaya Samiti' (Committee for Justice) that includes 'Peoples Courts' apart from various other developmental programmes that can reach basic facilities such as drinking water, health and education to the workers, peasants and the adivasis.

What then is the structural link between the political programme of the Maoists and the nature of violence of the state and democracy? Would it be appropriate to conclude that open and representative democracy is possible only when it is actively supported by unaccounted violence and extra-judicial 'exceptionalism' of the state, making exceptionalism not a mere aberration but a structural condition to allow representative processes to be made possible and acceptable to the ruling elite? The conflict between capitalism and democracy, expressed as a conflict between accumulation and legitimacy, is maintained and balanced by using coercive power against those political forces which raise issues that cannot be structurally accommodated within the limits of practicing open democracy that allows for incremental change. As we have argued, this balance has tilted heavily towards maintaining the hold of global capital, national bourgeoisie, landed gentry, professional classes and newly emergent neo-rich classes such as the contractor classes, with the use of growing extra-judicial and unaccounted violence by the state. This violence has, in fact, become endemic to the system and is no longer limited to its use against the Maoists but has extended to all forms of protest politics over the last two decades. It has even gone beyond controlling protest politics, seeping into the very form political power has assumed. To cite a few instances, the victims of the strategy of extra-judicial killings, referred to in the popular parlance as 'fake encounter killings', now include journalists such as Ghulam Rasool in Andhra Pradesh who was investigating illegal land dealings when he was assassinated in December 1991,[10] dealing with 'Islamic terror' that includes implicating in legal cases and attempt on the life of a Delhi University teacher Mr. Gilani, Ishrat Jahan in Gujarat,[11] the infamous Batla House Encounter killing young students registered at the Jamia Milia Islamia University,[12] and the Ansal Plaza encounter of a businessman in Delhi, among many other such incidents.[13] It has become endemic in the sense of growing violence by private groups, for instance a series of killings of RTI activists and killing of government officials, such as that of the Additional Collector of Maharashtra, who was burnt alive purportedly by the 'kerosene mafia', and a Superintendent of Police in Madhya Pradesh by the 'sand mafia'.[14] There has been, on the one hand, the rise of the so-called encounter specialists among the police, and on the other a veritable mafia led by the new lobbies of civil, liquor, mining, sand, petrol and kerosene, to name a few. The massive rise of 'righteous lawlessness' outside the 'high politics' of representative democracy has accounted for much of the social, economic and political processes in India, especially post-1990s.[15]

This then is no longer a strategy to contain the Maoists but a strategy that the state has made more generic to include all forms of resistance against the current model of development, and its lopsided implications.[16] For instance,

> existing Indian legislation on natural resources is premised on the colonial concept of Eminent Domain—which gives the state unrestrained power to use the natural resources of the people as it deems fit. ... In the absence of the right to have a say in the disposal of what lies on or below their land, local communities who oppose the plunder of natural resources in Odisha, Chattisgarh, Jharkhand, Assam and other states are called 'extremist' or 'secessionist' and their struggles put down brutally. (Raghavan 2012)

It needs to be noted here that it is not that the state has responded pro-actively towards struggles that have been non-violent either. In a glaring incident of protest against the raising of storage levels of the Omkareshwar dam in Madhya Pradesh, the people affected stood continuously in neck-deep water for more than a fortnight with the slogan 'drown but not move' to receive land-based rehabilitation. Finally, 'on a petition by the Narmada Bachao Andolan, the MPHRC considering the gravity of the situation, passed an interim order directing the State government to reduce the water level and ensure the safety of the oustees' (Singh 2012). It is therefore not merely about armed militants that the response of the state has been indiscriminate, but all forms of democratic and popular forms of protest have had to negotiate with a state that is increasingly dealing through its coercive apparatus. In another glaring incident that attracted the attention of the media was the anti-corruption struggle led by India against Corruption (IAC), one of whose activists Aseem Trivedi, who also happens to be a cartoonist, was charged with sedition for insulting national emblems in his cartoons.[17] Commenting on its editorial,

The Hindu, it reminded its readers that this provision was declared to be 'highly objectionable and obnoxious' by Jawaharlal Nehru himself; however, 'ironically, the sedition clause not only remains on the Statute book but is used periodically against human rights activists, journalists and intellectuals' (*The Hindu* 11 September 2012).

Exceptionalism, as a form and mode of governance in India, thus included the combination of use of extraordinary laws such as the TADA, POTA, AFSPA, and Sedition Laws, among many others, with extra-judicial killings, torture and cases of disappearance, custodial deaths and even sexual violence by the armed forces.[18] These modes of governance are aimed at militant armed struggles in Kashmir, Northeast India and Maoists in many parts of India, but they are also used against non-violent struggles led by peasants and adivasis affected by dams, farmer's displaced due to land acquisition, urban activists against corruption, civil rights activists, intellectuals, 'suspect Muslims', among other social groups. Basic rights are violated by state forces such as police, armed forces and paramilitary forces, but also power to inflict violence with impunity is 'outsourced' by the state to private mercenary and vigilante groups such as the Salwa Judum, Surrendered United Front of Assam (SULFA), surrendered naxalites in Andhra Pradesh, among many others. Thus, governance, outside of high politics representing democracy in the formal sense, is near-complete exceptionalism. There are, however, pockets where formal democracy works effectively, including, for instance, free and fair elections, and where the naxalite call for boycott of elections has been a near failure with an electoral turnout of near 60 per cent in most of the state and general elections.[19] There are pockets of growth, especially in urban and metropolitan cities that have seen an expansion of opportunities, rising income level for urban professional classes, social security measures and guaranteed employment schemes for rural and urban poor, and extensive affirmative action policies, which have been made possible due to the processes of globalisation and economic growth. The claims to India being an economic giant are accompanied by massive poverty statistics, including 50 per cent identified as below poverty line (BPL), and growing inequality and conflict between rural and urban areas, playing out the old conflict between *Bharat versus India.* It would not be an exaggeration, as some economists have observed that 'there is already a sub-Saharan Africa (SAA) within India—half of our rural population or over 350 million people are below the average food energy intake of SAA countries' (Patnaik 2005). Thus, India is assuming, at one level, the proportions of being a violent democracy marked by a structural link between the growing shift of the state to a model of governance based on 'righteous lawlessness' born out of its claims to legitimacy through functioning representative (electoral) democracy, on the one hand, and the insidious dependence of representative politics on the use of extra-constitutional violence with impunity, on the other.

In this context of India seeming to be a violent democracy, Chapter 1 titled 'Democracy against Maoism, Maoism against Itself' engages with and critically analyses the Maoist movement and its strategy of ushering a 'New Democratic Revolution'. Given this survival of Indian democracy at the extreme fringes, with pockets of formal processes, and a state that has managed to create a regime of neo-welfarism along with economic reforms, and a promise of inclusive polity that has found expression in its extensive programme of affirmative action policies, what is the possible equation of the Maoist movement with this kind of democracy? Has it succeeded in completely disengaging with its processes, institutions and policy? Or should it find new political modes to creatively resignify these practices to tilt them increasingly in favour of the dispossessed? Similarly, what has been the nature of political mobilisation by the Maoist movement itself? Has it been able to combine strategies of 'mass mobilisation', dialogue and accountability, alongside its focus on raising a militia and armed squads? What has been the equation between its armed squads and 'the party' and the various 'mass organisations' that reflect some of its core concerns? Chapter 1 argues that while the Maoist movement has waged a relentless battle in favour of some of the most dispossessed 'basic classes', including the landless, Dalits, rural poor, workers, and adivasis, and questioned the very nature of the economic model of development and political model of governance, it had to achieve this through an emphasis and somewhat singular focus on armed struggle. In course of such an armed struggle, the 'frames of war' have also structured the nature of political process initiated by the Maoist movement itself. It has failed so far to forge ties with other non-class political struggles in India, though it has been emphasising on forming a 'united front' with 'democratic struggles' across India. Neither it has managed to offer a new political language that can articulate these uneven social and political conflicts nor have 'other' democratic movements accepted the strategies and political vision of the Maoists. Part of the reason, as the first chapter traces, is to do with the discomfort that the Maoist party has in experimenting with giving autonomy to its own 'mass organisations' which are arranged in and through a strict hierarchy. This has disabled the movement from either developing a new organisational structure and culture or in expanding its understanding as to how to draw equivalence between class and non-class, or economic and cultural identities. Within the fold of the Maoist movement there has been a growing contradiction between class war and class politics. While the former requires the 'compression of space-time dimensions', the latter requires elaborate political experiments. These seem to have entered into an irreducible conflict bringing in stagnation. The Maoist party is also unclear in terms of its equation with available democratic institutions such as the courts, local bodies, among others. While it has shifted over a period of time to using courts and even contesting elections with local bodies in some states, these experiments have not found any sustained theoretical shift. These limitations and very strategies have arrested and suspended the Maoist movement between waging some exemplary battles against state violence and reduced political presence. Maoists have remained in pockets but those that have been among the most underdeveloped and where the reach of the state has been negligible. They continue to have very marginal presence in plains and cities. The first chapter raises some of these issues and opens up a debate of their equation with representative democracy that includes various forms of political mobilisation in the recent past by the middle classes, backward classes and the subaltern classes.

Democracy

The second section of the book deals with the nature of the changing democracy in India. It engages with some of the most vibrant forms of political mobilisation in the recent past, including the anti-graft movement led by Anna Hazare, backed primarily by the urban middle classes; 'second democratic upsurge' initiated by the reservations for the backward classes and the influence of this political activism by these relatively developed social groups on the agency of subaltern classes. Have these influential social groups taken over street politics from the subaltern? If so, what does it tell us about democracy in India today? What then is the role of the processes of globalisation in some of these contemporary changes to the way democracy is playing out?

In order to understand the dynamics of democracy and its interface with militant mobilisations on the one hand and global processes on the other, one needs to make sense of the unique global status that the language and discourse of democracy has come to enjoy in contemporary times. The most notable of this emergent change is the fact that

> democracy has historically unparalleled global popularity today yet has never been more conceptually footloose or substantively hollow. Perhaps democracy's current popularity depends on the openness and even vacuity of its meaning and practice ... we seek to capture democracy for yet-untried purposes and ethoi, we write of 'democracy to come', 'democracy of the uncounted', 'democratizing sovereignty', 'democracy workshops', 'pluralizing democracy', and more. (Brown 2012: 44–45)

The paradox of democracy seems to be in its celebration of popular sovereignty, voting and consent and even consensus, all of which assumes a certain singularity of the people, while they are vertically and horizontally divided across, caste, class, nationality and region, among many other fault lines. The cracks are now becoming more visible, which means that popular politics and mobilisation have taken shapes that are relatively new and their implications for the processes of democratisation are relatively unknown, as yet.

One of the most pertinent fallouts of the new shape democracy has taken is the emergence of the 'global street', which is imbued by protests of various kinds, but the most notable are those by the active middle classes. Sassen argues that

> the liberal state is in deep decay. And the social contract of the liberal state is with the middle class, much more so than the very poor and the very rich. Today we see a first generation in the middle classes since the World War II which is poorer and more hopeless than their parents and grandparents. One way of putting it is that the deal between the middle class and the liberal state has broken down. (Sassen 2013)

It is this breakdown of the social contract that has propelled a new theatre of the 'global street', whose performative aspects include holding candle light marches, blocking of traffic, holding fasts, occupying open spaces including the squares and public buildings; this is now a global phenomenon from the Occupy movement in the United States, to the Arab Spring in the Middle East, demonstrations against austerity in Spain and Greece, to the movement against crime, graft and sexual violence in India.

> The Street can, thus, be conceived as a space where new forms of the social and the political can be made, rather than a space for enacting ritualized routines. With some conceptual stretching, we might say that politically, 'street and square' are marked differently from 'boulevard and piazza': The first signals action and the second, rituals. (Sassen 2013)

The action, however, has its own marked difference in India. While it is signalling a new kind of politics of the middle classes to 'bring the state back', it has also demonstrated the potential to be a new kind of hegemony that carries its own kind of closures, making its equation with democracy and democratisation rather chequered. It is, precisely, against these closures that new militant politics have ushered in counter-mobilisation, and from their vantage point the demands of the new kind of street politics are to put more pressure on the state to protect the interests of urban middle classes that it has so diligently done in the past. Scholars have thus noted that

> it could be argued that the two most compelling forms of class politics in the present are the problem of widespread Maoist violence in a large swathe of central India, and the new politics of urban middle-class activism. ... Civil society is stratified by class, and middle class activism is exercising a new hegemony over civil society, generating a 'new politics' of neighbourhood associations which tends to exclude the lower classes in the informal sector and so to perpetuate inequality rather than interrogate it. (Jayal and Mehta 2011: xxvi)

Those championing the cause of the militant politics that organise the 'basic classes' have foregrounded this exclusionary aspect of the 'new politics'. Neither the modes of protest nor the purpose of these demonstrations takes into consideration the issues that concern the subaltern; on the contrary, they could actually be insidiously strengthening the same processes of exclusion that are embedded in the contemporary dynamics of democracy, in its tryst with global capital. Thus, Arundhati Roy, in her critique of Anna Hazare led anti-graft movement, argued that neither his protest nor 'the people' he wishes to represent take into account scores of issues that continue to plague the most underprivileged; instead the symbolic and substantive core of his struggle actually further delegitimises them and transfers the 'public' spaces that once belonged to them, to the now, emergent affluent middle classes. She, therefore, argues commenting on Anna Hazare's fast against graft that

> 'The Fast' of course doesn't mean Irom Sharmila's fast that has lasted for more than ten years (she's being force fed now) against the AFSPA, which allows soldiers in Manipur to kill merely on suspicion. It does not mean the relay hunger fast that is going on right now by ten thousand villagers in Koodankulam protesting against the nuclear power plant. 'The People' does not mean the Manipuris who support Irom Sharmila's fast. Nor does it mean the thousands who are facing down armed policemen and mining mafias in Jagatsinghpur, or Kalinganagar, or Niyamgiri, or Bastar, or Jaitapur. Nor do we mean the victims of the Bhopal gas leak, or the people displaced by dams in the Narmada Valley. Nor do we mean the farmers in NOIDA, or Pune or Haryana or elsewhere in the country, resisting the takeover of the land. (Roy 2011)[20]

The symbolic core of the 'new politics' seems to reflect the same discursive and performative spaces that have, in the past, delegitimised and stigmatised the struggles of the most marginalised that are forced into oblivion; they exist because they continue to be invisible. 'Meanwhile the props and the choreography, the aggressive nationalism and flag waving of Anna's Revolution are all borrowed, from the anti-reservation protests, the world-cup victory parade, and the celebration of the nuclear tests' (Roy 2011).

It is this paradox that is at the heart of the 'new politics' of the middle classes that is analysed in Chapter 2 titled 'Middle Classes: Urban Activism and Anna Hazare's Soap Opera'. This chapter, in essence, argues that while the 'new politics' has made a rhetorical use of available democratic protest forms, its substantive core seems to be nudging towards a new hegemonic frame that demands more law, more centralisation, more surveillance, more majoritarianism, less tolerance of deliberation, and in fact more contempt for the idea of democracy and vocation of politics itself. As Arundhati Roy rightly asks, 'Does the solution to the problems faced by ordinary people lie in addressing the structural inequality, or in creating yet another power structure that people will have to defer to' (Roy 2011)? The 'new politics' of the middle classes has raised, primarily, issues of corruption, urban crime and more lately sexual violence against women in metropolitan cities. While these causes are at the heart of both understanding and democratising processes of representative politics in India, the way they have, however, been framed by the new protest politics has something specific and is linked to the class location of those protesting.

This specificity has many characteristic features; however, in essence, they are not attempting a corrective action against the excesses in democracy but seem to perceive democracy—as in popular representation—itself as a problem. They therefore demand more legislation, more centralisation and more power being bestowed in 'experts', rather than elected representatives. While they wish to, in a rhetorical sense, instil more accountability by public representatives, this is accompanied by wanton contempt for the avocation of politics, and preference for those political figures who have demonstrated a similar contempt for democratic procedures and projected themselves as intolerant, and even authoritarian.[21] Similarly, another very notable feature of this mode of mobilisation has been its aversion to public debate, and abjured any attempts of reasoning out the causes—sociological and historical—for the spurt in urban crime, sexual violence and corruption; instead they have preferred quick-fix solutions, one-size-fits-all kind of modalities. Much of this hinges on the demand for more surveillance and more powers to the state, including more use of extra-constitutional force. In all the three above-mentioned issues, the protestors demanded death penalty, castration, public lynching, chopping of limbs and impunity to police forces and investigating authorities. They summarily declined the possibility that crime could be social, and not merely psychological, corruption could be systemic with these same classes patronising and being beneficiaries, and rape has something to do with our family system, masculinity in religious and social and cultural discourses, and in more complex ways linked to the brutalisation following abysmal living conditions of social groups, especially after the inauguration of the neoliberal reforms. This lack of reasoning, ironically, is the modality through which the 'enlightened classes' wish to engrave their social power, in lieu of their numerical strength to influence the representative processes.

They have demonstrated this very attitude, as a modality, in relation to issues of political militancy in Kashmir and the Northeast, and the growth of the Maoist movement. There is no public debate on the nature and character of the Maoist movement; the 'discussion' is devoid of facts often depending on falsity, in order to 'manufacture consent'.[22] They have, therefore, attempted to subsume the political dynamics under the social, civil and moral ones. Holding high moral ground on issues of public concern, in order to regulate democracy, seems to be an entrenched feature of the cultural capital of the middle classes. It is intriguing how substantive processes are relegated to their symbolic and rhetorical essence. These then do not instantiate at two different levels but are inextricably interlinked, in the very modality of the emergent 'new politics'. The subterranean logic seems to be one where, since these classes are carriers of 'traditions' of deliberation and best ethos of individual freedom, this cultural capital seems to provide them with rhetorical legitimacy to violate these very practices with impunity and demand institutionalisation of processes that are in substance a negation of those ethics.

Further, the 'new politics' has initiated a process of what could be referred to as the neoliberalisation of politics. As we argue in the second chapter, the attempts to disproportionately influence policy making and putting pressure on the state by the middle classes, and assuming the form of protest politics in the street, have installed a phenomenon of society 'seeing the state' as responding to a selective social base, rather than any claims to universality. The state itself begins to self-represent itself as actively representing the interests, language and symbols of certain classes and social groups, however, with an additional claim that this would eventually benefit all sections of the society. This is akin to the current development model, where sops to the corporate are justified as imperative for faster growth, which will eventually trickle-down to all social groups, in terms of better infrastructural facility, more social spending and more employment opportunities. The nature of groups being privileged and the way privileges are framed could differ based on the specific details of the nature of coalition, role of regional parties and their ideological underpinnings, but the logic seems to be one of state moving beyond from immediate claims to universality to serving fragmented interests that could eventually benefit from the trickle-down of democracy.

This mode of operating through the fragments has its impact on the various aspects of governance and the state–society relation. Among others, it is most tangible and palpable in the way law operates. While previously we observed, in relation to controlling the Maoist movement, the spurt in extra-constitutional violence of the state, here it could be that law itself begins to shift its terrain, in order to serve the new imperatives of this new kind of mobilisational politics of the affluent. This shift is marked in law moving from the realms of evidence to that of intention, as is visible in many of the anti-terror laws such as the TADA, POTA and AFSPA. Further, it moves from the realm of investigation and conviction to producing demonstrative effects, mandatory to quell the anxieties of the urban classes. It could be produced by 'carrying' out an encounter, disturbing the proceedings of the Parliament or creating 'simulated lawlessness' by physical assaults on the Speaker of the House, creating spectacles of various kinds such as the *Sadbhavana* and business meets in Gujarat, among others. The point is that they manage to create a rhetoric, which makes it increasingly difficult to find the social or discursive space to establish basic sociological and historical veracity of the claims, or the concrete impact and consequences of actions undertaken.[23] Media has undoubtedly played a formidable role, as we argue in the Chapter 2, in making these spectacles grander, allowing for 'drawing room politics', allowing for 'drawing room patriotism', reflected, for instance, in the 'cartographic patriotism', and serving the cultural appetite of the 'new politics'.

The 'new politics' of the middle classes contributes to the 'righteous lawlessness' of the state, through an activism that prides on contempt of politics and democracy. In other words, it is a paradox of using popular protest forms that are considered to be cornerstone of vibrant democracies, in order to undermine the legitimacy of democracy and politics, along with disapproval of militant modes of mobilisation, such as those initiated by the Maoist movement, and thereby they become the social base for the extra-constitutional governance of the state. Thus, the state and democracy are caught in a process of violence churning from both the ends. The two kinds of mobilisation that we have referred to, the Maoist and the urban activism in rather strange ways, converge in their attempts to 'overthrow' the state, and also democracy. As Arundhati Roy rightly points out,

> For completely different reasons, and in completely different ways, you could say that the Maoists and the Jan Lokpal Bill have one thing in common—they both seek the overthrow of the Indian State. One working from the bottom up, by means of an armed struggle, waged by a largely

adivasi army, made up of the poorest of the poor. The other, from the top down, by means of a bloodless Gandhian coup, led by a freshly minted saint, and an army of largely urban, and certainly better off people. (Roy 2011)

Chapter 3 titled 'Backward Classes: Reservations, Recognition and the Republic' in the second section of this book looks at the other side of urban activism that has emerged over the last decade; this activism is constructed not 'merely' around class, but that of caste, led by the mobile backward classes. Urban spaces have, along with the 'traditional' middle classes, have been occupied by the upwardly mobile backward classes and those caste groups that have been forcefully demanding to be identified as 'backward'. These are new kinds of elites, within Indian democracy, that are sociologically queer; they are economically and politically powerful, and socially backward, neglected and marginalised. There are heterogeneous sub-castes, which are vertically differentiable across their economic, political, social and cultural power, apart from their regional location across the rural–urban divide. Notwithstanding these divisions, they have managed to forge a common 'backward class movement'. It is a politically forged unity that is self-conscious of its internal differentiation. These social groups, along with those wanting to join them, including castes such as the Jats, Rajputs and Gujjars, have also occupied public spaces and imagination.[24] They have time and again expressed their 'reservations' against the urban elites—meaning upper caste/middle class—that are active with their urban activism. For instance, Mulayam Singh Yadav has expressed his aversion against the Bill that envisages 33 per cent reservations for women, by arguing that it will only benefit affluent, urban, middle-class women.[25] In the theatre of the 'global street', this is the new dimension constructed through a conflict between the urban/upper castes and the mobile/backward classes that are coming to constitute a 'new middle class'.

However, the challenge for the new middle classes is not merely economic but also very significantly cultural. Social and cultural stigmatisation has remained as formidable as questions of economic redistribution. For a democracy to actualise its potential in terms of allowing the participatory ethos, mobility and egalitarian concerns, it is important that various social groups extend mutual recognition, and not merely achieve redistributive benefits. The social and cultural practices of such groups need to be recognised as legitimate and dignified in the public sphere. The interface between a political community and a cultural community is pivotal to how political ideals play out in the real time of a nation's history. In India, the political ideals of constitutional governance and citizenship have been marred by cultural practices that run counter, whether it is with regard to gender, in relation to the *khap* panchayats or provisions of personal laws, or autonomous councils of the tribals, or the everyday practices based on caste discrimination. The civic ethos is integral to the imagination of the democratic spirit. The processes of criminalisation, in relation to the criminal tribes during the colonial time, or the practices of stigmatisation and humiliation with regard to the Dalits and other lowered castes have been very significant in arresting the emergence of a 'sense of self' that can enjoy self-confidence and self-esteem (Gudavarthy 2013a).[26]

Chapter 3 precisely addresses this question of overcoming stigma that has been attached with the various caste groups, in order to achieve mobility and access modern amenities, including the urban spaces. This chapter argues that this aspect of stigma is set to undergo a significant shift with the implementation of the reservations for the other backward classes (OBCs), around the recommendations of the Mandal Commission. The new mobilisation by the backward classes and other caste groups in urban spaces, it is argued, will lend a new legitimacy to all those groups that have been the beneficiaries of the protective discrimination. There are already moves to make provision for protective discrimination beyond caste, for religious minorities, women, and even the poor among the upper castes, including the Brahmins. It could also be argued that the new legitimacy gained for the policy of reservations has pushed the new debate for quotas in promotions for the Dalits. It has also expanded the debate beyond mere provision of opportunities into how new social relations can be realised for these new entrants into higher education and jobs. In other words, with the discourse of reservations itself being de-stigmatised, these new entrants can now influence the system in raising issues regarding what have been referred to as the necessary 'background conditions', such as universal education, land reforms, among others.

Liberal social scientists and the Left-of-centre political parties, including the Maoists—representing another kind of convergence—have for long rued the fact that reservations only address the symptoms but not the more basic conditions that are continuing to create social and economic inequalities. Pratap Bhanu Mehta argues:

> Reservations, even when it works, deals only with symptoms, not causes. Real equality of opportunities will require a change in a whole range of background conditions: from access to primary education to access to public goods, financial support, and a robustly growing economy that provides opportunities for mobility. They may not address all the problems of discrimination. But they will create conditions for genuine empowerment. That larger churning and mobility is necessary for what Ambedkar called 'endosmosis'. (Mehta 2012)

However, he does not raise the question as to who will demand these larger and 'background conditions' in a Republic? Under what conditions will the elites respond to the marginalised groups? It is in this context of an endemic prejudice and utter lack of participatory avenues that reservations become a pertinent tool to empowerment, and these demands need to come from these very groups and from the changes initiated by the policy of reservations itself. Thus, these changes—mobility by reservations as against achieving 'background conditions'—cannot be imagined as mutually exclusive; rather they ought to be legitimised as mutually reinforcing transformation. Here, the change inaugurated by the reservations to the OBCs, it is argued, is laying the grounds for such mutually reinforcing transformation. How do the Maoists raising issues of 'economic structure' negotiate with these changes that are initiated in and through representative democratic processes? Can they simply see them as methods of co-option into the 'system', especially when lower castes themselves perceive these changes, in terms of new class formation and this kind of mobility as empowering? Class, therefore, is not just a static or a monolithic structure but needs to be understood in terms of a process, in relation to the cultural practices (here imbrued with the practices of caste system). Will sustained mobilisation and new 'politics of recognition' influence new ideological and discursive changes in the understanding of the politics of the Maoists? If they continue to remain disengaged—disconnected—from these changes, what will be the contours of the tension between Maoism and democracy? This assumes significance, especially in light of the fact that the sense of mobility provided by reservations continues to be the strongest link, in an otherwise weak chain called democracy.

These questions assume significant proportions in the workings of a democracy and radical left politics, when we account for the fact that caste-based discrimination in India has not only led to insidious discrimination but bloody violence, and massacres against Dalits, across the country; the latest among these is the one on 29 September 2006, in Khairlangi, Maharashtra. The editorial in the *Hindu* brought into relief the facts of the massacre; it said:

> The victims, members of the Bhotmange family, were bludgeoned to death in full view of people of the village. Their mutilated bodies were dumped in a nearby canal. The 'provocation' for the bestial killings was that Bhaiyalal Bhotmange's wife, daughter, and two sons were educated and asserted their right to a life of dignity despite their poverty. (*The Hindu*, 20 November 2006)

It further reminded that

> Dr. Ambedkar defined democracy as 'primarily a mode of associated living ... [and] essentially an attitude of respect and reverence towards our fellow men.' His searing analysis of the distinction between 'political democracy' and 'social democracy,' and of the huge social democracy deficit in India, is as truthful and relevant today as it was in his lifetime (1891–1956). (*The Hindu*, 20 November 2006)

The transformation is partial because the rise of the backward classes has on the one hand lent a new space and legitimacy for the policy of protective discrimination, and in that might initiate a new set of terms for the legitimate claims to recognition by all marginalised caste groups, and on the other hand has also resulted in a spurt of intra-subaltern conflicts, including those between the OBCs and Dalits, OBCs and urban women, and between the various sub-castes within the Dalits, among others. For instance,

> on the evening of November 7, 2012, a crowd numbering over 1000 people burst into three Dalit settlements in Dharmapuri northwestern Tamil Nadu, and laid them waste. Over a period of several hours, they looted, smashed and burned. ... The immediate motive for this sustained attack was said to be an inter-caste marriage between a Dalit man and a backward caste woman. (Gorringe 2013)

Alongside such anti-Dalit attacks the OBCs have also remained a potential social base for the right-wing mobilisation by the Bharatiya Janata Party (BJP).

Co-existence of forms of mobility with modes of intra-subaltern conflict folded into the same political process makes the emergence and workings of a violent democracy ever more insidious. The modalities of violence are top-down, bottom-up and also horizontal in nature, making it incumbent to keep the conclusions regarding the possible consequences of such a double-edged process open-ended.

It is in this context of the growing shift of popular mobilisation and occupation of the streets by the old urban middle classes and the new middle classes represented by the OBCs on the one hand, and growing intra-subaltern conflicts on the other, Chapter 4 titled 'Subaltern Classes: Governmentality, Resistance and "Political Society"' in the second section turns to conceptualising the question of subaltern agency in contemporary Indian democracy. What has then happened to the subaltern agency in the insidious working of a violent democracy? It can be observed that the poor, including the landless labourers, marginal farmers, migrants, among others, have moved away from popular mobilisation. They have, over a period of time, either moved towards the militant mobilisation by the Maoists or remained powerless, taking recourse to suicides, as farmers did in many parts of India due to the agrarian crisis, or remained demobilised as migrants from the North India in Maharashtra. Between *militancy and powerlessness*, democracy has been vying to be meaningful for the subaltern classes.

Postcolonial theorist Partha Chatterjee, in this context, has attempted to conceptualise the interface between democracy and the subaltern groups through his formulation of 'political society'. Between *militancy and powerlessness*, he believes, 'the ordinary stuff of democratic politics is about constant tussles of different population groups with the authorities over the distribution of governmental services' (Chatterjee 2012: 47). He now argues that the Subaltern Studies, as it framed the question of subaltern agency in the context of peasant rebellions during the anti-colonial period, is no longer relevant. He says, 'the question of the mass political subject was posed by Subaltern Studies, but given the form that question has taken today, it cannot be answered any more within the conceptual framework of that project' (Chatterjee 2012: 47). In other words, from a mass political subject, the subaltern has now become a subject of the governmentality of the Indian state. It has now invested more in carrying out 'contextual negotiations' with the state to get benefits, and this is its predominant mode of political subjectivity.

The problem, as is suggested in Chapter 4 of this book, with the formulation on 'political society', is that it does not sufficiently interrogate the link between the subaltern being pushed to the periphery of the system in taking to distress suicides or militant armed modes of protest, and their perennial dependence on 'survival strategies' provided by the governmentality of the state. The idea of political society also intriguingly argues that taking to 'survival strategies' is a mark of subaltern agency, rather than the domination of elites and the structures they operate through. Further, the interlink between the subaltern and urban middle classes is conceptualised as one of subaltern working their way through by converting the middle classes into 'middle-men-like' groups, and taking advantage of the social and cultural capital they are in possession of. In other words, the subalterns have moved beyond the 'traditional' patron–client relations, and instead through the 'creative power of the community' relations have transmuted them into an active subaltern agency. These tenuous, everyday and 'contextual negotiations' are then understood as the stuff of democracy in India.

Contrary to these formulations, Chapter 4 argues that the changes, in terms of the rise of urban elites to the centre stage, and the new development model have resulted in thinning of the agency of the subaltern and increased their dependence on survival strategies, since beyond a level of distress subaltern cannot afford to protest. Thus, protest has become the weapon of the affluent, while 'contextual negotiations' have become a mode of survival for the subaltern.

Similarly, the dependence on elites and middles classes far from questioning the patron–client relations is a new mode of 'refracted patronage', where subaltern is accommodated in order to create new spaces of negotiated peace. If subaltern agency is to be sought in its workings through the governmental mechanisms of the state, it will have to be explained why the subaltern still continues, in large swathes of central India, to wage a bloody battle against the state and the corporate-driven economy, in the same breath it also needs to be explained why the subaltern is extended sympathy, by urban elites and even the media, in times of distress while face contempt in taking to protest politics.

Thus, in the passive governmental operations of the subaltern, we need to factor in the structural coercion that has now become intrinsic and endemic. Partha Chatterjee undermines much of these characteristic phenomena;

instead, in foregrounding 'what is new in quotidian', randomly, Chatterjee produces an upside-down narrative of an expanding subaltern agency, while it seems to actually be shrinking.[27] This shrinking agency gets reflected on the one hand in the withdrawal of the subaltern from active protest politics and on the other shifting their terrain of operation towards adopting survival strategies and in unprecedented spurt in intra-subaltern conflicts. Conflicts within subaltern groups have become the stuff of the 'politics of everyday life' and 'politics of the possible'; they adopt what is feasible, to that extent subalterns do make a concrete 'choice', but to argue that this is beyond 'hegemony', and represent new forms in which democracy is being practiced and celebrated, looks conjectural to the contempt for democracy and politics among the urban middle classes. Political processes thus seem to create a sense of powerlessness amongst those subaltern groups that are less mobilised, which then might eventually take more militant armed modes of protest. The story of democracy for subaltern seems to be inextricably caught between *militancy and powerlessness*. What would be the emergent nature of the relation between these variedly located social groups then forms the stuff of the relation between Maoism, democracy and globalisation.

Globalisation

Finally, the last section of this book opens up a debate on the new political dynamics that was inaugurated, especially with the emergence of a new global world. Globalisation has been scrutinised closely more in terms of its economic impact, rather than its political dynamics. While it is well documented as to how neoliberal reforms were part and parcel of current globalisation, and how they have exacerbated inequalities between the Global North and the Global South, between nations within North and South, and then between social classes within a nation (Stiglitz 2000). However, what needs to be done, especially from the point of view of the South, is to explore what kind of political possibilities the phenomenon of globalisation throws up. Does it, in any way, allow for new political momentum to abate the growing structural inequalities between the nations? What then is the equation of such political dynamics with the nature of democracy in India and with the kind of political changes, with reference to various classes—middle, backward and subaltern—that have been mapped so far?

In the final section of this book, we shall limit our exploration to two seemingly radical political possibilities that the current phase of globalisation has opened up, namely the discourse of human rights at the global level and inter-regional organisations at the regional level. These two political dynamics promise to not only moderate global inequalities and provide for avenues to realise transnational justice but also tend to offer a new political language to the marginalised social groups within the nation.

> Globalisation raises difficult questions concerning how justice must now be rethought beyond the national frame which successfully routinised shared understandings of justice as relevant only to fellow citizens. Human rights are themselves globalising as they are deployed in strategies to end human rights violations or to condemn states which resist international pressure to comply with human rights norms. ... However, at the same time, human rights also seem to stand above globalisation, to represent a framework through which globalisation itself might be regulated and global governance organised. (Nash 2009: 2)

In other words, globalisation has heightened the role of human rights in two senses, on the one hand the processes of globalisation have allowed to expand the reach of human rights across the globe, which in turn influenced the content and nature of globalisation that we are currently witnessing. The specific context, as Samuel Moyn points out, has to do with the fact that human rights have emerged as globally acceptable practices that can concretely and not merely ideologically guide the practice of nation states. In addition, they have filled in the gap created by the implosion of various ideological systems at the turn of the century. As Moyn argues,

> there is no way to reckon with the recent emergence and contemporary power of human rights without focussing on their utopian dimension: the image of another, better world of dignity and respect that underlies their appeal, even when human rights seem to be about slow and piecemeal reform. But far from being the sole idealism that has inspired faith and activism in the course of human events, human rights emerged historically as the last utopia—one that became powerful and prominent because other visions imploded. (Moyn 2010: 4)

Human rights are the new universal language that allows societies that are differently placed, in terms of economic development, political systems and cultural orientation, to speak to each other. They have allowed a complimentary and utterly essential political language to the process of economic globalisation. As Moyn rightly observes, though they took centre stage after the scepticism about meta-narratives, 'incredulity of meta-narratives', they have now come to stand for the new kind of grand vision themselves, which he refers to as the *Last Utopia*. He argues,

> Though they were born as an alternative to grand political missions—or even as a moral criticism of politics–human rights were forced to take on the grand political mission of providing a global framework for the achievement of freedom, identity and prosperity. They were forced, slowly but surely, to assume the very maximalism they triumphed by avoiding. (Moyn 2010: 9)

In Chapter 5 titled 'Politics of Global Human Rights in India' in the last section of this book, we attempt to explore the new spaces created in the political dynamics through the global human rights discourse. In turn, we ask how the various political formations in India, around caste, class and gender, transmuted the available global practices of human rights for the imperatives of the ends they wished to achieve. In what sense these new discourses interpellated the already existing democratic practices in India? With regard to the kind of exceptionalism, we pointed out earlier that the state has now made integral to its mode of governance the international human rights discourse, since the Universal Declaration of Human Rights (UDHR), and the International Covenant on Civil and Political Rights (ICCPR), has been very proactive in highlighting the need to protect the citizen against the human rights violations by the state. Various international human rights organisations, including the Amnesty International and Asia Watch, among others, have repeatedly pointed to the rise in extra-judicial killings by the Indian state, especially in handling the issues of the Maoist movement, Kashmir and the ethnic movements in the Northeast India. Independent Citizen's forums have been making the demand to declare the 'war' in central India against the Maoists as 'internal civil war', and both the Maoists and the Indian state need to abide by the provisions of the Geneva Convention, especially in relation to the issue of 'collateral damage'. At the other end of the spectrum, especially by the urban elites, there has been the growing anxiety about the constraints imposed on the state by the imperatives of rule of law and democratic procedures in controlling the phenomenon of 'private violence' and terrorism. There has been an undeclared consensus among urban elites that Criminal Justice in India is weak, and therefore it has resulted in low conviction rate and rise in crime. It is this sentiment that gets reflected in the demand for more centralised institutions such as the Lokayukta, or demands for death penalty for rape. This sentiment also gets extended to the use of extra-judicial methods against 'Left-wing Extremism', 'Suspect Muslims', and 'Hardcore Criminals'. It is in this context that there have been attempts to change the procedural and substantive aspects of the Criminal Justice System in India. As this chapter points out, the provisions of the *Justice Malimath Committee on Criminal Justice Reforms* respond to this kind of growing sentiment among the urban elites. In this ongoing debate between these two parallel discourses of more accountability on the part of the state, and stronger laws and more conviction, international human rights discourse has served as a constant reference point.

Similarly, globalisation has opened new spaces of activism. Those social groups that have been pushed to the peripheries of social existence, as we pointed out earlier, have now turned to exploring these new global spaces. Also, the growth of new middle classes within these subaltern classes and castes that we alluded to before has allowed them to intervene in the emerging global debates and frame the questions of marginalisation through novel discourses and politics. One such very glaring example is that of the demand by the Dalit organisations in India that caste be equated with race. In the 'Caste is Race' debate, it has been demanded that the provisions of Convention for Elimination of All Forms of Racial Discrimination (CERD) be made applicable to caste-based discriminations. These groups have also sought to forge new alliances with groups pursuing similar politics, such as the Black movement, in other continents. The Indian state has resisted these moves, as we shall discuss in the chapter on global human rights, since it believes that they might erode its sovereignty and therefore they need to be treated as issues internal to India, and cannot be discussed on international forums.[28] The visible tension seems to be one between consequences of economic globalisation and anxiety of political sovereignty.[29]

Thus, whereas the various militant movements are challenging state sovereignty through their armed struggles, the other marginalised groups, such as the Dalits, have taken the route of contesting sovereignty by framing issues and accessing international human rights law and institutions. As Partha Chatterjee rightly points out,

> There are indeed territories and peoples in India that may be described as challenging the Indian state's sovereignty over them: the insurgent movements in Kashmir are a clear example, as are the periodic insurgencies in some of the north-eastern states. The continued insurgency that has simmered in the forest regions of central India since the 1970s also has, at least in the recent phase of the Maoist-led war on the Indian state, the characteristic of a contest over sovereignty. (Chatterjee 2012: 47)

So now the Dalit movement has joined the contest, through the international human rights provisions. This, yet again, is a new kind of convergence that is emerging, in the context of the current phase of globalisation, moving towards post-Westphalian modes of justice. However, nation states are still not willing to concede erosion of political sovereignty, even if much of the economy has been deregulated.

Finally, this chapter points towards the new dynamics that exist between the global and local even if they are not consciously articulated by the political movements. The discourse/philosophy around indivisibility of rights—between civil/political and social/economic—that has been at the core of human rights, since the days of the UDHR, has been reinvigorated by the more contemporary articulations such as the Right to Development. The declaration on Right to Development lays thrust on the fact that development cannot be envisaged merely through growth rates and GDP; instead it needs to take into account the expansion of civil and political freedoms and how they are in turn dependent on social and economic rights. In essence, one cannot be achieved without the other. It is this emphasis on indivisibility that is visible not in the policy frame of the state but that of the political movements. This chapter explores the women's movement for prohibition of liquor and argues how at the core of the movement was the emphasis as to how political, legal, social, cultural and economic dimensions are closely interlinked, in order to ameliorate the position that there is a need to advance on all these fronts. Thus, global debates have resonance at the local level, and globalisation has made it possible for us to realise that these are not two separate domains. This, in effect, is further realised through the other major political current of globalisation, forging new regional organisations.

The last chapter of this book titled 'Globalisation and Regionalisation: Mapping the New Continental Drift' focuses on the emerging new regionalism. Globalisation has itself initiated a process of regionalisation. The process of formation of regional organisations has had an interesting trajectory of beginning with organisations between the North and the South, from there it moved towards new organisations being forged within the various continents of the global South, and the current phase of regionalism is witnessing a new regionalism of organisations between countries of different continents of the global South, from intra-continental to inter-continental. In this chapter, we attempt to understand this phenomenon of new regionalism across Asia, Africa and Latin America and what are the new avenues that open up for India at the global level, and its impact on the some of the political currents we have discussed so far.

New regionalism has emerged in light of the new-found economic status and political space for the 'developing' countries. The phenomenon of regionalism paradoxically is itself the result of the current phase of globalisation. The issue that centrally concerns us here and which links up to the processes of democracy and militant modes of protest is the growing economic inequalities between nations and between social classes within the nation. In other words, whether or not the neoliberal model of development that in many ways runs counter to the spirit of the newly de-colonised nations that was part of the vision of New International Economic Order (NIEO), which was envisaged as part of Non-Aligned Movement (NAM) in the 1970s, is being questioned through the new regional organisations. How do issues of global poverty, climate change, human rights violations, illiteracy and unemployment, among many others figure in the deliberations of the new regional organisations? Finally, will they therefore have a positive impact on the expansion of democratic practices within the nations by allowing for wider participatory frame and moderate the various kinds of militant struggles and violence (including in many countries of Africa and Latin America) by addressing issues of economic inequality?[30]

The development momentum has shifted in the last decade or so to the developing countries of the South, including India, Brazil, South Africa and China. This has brought to the fore various socio-economic inequalities between nations that can be corrected through 'alternative regionalism'. The focus has shifted from the North–South relations to the inter-relations between various nations of the South. This has also led to a growing comparison between the nations of the South; the most glaring among these has been that between India and China. This comparison has raised questions regarding how to develop more sustainable economies, whether a nation needs to have a strong manufacturing or industrial capital like China does or it is sufficient to get integrated into the global market through the expansion of service sector and financial capital like India does. Similarly, there has been public debate regarding India having an advantage because of its 'demographic dividend', where more than 65 per cent of its population is less than the age of 35 years.[31] However, it remains a fact that this 'demographic dividend' can become a 'demographic disaster' if India fails to provide employment opportunities, skill upgradation, literacy and basic health facilities to this young population. It might lead to a 'reserve army of labour force' and growing 'disguised unemployment', adding to the already existing staggering poverty figures in India.

> There is nothing inherent in demographic patterns that guarantees economic success: whether a certain set of preconditions eventuates into socially widespread and meaningful growth depends, as always, on state policies that prioritise human capital (the health and education of its citizenry); on efficient state and political party institutions to deliver these programmes to the people; and on the ability to insulate these programmes from being hijacked by elites and middlemen. (Krishna 2013)

In this context, it is being debated that labour policy has to be integrated, on the one hand, nationally with policies related to fiscal, industry and technology and, on the other hand, globally with trade and regional integration. Without this new frame, it could lead to lopsided development, which could result in both internal distress migration and illegal migration across the borders. For instance, economists have observed that in India bulk of growth and economic initiatives are concentrated in the west and the south, leaving behind regions of the north that has huge population growth. This has resulted in large-scale migration to western parts, into states like Maharashtra; this has also led to the emergence of backward regions such as Vidharbha in the west and Telangana in the south.[32] In essence, this new-found growth story might not necessarily translate into better living conditions for the majority of its people.

There is probably no other example in the history of world development of an economy growing so fast for so long with such limited results in terms of broad-based social progress. Sen and Dreze were referring to the fact that for about 32 years now (since 1980), India has averaged annual GDP growth rates of approximately six per cent—whereas, the nation's ranking in terms of the Human Development Index has remained unchanged over that period: we were ranked an abysmal 134 in 1980, we were ranked exactly that in 2011. (Krishna 2013)[33]

It is therefore not merely about achieving growth but also about the nature of development that is aimed for. It has always remained debatable whether corporate economy generates sufficient employment, and the model of 'crony capitalism' that India has adopted is the reason behind growth not translating into better human development. In this context, the FDI led growth has failed to generate consensus in Indian politics.[34] Recent controversy regarding FDI in retail sector opened up debate on some of the adverse impacts it might create. Interestingly, the fault line was drawn between a corporate-driven central government and local economy being protected by the regional parties in the states. Almost all the important regional parties remained opposed to the entry of FDI into the retail sector—maintaining their support in the era of coalition politics was often referred to by the ruling Congress party as dealing with the 'constraints of democracy' in managing the economy—highlighting an interesting conflict, so to say, between democracy and globalisation.[35]

Further, the model of 'crony capitalism' has also led Indian economy to a large-scale export of raw materials to the developed countries of the North. This has resulted in unprecedented mining of raw materials such as iron ore, bauxite and mica, among many others through various MNCs. This in turn has had consequences for tribals living in these mineral-rich areas of central India, including Chhattisgarh and Odisha, among other parts of the country, 'where natural resources are being over-mined for the benefit of the few and at the cost of the local people and the environment' (*Economic and Political Weekly*, Editorial, 2012: 8).[36] Not only has it led to the wide-scale displacement of the tribals but also concerns regarding the adverse impact on ecology of these regions. This crisis is reflected in the ongoing protests against the Korean company POSCO in Odisha, which constitutes 'the biggest foreign investment ever in India', yet the project has been in limbo for more than six years now. In 2005, the central government commissioned the Hoda Committee on Mining reforms, 'which laid the ground for India's National Mineral Policy, 2008 and the MMDR Bill'. However, the focus of policy making and legal reform has been more on economic development rather than social justice, for those affected by these projects. The preamble of the National Mineral Policy is silent on issues of social justice; it instead focuses on the role played by the mining industry in the country's economic development as a provider of 'vital raw materials for infrastructure, capital goods and basic industries. The policy does address environmental and displacement issues … but the primary focus of the document seems to be economic development' (Maddox et al. 2012: 77). Policy provisions have only acknowledged the need to pay compensation but not provide terms of reference for employment or share in ownership through equity participation. It is in these regions and around these issues that, as we pointed out earlier, the Maoists have been mobilising the tribals against the MoUs signed by state governments of Chhattisgarh, Odisha and the rest of the 'Red Corridor'; the state and central governments have governed as a response to the protests through an exceptionalism represented by 'Operation Green Hunt', bringing into relief, so to say, the conflict between the Maoists and globalisation.[37]

It is in this context of the conflict between democracy and globalisation on the one hand and the Maoism and globalisation on the other that the last chapter of this book raises the question as to whether or not the 'alternative regionalism' between the countries of the South offers a paradigm shift. Can it offer resistance to the neoliberal order and promote social welfare with human development as its central concern? The final chapter attempts to trace the basics of how to conceptualise alternative globalisation and models of development and in light of that maps the history of regionalism in Asia, Africa and Latin America. It traces the history of African Union (AU) and New Partnership of Africa's Development (NEPAD) in Africa, South Asian Association for Regional Cooperation (SAARC) and Association of Southeast Asian Nations (ASEAN) in Asia, and MERCOSUR and ALBA in Latin America. In comparing the regional organisations within the three continents of the South, it argues that regionalism in Africa is primarily being driven by the global governance paradigm offered by international financial institutions such as the IMF and the World Bank; regionalism in Asia continues to suffer from cultural entrapments and political conflicts, even if it has managed to, as a rhetoric, live by the spirit of NAM; finally, it is the ongoing experiment in Latin America, instantiated primarily in forging a Bolivarian alternative for the Americas that offers an alternative paradigm in keeping human development as its central focus. The chapter concludes by looking at the policy frame and role India is playing in the emerging inter-continental regionalism that is initiated by the formation of the Brazil–Russia–India–China–South Africa (BRICS) and India–Brazil–South Africa (IBSA) groups.

BRICS in its recent 'Delhi Declaration', following the Latin American experiment, also attempts to set up a new 'development bank'.

> On the economic front, the one measure of some significance, though hardly a challenge to existing structures of global economic governance, was an agreement on intra-BRICS credit provision in local currencies for promoting intra-BRICS trade. There would be greater inter-bank cooperation as well as facilitation of more cooperation in capital markets, financial services, treasury transactions, stock exchange investments and the issuance of local currency bonds according to national laws, that is, minimising transaction costs in intra-BRICS economic activities. (Vanaik 2013)[38]

While these groups are shifting the initiative towards the countries of the South, if they fail to step outside the existing international order, then the ensuing conflict between democracy, globalisation and militant movements led by the Maoists in the countryside is bound to sharpen.

To conclude, various political patterns have pulled the society in different directions and remain disconnected. This is marked by a growing generalisation of exceptionalism as part of governing democracy, which includes an unprecedented rise of violence by the state and those countering it, which is in turn structurally linked to the functioning of a representative democracy, even as there is a visible expansion of neo-welfare policies; growing clout of the urban middle class has taken democratic forms of street protest politics, even as they have demonstrated contempt for democracy and the avocation of politics itself; mobility of lower castes that have come to constitute the new middle classes is marked by new modes of access to public sphere and overcoming caste-based stigma with the possible expansion of affirmative action policies for newer social groups, even as there is an increasing possibility of these social groups moving towards a right-wing-oriented Hindutva politics on the one hand, and militant modes of mobilisation by the Maoists remaining disconnected from the new modes of mobility, on the other; shrinking of subaltern agency marked by their displacement from traditional forms of protest politics, accompanied by the emergent phenomenon of growing intra-subaltern conflicts at one end, and a negative dialectic of increasing representation in democracy leading to a less responsive state, and 'neoliberalisation of politics', at the other; emergence of global neoliberal order and corporatisation aided by a new 'global imperial state' that have constrained the emergent forms of 'alternative regionalism', even as global human rights has remained the 'Last Utopia' for various political movements to continue to articulate radical democratic agendas—stressing on the aspect of indivisibility of rights—at international forums through global human rights conventions, chipping at the claims to sovereignty by the nation state.

Endnotes

1. I have elsewhere referred to this as the 'logic of circularity' (refer to Gudavarthy 2013a).
2. Economists have repeatedly suggested that the only option for improving India's BOP crisis is to have more FDI; they argue that 'growing external imbalances can be resolved by various reform measures and by 'stepping up non-debt creating inflows, especially in the form of FDI' (Shetty 2012: 84).
3. Kalyan Sanyal in his book *Rethinking Capitalist Development* has, in effect, argued that the process of primitive accumulation in India is different from that of Europe because the excesses of dispossession and displacement are moderated by the imperatives of representative democracy, wherein the state is bound by the pulls of legitimacy in extending its governmental machinery in implementing far-reaching welfare policies such as the MGNREGA, Food Security Bill, among others.
4. It is estimated that in Rowghat Hills in Chhattisgarh, where the Maoists have the most powerful presence, there are iron ore deposits worth 731.93 million tonnes; however, Chhattisgarh continues to suffer with the worst human development in India, due to the abject neglect of tribals.
5. These figures have been questioned by other reports. Some have put the figures at 119 districts in 20 states, based on the operations of Maoist front organisations. Districts are classified into two categories—'affected' and 'under left-wing extremist influence'—based on the extent of violence (refer to Reddy 2012).
6. The report by the civil rights groups also points out that 'a total force of roughly 13–16,000 is currently deployed to fight naxalism in a district [Dantewada in Chhattisgarh] with a total population of merely 7.2 lakhs (2001 census);

in other words, forces to people ratio of 1:45!' (PUDR et al. 2006: 33). It was also as part of this strategy that former DGP of Punjab K.P.S. Gill was appointed as a special security adviser between 2008 and 2010, based on his track record in quelling the 'terrorist' upsurge in Punjab.

7. There were many other significant fact-finding teams that visited Chhattisgarh during this period when Salwa Judum was at its height, between 2004 and 2010. However, the activists of Salwa Judum did not spare even these teams from their attacks, with support from state police, which highlights that constitutional protection is not guaranteed to those who wish to step outside the 'legal activity' as understood by the state and forces supported by it. For instance, another fact-finding team that called itself Independent Citizen's Initiative (ICI) was disallowed to investigate and find details about the 'ground situation in Dantewada'; it reported that 'it is critical to note that the movement of the Citizen's Initiative was physically curtailed through acts of violence and threats of further violence by Salwa Judum activists. ... This was a regrettable omission, especially since the numbers with the Maoists appear to be increasing rather than decreasing after the Salwa Judum and it is important to understand why' (ICI 2006: 7).

8. If it is a question of mere scale of violence, according to official sources themselves, the Maoist Party since it started its armed struggle in the 1980s initially as the People's War Group (PWG), it has not killed more than 3,000–4,000 individuals. These killings took place within a week during the anti-Sikh riots in Delhi in 1984 and the 2002 riots against Muslims in Gujarat.

9. 'The Maoist organisational structure has at the base the smallest 'two-man' village unit and then area secretary and area commander. The sub-zonal committee is overseen by the zonal committee and zonal commander. There is a people's Revolutionary Committee called the 'Janatana Sarkar' elected by a cluster of three to five villages. Maoists have regional bureaus which send representatives to the central committee and highest being the politbureau. The Maoists have their armed militia, the special guerrilla squads- 'dalam' and the People's Liberation Guerrilla Army (PLGA), with strength of 50,000 militia men and 10,000 PLGA members. The Maoists have an unofficial body called the 'Sangham' in the villages to check events in the villages (Chenoy and Chenoy 2010: 60).

10. A report of the People's Union for Democratic Rights (PUDR) (January 1992) investigated the 'encounter' death of Ghulam Rasool, who was then working as a journalist with the popular Telugu daily *Udayam*. 'Among the more well-known of his stories were ... police harassment of villagers in his area, misuse of TADA, role of police in the land grabbing and eviction of slum-dwellers in NTR Nagar in the city. In the latter story Rajaiah, DSP of Saroornagar was named' (PUDR 1992: 1). This investigation, in effect, led to the 'fake encounter' killing of Ghulam Rasool, and the police claimed that 'Rasool was involved

in the extortion of money on behalf of Naxalites, was a member of the armed squad of the CPI (People's War Group) and was involved in a murder case' (PUDR 1992: 1). Such claims by now had become routine in the 'Maoist-affected states'.

11. After the alleged encounter of Ishrat Jahan in 2004 in Gujarat, the case was being pursued by the CBI. The Gujarat High Court on May 10 warned the Gujarat Government for shielding the police officers involved in the encounter. Justice Patel stated that 'It has come on record that some officers of state government are obstructing the investigation' (*Indian Express*, 11 May 2013). Similarly, a case has been filed by Zakia Jaffrey, whose husband Ehsan Jaffrey, a former MP, was also killed during the 2002 riots in Gujarat. This case directly implicates Narendra Modi as an accused.

12. Refer to the report titled 'Framed, Damned, Acquitted', brought out by the Jamia Teachers' Solidarity Association (JTSA) on the Batla House 'encounter'. It can be accessed at www.teachersolidarity.org.

13. Much of the Northeast India is considered a 'disturbed area'. The strategies are pretty much similar to the ones we have been discussing. Another independent citizen's fact-finding report explains a similar kind of 'righteous lawlessness'. The report states, 'The DGP confirmed over 260 people have been killed since January 2009 and affirmed that all of them were underground militants/ activists/insurgents'. The state in Manipur does not recognise any such thing as 'extra-judicial killing'. According to the DGP, there had not been a single proven case of this. He said that they had fool-proof hundred per cent evidence that those who were killed were members of the underground; none of them was innocent. However, his contention left unanswered why they could not instead be arrested and faced with trial. The IG prisons, in the context of combating insurgency in the state, stated, 'When a surgical operation takes place, there must be pain' (Independent Citizen's Fact-Finding Report to the Nation 2009: 19). There have been umpteen numbers of fact-finding teams of the civil rights organisation looking into the situation in the Northeast India, rallying around a demand to repeal Armed Forces Special Powers Act (AFSPA). This demand took a sharp turn after 'Thangjam Manorama was picked up from her home in Imphal at night [July 11, 2004]. She was tortured, raped and her corpse abandoned in a deserted stretch of the highway the next morning' (Committee for the Repeal of the Armed Forces Special Powers Act 2005: 1). Irom Sharmila, a political activist, has been on hunger strike for the last decade (being force fed by the officials of the state) demanding the repeal of AFSPA, given the grave nature of human rights violations it aided. More recently, the Chief Minister of Jammu and Kashmir, Omar Abdullah, himself has demanded its repeal by the central government.

14. The report by the Asian Centre for Human Rights (ACHR) titled 'RTI Activists: Sitting Ducks of India' stated that 'from January 2010 to August 2011, at least 12 activists including Masood were killed for seeking information to "promote transparency and accountability in the working of every public

authority" in India' (available at www.achrweb.org/ihrrq/issue3-4/India-Sitting-Ducks-2011.pdf [accessed on 12 January 2013]). Finally, it was the killing of RTI activist Shela Masood that led to a furore and demand for special legislation for the protection of RTI activists.

15. *Indian Express* reported, 'Twenty nine RTI activists have been allegedly killed since May 2008, and around 164 cases of assault and harassment of RTI activists have been registered across India'. These killings have in fact led to promulgation of the Whistle-blower Bill, which is yet to be cleared by the Rajya Sabha despite being passed by Lok Sabha in 2011 (Mallikarjuna 2013).

16. It is often argued by various political activists that while 'Islamic terrorism' was a bogey to arrest those associated with various kinds of protest politics for the NDA regime, 'Maoism as a security threat' is the bogey for the UPA-I, and conflating the two—terrorism and Maoism—the strategy of UPA-II.

17. Under Section 124(A), Sedition was introduced by the British Government in 1870. Some of the famous trials under this provision included those against Balangadhar Tilak, Gandhi, more recently Dr Binayan Sen, an activist of the People's Union for Civil Liberties (PUCL) and Arundhati Roy in 2010, for speaking against the human rights violations in Kashmir.

18. Prevention of Terrorism Act (POTA) was repealed in 2004. For an extensive debate on the ACT and its consequences, refer to Singh 2007.

19. The Assembly elections of Karnataka in May 2013 attracted a record 70 per cent of voter turnout.

20. It is significant to observe that Irom Sharmila had to appear before the Court as she was framed for 'attempt to suicide', while the Supreme Court cleared the Kudankulam nuclear reactor in a Judgement made on 7 May 2013.

21. It is therefore not surprising that those protesting against rape and sexual violence or against graft are also the same social groups who have celebrated the rise of Narendra Modi in Gujarat, who was himself held responsible for pogrom against minority community. Our survey, presented in the second chapter, clearly shows this trend of those who were active with the anti-graft movement in Delhi. They showed considerable admiration for Modi and T.N. Seshan, apart from Anna Hazare himself endorsing the 'Modi brand' of development.

22. In fact, in much of the media, looking for a reasoning for movements such as the Maoist or the discontent in Kashmir is itself a justification, and therefore anti-national and anti-social. It is however duly recognised as 'politicisation' of the issue. These codes insidiously also dictate how law itself works or does not work, providing public justification for slapping cases of sedition and carrying out fake encounters.

23. For instance, the IT talk is always more than the real contribution of the IT sector in terms of creating jobs, or the salary structure and work conditions that are invariably modest, in comparison to the rhetoric of the high pay structure in the private sector. The fact that Gujarat has always been relatively developed, and in fact has gone down in the human index, is difficult to establish given the context of massive demonstrative propaganda of the state.

24. Recently, in May 2013, the former Chief Minister of Punjab, Amarinder Singh, demanded that the Jat community should get reservations as OBCs. He said: 'the educated youth belonging to the community were not finding jobs, and as a result getting trapped in various social evils like drug addiction' (http://www.firstpost.com/politics/jat-community-should-get-reservation-under-obc-says-amarinder-singh-775729.html [accessed 13 May 2013]).

25. Mulayam Singh argued that 'with it (Bill) coming into effect women belonging to the affluent class would march ahead while those of the poor sections would be further pushed behind'. The Bill, proposing 33 per cent reservation for women in the Lok Sabha and State Assemblies, was passed by the Rajya Sabha in 2010. SP, RJD and JD(U) are opposed to the bill (http://post.jagran.com/Women-Reservation-Bill-to-cater-affluent-class-Mulayam-1352388492 [accessed 20 January 2013]).

26. For an elaborate discussion on how the politics of recognition have panned out in the Indian context, refer to Gudavarthy 2013a. Here, I have tried to argue how the Dalits have been stigmatised by the practices of civil society, in offering them space for caste-based mobilisation, on the one hand, and how these very processes have been stigmatised for being 'sectarian', on the other.

27. More elaborate version of some of the arguments made here is discussed in the book that I edited with a set of critical essays on the concept of political society (Gudavarthy 2012a).

28. The nature of the debate is not new to India. The issue of Kashmir was also put through a similar churning between discussing the human rights violations in Kashmir, and the need to maintain it as an internal issue, especially in terms of not taking it to the United Nations, and the need to maintain it as an internal issue of India respecting its sovereignty.

29. It would not perhaps be inappropriate here to think of the possibilities of political globalisation through the discourse of human rights and economic sovereignty that allows for protection of local markets.

30. There has been a spurt of violence of various kinds in many parts of Africa, including the recent events in Congo and Rwanda. Similarly, there were large-scale deaths in Mexico (approximately 50 beheaded bodies of unidentified persons were found) involving drug mafias, along with the continued militant struggles, very much like the Maoists in India, of the Zapatistas.

31. For instance, the Union Minister of State for Human Resource Development, Daggubati Purandeshwari has emphasised on 'demographic advantage' that India has, on more than one occasion, reflecting the policy significance of this factor. Speaking at a function held in K.L.N. Memorial Polytech college at Madurai, she opined, 'India's demographic scenario will be advantageous by year 2030 since the country will have 95 crore young people by then. On the other hand, China's demographic profile would be at a disadvantage due to its aged population by that time' (*The Hindu*, 26 August 2012).

32. This was the observation made by economists Nitin Desai and Deepak Nayyar at a book release function at India International Centre on 2 April 2013.

33. Krishna, further, argues that 'In 1980, about 80 per cent of the population subsisted on less than two dollars a day, and that percentage has declined by as little as five per cent since then' (Krishna 2013). In terms of health standards India has had for a very long time the worst track record. For instance, India ranks number one in terms of first day of birth mortality; its share in global first-day deaths stands at 29 per cent. The next in the list is Nigeria, which is a distant second with only 9 per cent of global deaths. Bangladesh has one the lowest first-day deaths at 28,000, with less than 3 per cent of Global share.

34. While there is near consensus within national parties on economic reforms, it is the regional parties that are contesting global capital flows, opening up new possibilities such as the 'Third Front' experiment in upcoming general elections. For a more detailed analysis, refer to Gudavarthy 2013c.

35. Parties such as TMC in West Bengal, TDP in Andhra Pradesh, Samajwadi party in Uttar Pradesh, among many others vehemently opposed the entry of FDI in retail sector, finally pushing the national party BJP to follow suit. Instead, it needs to be debated how to strengthen small and medium enterprises, which did not happen. It is interesting to observe the conflict between federalisation of the polity as against the globalisation of the economy.

36. The Editorial in *Economic and Political Weekly* (EPW) noted that Justice M.B. Shah Commission report on illegal iron ore mining in Goa had identified the loss to the state revenues to the tune of 35,000 crores between 2006 and 2011, along with 'irretrievable' damage to the ecologically fragile zones. The story is very similar with regard to the mining of Bauxite in Chhattisgarh and Odisha, iron ore in Karnataka and Andhra Pradesh, among other states. This is being carried out with a nexus between the mining lobby, political and bureaucratic classes.

37. It is important here to observe that while conflict over FDI splits centre and state, conflict against the Maoists in favour of global capital and MNCs brings them together within a single policy-frame. There is certain 'globalisation of language' that is visible in negotiating with the Maoists, making them comparable to global terrorism. The media often referred to them as 'Red Terrorism' or 'Talibanisation', or protests in Manesar by workers were referred to as 'industrial terrorism'. This is part of the language of 'global war on terrorism' not only against Islamist militants, but also against those protesting against various modalities of global governance. For instance, Joe Biden refers to Assange of Wikileaks as 'high-tech terrorist'. In opposition to this radical economists such as Amit Bhadhuri have referred to the new development model as 'developmental terrorism', or left groups have referred to state violence as 'state terrorism'. More on this is given in the Chapter 5 on human rights.

38. Fourth summit of BRICS took place in New Delhi on 29 March 2012, followed by the recent summit in Durban in March 2013.

Maoism

1

Democracy against Maoism, Maoism against Itself

Maoist movement in India is as intriguing as it is predictable. It is intriguing for the way it seems to so resolutely mark itself against the current spirit of our times that favour localised protest, unorganised, autonomous and leaderless struggles against dominant and received notions of representative democracy; and for its clarity of purpose with a definitive focus on what needs to be achieved for the 'basic classes' and for doggedly questioning some of the very 'fundamental' aspects of power. But it has also in so many ways remained unchanged, its ideas look fairly rehearsed and repetitive, and its strategies have set in a degree of ennui.

It is always difficult to reflect on a movement that defines itself in such clear and categorical terms that there is always the possibility of one's reflection going beyond the parameters the movement has set itself. The issues on which one wishes to engage them could well be beyond their immediate concerns. The strategy of armed insurrection—based on Mao's strategy of 'surround the cities'—is so well defined that its interrogation in a proper sense looks possible only after its goals are realised. A critique that is based on prompting, with good reasons, the limitations could always be brushed aside as a mere intellectual activity or way too abstract for the movement to be so privileged to take them up here and now. Thus, the movement's belief that practice—as in political action—alone can guide, though Lenin had in so many words declared that 'there cannot be revolutionary practice without revolutionary theory'.

The challenge for intellectual activity really is to frame questions that have relevance in their immediate practice that can translate into what those in practice can be convinced or seen as being of some 'use-value'. The gloss that generally accompanies an intellectual activity for itself is looked upon contemptuously, even if it has a value for exploring the 'not-yet-known' dimensions of the very materiality in which politics find their vocation. The onus here, unlike what we generally believe, is on those offering the analysis, and not on those for whom we seem to offer our analysis. The movement and its politics refuse to be a passive subject matter, and therefore it is with some trepidation that one needs to take up this exercise of writing and reflecting on the Maoist movement and its rather enigmatic understanding of a theory of politics. It is within its own set of terms that one needs to disturb some of its settled and self-assured understanding of the project of revolution. Critical engagement needs to mirror their practice to allow them to appreciate the political nuances.

The Maoist movement has, in a sense, remained at one end of the political spectrum in questioning the nature of democracy in India. It has raised questions, without circumventing the most brutal aspect of state power—its monopoly over the use of physical violence. It does not either postpone this issue for posterity to take up nor does it believe that it would get resolved on its own as many who are otherwise critical of anything 'automatically' changing believe when it comes to the issue of state repression. It rather begins with this question, and in that it actualises the class perspective, which is at the core of self-defining itself. In beginning with this rather condensed political question, the Maoist movement has perhaps in its own way opened up spaces for political mobilisation keeping the state and capital at bay (Myrdal 2012). This has its own political impact, even if in strangely less tangible ways, in practicing democracy. If the movement has succeeded in stalling the actualisation of a series of Memoranda of Understanding (MoUs) in Chhattisgarh, and held to ransom the state and the corporates from making any inroads, it cannot be without any impact on the content of democracy and democratisation.[1] This violent yet intangible dimension of democratic practice has a certain difficulty in finding for itself an appropriate political language to make a case for itself, as against the 'high politics' in representative democracy. Class war, as it closes certain known ways of pursuing democracy, also opens certain other routes of pursuing the same paths in exposing the convergence between the state in a democracy and the capital under globalisation. While movements that are local, autonomous, non-violent and open could well be defining the spirit of the way we understand democracy today, the forms adopted by Maoists contribute to democracy—as in democratisation—in their own set ways. While many a criticism of such a centralised movement is absolutely essential as a caution against its possible rigidification, there is perhaps also a need to critically analyse why non-violent and dispersed movements often led by the NGOs fail to stall the red-carpet walk of the corporates. The state works itself in many ways; the Maoist movement in stalling the corporatisation of the economy is also blocking the statisation of democracy (Pandita 2011). The near convergence between the state, market and civil society can construct spaces that work 'as if' they were democratic.[2] In seeing and beginning with the convergence, the militant forms adopted might look undemocratic—essentially for those in civil society—but in intangible ways might be contributing to the democratisation of social spaces and relations. It is not in questioning the militant methods but in questioning what is happening in those less structured and politically tenuous spaces that open due to the very 'deployment' of such militant methods by the Maoist movement that one can, and one should, engage the Maoists. Any engagement needs to make this rather unencumbered distinction. It is quite possible that Maoists could still remain non-dialogic in mistaking it for being uncompromising, as in democracy we mistake naivety for simplicity (what better example than Anna Hazare that we focus on in the next chapter). While democracy is increasingly turning against Maoists, they could turn against the very spaces their politics potentially create. How do they then create new spaces by negotiating centralised structures, yet do not centralise themselves and allow for diverse voices, remains the most crucial question, and it is this issue that we shall attempt to explore here.

The Maoist movement has questioned the legitimacy of the state where it matters the most, in questioning the legitimacy of the state's monopoly over the use of violence, to control, govern and maintain order. Azad (long-time spokesperson of the Maoist party in India) reflecting on this issue has concluded that

> thus, the question of how you look at violence is coloured with a class bias. The violence by the ruling class parties is considered legitimate while those by the oppressed masses and their organisations are dangerous and a threat to the security of the rulers. This has been true right from the time of Charvakas. (Azad 2010: 102)

He asks a simple but formidable question to those who have a problem with using violent means to counter the power of the state: 'what answers do the writers (in the EPW special issue on the Maoist movement in India) have to put an end to such endemic state violence on different sections of the struggling people? How should these people organise to improve their lives? How should they fight back?' (Azad 2010: 2).[3] This is really a tough question to begin, since it makes one realise that at the rock bottom of all political questions is the issue of physical violence. From the most complex and abstract of issues of power to the most simple and banal issues of everyday conflicts they are haunted by the prospect and possibility of breaking into physical violence. In that state and capital have come down with brute force, without hesitation and with impunity. This remains essentially a question that draws equivalence between various dominant structures—from local to the global.

Even the most ardent of anarchists, autonomists, those reposing faith in civil disobedience, and critiques of modernity, do not have a definitive answer for this. They either circumvent the question, do not want to begin with this question, or offer solutions that yield no results—Deleuze and Gauttari talk of 'lines of flight', Holloway speaks of 'proliferation of multiplicity' and 'community gardens' or anarchists like John Zerzan argues:

> [F]or me, words are a better weapon to bring down the system than a gun would. This is to say *nothing* about anybody else's choice of weapon, only my own. So that's why I do what I do'—'right now I am Ok with my form of resistance, which is through a cultural critique. (Zerzan 2000)

There are contexts that have no easy alternatives. We cannot have a state with police, army and prisons and expect it not to use them—30 years of strident human rights activism in India has failed to put an end to 'fake encounter killings'. The state today not only violates the law but would also want its subjects to understand in no unclear terms that law is indeed being violated—fear cannot be but generated through lawlessness. This is an 'exceptionalism' of a different kind from what Agamben or Carl Schimdt have come to conceptualise, where what it wishes to re-impose is not the norm but to generalise normlessness itself. Sovereign power is sought in the wilful and abject use of state power without norms. Normlessness is the only way state power actualises itself. In other words, in the regions where Maoists have hold, *normlessness is state power*. State power is marked and identified by the extent to which it can create lawlessness—law here has only an 'absent presence'.[4] Further, the state itself intends that 'citizens' should comprehend that lawlessness is not an 'exception' but is the only way it knows how to govern. In other words, the state does not seek to legitimise its lawlessness as an exception but seeks to demonstrate its capacity to be lawless without seeking legitimacy. In not seeking legitimacy, 'exceptionalism' becomes real and comes to have its intended effects. It is no longer a condition where 'state of exception appears as a threshold of indeterminacy between democracy and absolutism' (Agamben 2005: 3). On the contrary, the state itself intends to be understood as 'absolutist', and this absolutism is beyond the imperatives of legitimacy and democracy—the political obligation of the citizen to remind the state of its absolutism is already taken over by the state. It is a state that is immune to both real and perceived 'crisis of legitimacy'. This is more than sufficiently demonstrated not only in the number of extra-judicial killings that state indulges in but also the sheer brutality of these, in order to make the point that challenging the sovereign rule of the state in any manner legitimises taking resort to 'righteous lawlessness'. Among many other such killings, the more recent of them includes the brutal torture and killing of a popular Maoist leader Kishenji, who had played an important role in building resistance, in West Bengal, against wanton land grab by the state and displacement of the peasantry. He had, by what could be perceived, a fair degree of popularity following the local areas of Singur and Nandigram. He, as the Maoist party has claimed, was 'captured', put to third-degree torture and was later announced as a death in a fierce encounter that took place between the paramilitary forces and the Maoist squad. The photographs 1.1 and 1.2 clearly seem to support these claims by the Maoist party. It is this practice of absolutism beyond the imperatives of legitimacy that is at the core of the emergent violent democracy in India.

In fact, the 'crisis' of legitimacy understood in terms of democratic practice is seen as a modality—a precondition—through which absolutism is actualised. This is somewhat akin to capitalism today, which expands not bereft of crisis—in growth and development—but precisely because of crisis. It is crisis that compels us, not to resist but hold on to the system to survive, because we need to survive to protest. Although the protestors of the Occupy movement declared 'Capitalism is Crisis', it could well be read the other way round as 'Crisis is Capitalism'. Beyond a level of distress the subaltern resists protest, and state and capital understand this better than before and can therefore fine-tune their methods, as and when it is required doing so.[5] New modes of governance have allowed rulers this kind of transparency: 'Thus Salwa Judum was formally launched on 5 June 2005, the very day Chhattisgarh government signed an MoU with Tata

Photograph 1.1:
Kishenji wearing the party uniform

Disclaimer: This photograph first appeared on the cover of Kishenji Yadilo published under Erra Nakshtram Publications by Varavara Rao. Published with due permission.

Steel. Coincidence?' (PUDR 2008: 6).[6] Thus, capital has come a full circle where it does not 'dig its own grave' in creating a crisis but constructs trenches for itself *in* and *as* crisis.

Crisis does not expose capitalism but condenses it, makes its growth indispensable and thereby invites compromise, accommodation, and further governance and governmentality—it invites 'passive revolution' (Kaviraj 1988). Crisis is so all-pervasive that alternatives look untenable, unrealistic and, of course, utopian. But this is part of the very materiality of the politics that is 'historically constituted' (Carlos 1996). Going beyond

Photograph 1.2:

Kishenji's body inside the mortuary. Seen here are torture marks, while police claimed he was killed in an encounter.

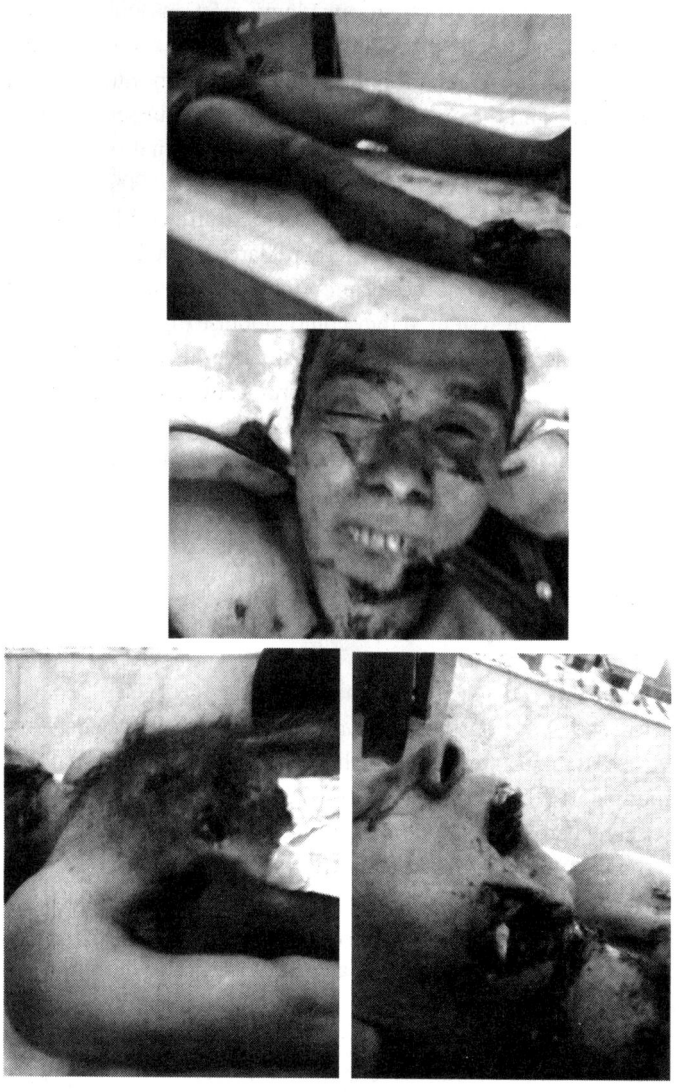

Disclaimer: A team of activists was present at the mortuary when the body of Kishenji was shifted to his native place. This photograph has been taken inside the mortuary and is being published here with due permission. The quality of these pictures is as it appears in the source document.

cannot escape this but one needs to negotiate this reality. Negotiating it needs counter-force and counter-violence, but it is invariably accompanied by the question: how much or how long? Same questions look out of place when we ask them of state power and unprecedented encroachments of capital. Therefore the search for radical subjectivity continues in looking at the 'primitive' and the indigenous who might have missed history and have continued to live on the fringes of state and capital—the itinerant communities, tribal, adivasis, indigenous peoples (Scott 2009)—the status that was once given to the blacks, peasant of the 'third world', women and students (by New Left theorists like Herbert Marcuse 2002). Maoist movement, for one, believes that these communities continue to be the nerve centres of the current system. If they could mobilise them, then history of violent democracies can be still rewritten and neo-liberal globalisation is not irreversible. It is this storyline that is ironically unbelievable and yet predictable. Its strengths, as much as its limitations, live and breathe in the interstices of this irony—the irony about which the movement itself has little gestation and privilege to self-reflect on.

Maoists and 'Frames of War'

If there is a certain degree of inevitability in class war when democracy turns against the Maoists, the questions have to be raised elsewhere to test if the spaces that open up due to such militant resistance remain political and not militarised, and this is where Maoism can turn against itself. This is precisely where our search for the new kind of politics begins—point where the knowledge of inevitability has to be combined with the search for the novel, and not slip into reliving the inevitable to the point of becoming politically and 'ideo-logically' (as Alain Badiou puts it; refer to Badiou 2005) dependent on it. The larger challenge is to realise, amidst this grave situation, that resistance in itself does not necessarily lead to creating new forms of politics; it could well recreate the old. History, unfortunately, has repeatedly stood as witness to this, and it might be something little more than a 'petty bourgeoise' pre-occupation if one sees a crooked line between resistance and emancipation. Judith Butler observes that 'frames of war' are the 'ways of selectively carving up experience as essential to the conduct of war. Such frames do not merely reflect on the material conditions of war, but are essential to the perpetually crafted animus of that material reality' (Butler 2009: 26). This anti-politics militarisation—as frames of war—is expressed in subtle but formidable social, political and cultural practices that become integral to the way politics itself begins to be pursued. Thus, it is not—militant—class war that is the issue but the accompanying statisation and creation of imaginaries of 'war zones' that arrests politics and converts the political into the moral, and the material into the abstract—outside any historical constitution—that Maoists themselves otherwise abhor. As neo-liberalism is 'privatising the public', militant politics could statise the public. Statisation is not necessarily only about 'capture of state power', but it can be found—and founded—in places and practices one might be unsuspecting.

Within the realm of the politics, this is visible when it is often considered that one's commitment to Maoist politics should be demonstrated by 'abjuring' (the simile with the former Home Minister P. Chidambaram's fascination for this word is not to be missed) any public criticism of the movement; instead its well wishers should or can always raise criticism in close(d?) circles.[7] Contempt or suspicion of public criticism is fundamentally anti-political; imagining vibrant debates in 'close circles' without accompanying public debate is nothing short of fiction. Even if this were to be practised by the ideologues and public intellectuals of this movement, this is what construes to be political elitism, with a distinct Maoist tinge. Public criticism, of all hues—good, bad and ugly—is politicisation; to have contempt for those wishing to engage in critical terms and not through the frames of loyalty—social version of frames of war—is nothing short of germination of Etatism in its nascent form. The secrecy code, integral to state and corporate, is not very different in its replication in the contempt for public criticism.[8] One can well imagine a good Maoist to be someone who critically engages with the movement in public; public debate and course correction where needed are necessary political processes and this 'drama of history' has to be played in public. The trial and error is how politics—of 'mass line'—take shape, and not the instantiation of a non-existing 'correct line'. This cannot be realised through the way the Maoist party operates currently in offering an absolutist critique of the 'system' on one hand and putting a blanket ban on any public criticism against their politics on the other hand. This raises genuine doubts about the democratic credentials of the movement, given the route socialist and revolutionary experiments took in the past, and what, in some sense, is distinct about liberal democracies across the globe.

Secrecy and loyalty, as social practices, are close cousins of the moral language, which takes precedence over the political, as part of Maoist politics. Such moral talk cannot be differentiated in any meaningful way from moralisation. Every uncomfortable question finds a moral answer, either in foregrounding repression by the state (repression itself can be raised as a political issue, distinct from a moral issue) or alternatively in bringing into relief the tremendous sacrifice those with the movement make. Sacrifice, while inspiring in itself, does not necessarily answer political issues of power or fraternity. This in turn (e)merges with an unwritten organisational law of hierarchy between 'mass organisations' (those that work legally and in the open) and 'the party' (read-armed squads). There is no reason why 'the party' has to have a better understanding of contexts that are markedly different from the political terrain it works in. Further, such structured—disciplinarian—hierarchies perhaps have something to do with the way bulk of creative energies of Maoist movement found expression through literary forms—song, dance, poetry, short stories—rather than social and political analysis.[9] While these forms cannot be hierarchised, they do work through distinct analytical tools. While it is commendable that the movement has inspired a retinue of singers, poets, balladeers and artists, the literature that has emerged from the rank and file of the Maoist movement reproduces the popular imagination of either/or and 'us' versus 'them' that is integral to the imaginary of the 'war zones'. Japanese Marxist Philosopher Karatani further argues that literary mode emerges as a dominant form in conditions of political failure. To put it in his words,

> This sort of thinking always comes from political failure. It seems revolutionary, but underneath it lies political impotency. Similarly, during the 1960s there was no possibility to go beyond the cold war. Then people tried to go beyond it by imagination, that is, literature. This was why philosophy or any other thing had to be literature... modern literature is a product of such inversion, or the internalization of political failure. (Karatani 2012: 35)

Thus, the equivalence between secrecy–loyalty–morality/moralisation–organisational hierarchy–literary forms is the modality through which 'frames of war' reproduce themselves. We need to open up this 'structure' that emerges around or along with the strategy of an armed struggle that is essentially waged in and against the emergent violent democracy. It is important to recognise that practices internal to a violent democracy have the potential to reproduce themselves by mapping themselves unto the modes of protests that essentially begin by questioning the structure and nature of such violent democracies. Invitation for public criticism, critical engagement rather than loyalty and moralisation, new organisational culture rather than hierarchy, and political analysis and not just literary expressions need to be interrogated as the new modalities in their complex relation with 'alternative' radical politics.

The Question of United Front

Maoist movement and its leaders of late have expressed concerns about the fact that the movement is weak in plains and urban areas, and also the need for a broader united front with various other struggles, including that of the Dalits, nationalities and religious minorities. Again Azad argues that

> moreover, the problems in the advanced areas and plains and in the urban areas are of a different nature and we admit our party has not been able to address the problems of the poor living there. Thus, whatever has been achieved in a few pockets of the backward areas does not provide a wide-ranging viable alternative model by itself. A lot more has to be done to convince the people about a viable alternative model. (Azad 2010: 43)

Similarly, Kobad Gandhy is of the opinion that

> as far as India is concerned, though the Maoist movement has spread probably wider than the parliamentary communist parties, today, even after 40 years, it is mostly confined to the most backward forest areas of the country. There seems little presence in the rural plains, let alone the cities. (Gandhy 2011: 107)[10]

Now these two issues of spreading in plains and urban areas and forging united fronts are closely related issues. What are the new ideological and organisational forms necessary for such an exercise? How did Maoist movement so far respond to these imperatives? What are the causes that they locate for the absence of the movement in plains and urban areas, as much as their absence in playing any significant role in bringing various democratic and progressive political organisations unto a 'single' platform, around certain core issues that they might collectively identify? The obvious ideological problem that Maoist movement faces is the extent of changes that are necessary in its own ideological, strategic and organisational orientation, for both the above-stated agendas to fructify. There seems to be deep lack of clarity as to how far they need to go? There have been attempts in the past to forge such unity, but only to quickly retreat. For instance, on two occasions when Maoists had agreed to hold peace talks with the government, led by 'neutral' teams of public activists and intellectuals, the process began by Maoist movement itself floating parallel 'fronts' that have offered to mediate between the government and Maoist party (refer to CCC 2006).[11] There is an innate insecurity about the problem of 'diluting' their 'core focus' in becoming either part of or going along with other progressive and democratic organisations. That idea of core is invariably tested in terms of the preparedness of other movements to face state repression, and whether or not they are willing to take a principled position on armed struggle. This then is the final and the most authentic litmus test, as far as the Maoists define their relation with other political movements.

The problem of its chequered relation with other non-Maoist, non-class movements is marked by the dilemma that while on the one hand they recognise them to be democratic and progressive, on the other they have deeper problems in being part of these fronts. Where do these problems emerge from? Such an exercise undoubtedly requires new ideological orientation as much as new and creative modes of building new organisational culture. The urban organisations that are ideologically and organisationally close to the Maoists need to enjoy real and genuine autonomy from 'the party' leadership, essentially constituted by armed militants leading armed squads, for such an orientation and culture to emerge. However, what one witnesses, on the contrary, is a culture of simulation. There is no real philosophy of respecting autonomy of other struggles and organisations. This has emerged among the leaders of the Maoist movement, more so their more publicly visible ideologues and those associated with their 'mass organisations'. There is no clarity partly because Maoist movements' own 'mass organisations' do not themselves enjoy autonomy of any sort. Often, organisations operate in real terms as fronts, but 'tactically' it is denied that they are fronts. For instance, most of the civil liberties organisations have individuals exclusively with an orientation close to the Maoist movement; they are however projected as 'mass organisations' and not direct fronts. In fact, when these organisations begin to, in real terms, function as more autonomous organisations, they often witness internal splits.[12]

What does autonomy then mean in real terms? Will these organisations have the freedom to critique the Maoist movement or at least critically engage, in public and not close-door meetings, or will they have to remain silent on issues that they may differ with? For instance, the strategy of 'cover organisations' in part is due to repression but also as much due to their ideological and strategic position on how to spread the Maoist movement in plains and urban areas. Invariably, the individuals associated with the various 'mass organisations' of the Maoists are prone to simulated guerrilla warfare. Their language, including body language, and various other performative aspects resemble those of the guerrillas in armed squads. There is seldom any dialogue possible. It is not a coincidence that invariably individuals who assume important positions within these organisations are those mostly without a critical engagement to the new developments. Internal differences seldom lead to dialogue but are often evened out with disciplinary action, questioning the intention of individuals with differing perspectives. Questioning intention—or explaining political positions through intentions—as K. Balagopal had once observed, is necessary for every 'totalitarian' philosophy, since it needs to also account for that which is not visible—but how do we make a distinction between that which is invisible and that which is not present?[13] It is intriguing to observe here that the location of intention in settling political differences has parallels with the manner in which the state in democracy settles dissent through pegging on this very notion on intention in its extraordinary laws. Modern democracies and militant modes of protest converge on the centrality accrued to intention supplanting the role of dialogue and outcomes.

What is the kind of a change that is possible, without the Maoist movement feeling the danger of dilution and reformism seeping into their ranks, when they begin dialogue and forge links with political groups that are distinct not merely organisationally but also in terms of strategy and even in terms of an imagination of the alternatives? What is the new organisational culture that is necessary to allow for newer forms of 'struggle and unity' to emerge, beyond a culture of disciplinarian expulsions and splits? How do we, for instance, explain the fact that in the state of Andhra Pradesh, invariably individuals who have assumed important leadership roles in every other type of political mobilisation, including that of the Dalit struggles, sub-caste within that frame, movement for a separate state of Telangana, and independent human rights organisations, have in the past been part of the Maoist movement? This is as much a compliment to the movement as a vexed question. For instance, with regard to the ongoing struggle for the separate state of Telangana, Maoists have maintained a tactical silence, since they perceive the possibility of disallowing the legitimate demand for a separate state showing the perceived 'threat' of Maoists.

However, what is needed is not tactical silence but privileging the demand on its own terms; seeing and accepting the real possibility of achieving this demand without the need for an armed struggle; a critical engagement with the movement to include within its fold demands such as the redistribution of water resources, plight of Muslims, creation of new jobs, and so on. There are demands that can be achieved without armed struggle, as there are demands that an armed struggle alone seems to be able to achieve. While those opposing the armed tactics (de-)moralise the issue of armed methods and the violence it brings along with it, those supporting the armed methods seem to also glorify and moralise such methods. Armed struggle is only a strategy and not a moral position that needs to be glorified. Would a Maoist movement, in principle, accept the need for other forms of struggle? Would they therefore accept that armed struggle cannot achieve certain demands and is not the mode that needs to be pursued for all forms of political demands? Therefore, there can be movements better equipped to achieve certain issues outside the fold of armed tactics, and also then that support or opposition to armed methods cannot be the litmus test in deciding the degree or content of the revolutionary potential of other democratic struggles. Moralisation, as against political engagement, is yet another convergence that is becoming increasingly visible between the new dynamics in democracy with the rise of middle classes, and the entrenched practices of the Maoist movement.

What is, perhaps, most poignant about the current situation in Telangana is that the political mobilisation by the Maoists in the past has today enabled political mobilisation for a separate state—mobilisation of unprecedented kind in the post-independence history of India. How can the Maoist movement link these two moments in which struggles that have happened in the past are linked—through memory and political consciousness—to those in the present? It seems almost always that the Maoist movement provides the fillip for various struggles but dithers in either engaging with them when they take forms that are different from their own. It therefore looks like that the Maoist movement plays the role of clearing the ground and accompanying hardships in people mobilising themselves, only to retreat when it takes creative forms that are different, and even critical of armed methods. It almost looks like that Maoist movement would play this role for a long time to come and it all depends on how it reconfigures its own strategies to positively identify and align with such movements 'outside' its fold.[14]

It could also be possible, as again Balagopal in course of personal conversation had observed that when an armed movement retreats it could also make collective struggles difficult as people would have been vexed with struggle and the consequences they face in light of waging them. E.P. Thompson once remarked that struggle is not a reality or a form that subaltern adopt every morning; they like any one of us also wish to lead lives that are as passive as any other class. This again is not something that has missed Maoists completely because it was this realisation that had prompted them to accept going for 'talks' with the state, but whether they are prepared to draw more generalised political lessons from it remains a moot question. The prominent leader of the Maoists, Ramakrishna (alias Haragopal, heading North Telangana), in course of the peace talks once remarked that 'limitations of the people are the limitations of the party'; but instead of looking at them as limitations, there could well be the need to combine various forms of struggles; and there could well be the need, which is political and not merely tactical, to privilege and not merely acknowledge, other forms of non-armed struggles, other modes through which class politics need to be actualised—because class is not just a structure but needs to be made sense of also as a process'; it is not merely economic but also necessarily cultural.

Class War versus Class Politics

Class as a process, as against a 'given' structure, throws up complexity of its own kind, which could belie the restricted and reduced understanding of class as a structure. Structure is bounded but not its effects. They can spill over and create a political 'excess' that needs to be creatively re-linked as much as resignified. 'Frames of war' often nudge politics towards a reality that suits such frames. Since it requires two opposing parties, reality is constructed in such a way that the 'frames of war' look more legitimate. There is a difference, subtle but significant, between class war and class politics. The former is metaphorical in nature and can inform the latter but it cannot replace it. One is not sure if the Maoist movement makes this distinction and even if it does whether that guides its politics. For instance, Marx's famous reduction of classes into two opposing poles in the *Communist manifesto* was more in order to explain the nature of classes in the broader sense—bourgeoise and working class—and not to undermine the nature of complexity and conflict within, and not just between, these classes or to argue that politics will 'naturally' move in that direction of getting vertically split between two opposing camps. In any case, Marx's prediction about the middle classes dissolving themselves into the proletariat class was far from the target, and since Marx realised the complexities that emerge in course of pursuing class politics, as against his metaphorical use of class war, his exposition of the nature of class and state was far more complex and detailed in *18th Brumaire* and could well be the reason behind the missing pages on 'classes' in *Capital*. Maoists, however, continue to collapse one into the other, which serves well, not only to legitimise their war but to actually extend its form. To put it differently, class war becomes synonymous with armed struggle; all other forms are either tactical innovations or compromises necessary in course of the war and seldom constitute the 'war' itself.

Again, Azad believes that any offensive by the 'enemy class' will reduce the society into two polarised warring camps:

> The enemy class cannot deciminate us without deciminating the entire population in the regions we control. And if it dares to go into an all-out war of extermination of the tribal population the entire socio-political scene in India will undergo a fundamental shift and will witness a radical realignment of class forces. All peace-loving, democratic, patriotic, secular forces, all the downtrodden sections of the society will polarize into one pole while the most reactionary, anti-people, authoritarian, traitorous, jingoist counter-revolutionary forces will end up at the opposite pole. Such a polarization is bound to take place as the war advances mercenary forces attempt to turn central and eastern India into a graveyard. (Azad 2010: 49)

This mode of pursuing class politics has much to do with capture of state power through an armed insurrection. It emanates more from understanding the nature of state power and its dependence on brute force than from 'annihilating' class itself. For instance, in the Indian context we have argued all through that caste is also class, but it is not self-evident in this understanding that class then is also caste. Class politics then would get mobilised not in class terms alone but could manifest through various other political and cultural forms. It not only encompasses within itself notions of recognition, dignity and mobility, but also these notions can have different meanings or political effects in different socio-economic contexts (Sayers 2005). Therefore, the point that class understood in course of political process comes through differently from class understood as a stand-still structure is absolutely significant. For instance, Dalit movement for long has been arguing that formation of new classes within Dalit communities is the sign of mobility for Dalits, while, at the same time, the break-up into the sub-caste movement has led to a debate on 'classes within caste groups'. This is one way to argue how class mobility manifests itself, as an empowering—creation of new elites among the Dalits—and in another context as a disempowering structure. The imperatives of representative democracy have made it possible to put in place an elaborate policy frame of reservations, which has introduced a new political dynamic into caste and class structures. What type of engagement Maoists would have with such political processes of a democracy depends on how they understand class.

Maoists, however, could well argue that the structural understanding of class lends us clarity to grasp the new classes within Dalits as not emancipation of Dalits but co-option into the bourgeois democratic system through generating certain classes without actually doing away with either caste or class. There is, in principle, nothing wrong with this understanding, but that there is a historical process into which this understanding needs to be read, which is a political exercise in itself. Without this weaving, Maoist politics would either be eternally playing a catching-up game (i.e., waiting for other Dalit groups to realise this 'pure' class point of view) or have to depend on wanton use of force, as they did during the Vempenta massacre in Andhra Pradesh, where the Maoist mobilisation though based on class as the fault line ended up flaring sub-caste violence between Malas and Madigas.[15] If a structured understanding of class alone offers a guide to a neat and 'pure' class politics, then the same kind of analysis needs to be applied to the Maoist movement itself. The question that Balagopal raised, as to why do all militant struggles end up killing more of their own social base than that of the 'enemy class', needs to be answered here and now, and cannot be then given the leeway of being made sense of in terms of a revolutionary process (Balagopal 2006). In terms of a 'pure' class understanding, this phenomenon of killing the poor becomes condemnable. Or, take it the other way round, one can observe how class does not leave one, just like caste, even in death, and even if one has self-consciously overcome all privileges that come with it. At a time when the deaths of Maoist leaders and cadres almost go unnoticed except for a mandatory story of an encounter, it is intriguing to see the coverage and even if one may say outrage at the killing of Azad and the arrest of Kobad Gandhy. While *Outlook* carried a special issue condemning the killing of Azad in a fake encounter, the *Times of India* carried a detailed biopic of Kobad. This has everything to do with their class, which they perhaps left behind but it does not leave them.[16]

Class consciousness, as annihilation of caste, is more of a concrete historical question set in a specific socio-cultural context than something given. What does overcoming class as a social criterion means has to be part of the debate of class politics, 'relatively autonomous' from a class war. Again, a demand such as land reforms is not *ipso facto* a demand against class structure. Even if the party succeeds in redistributing land, it would not be able to guarantee that those benefitting from the redistributed land do not perceive land as property and themselves as the new land owners. Land redistribution can, strangely, reinforce and reify property consciousness and property fetishism and does not necessarily lead to a classless society or revolutionary consciousness. Now how do we combine the redistribution of land and ensure revolutionary consciousness is a question that needs a more historical and primarily a cultural understanding of a specific context. What values, social mores and cultural symbols of dignity structure consciousness becomes the moot question. There is nothing in the consciousness of the propertyless that makes them 'naturally' radical, as Marx believed when he gave his clarion call: 'Workers of the world unite, you have nothing to lose but your chains'. In what forms this new consciousness emanates is a question in itself, and essentially a question of class politics and not class war. While the former needs an elaborate historical time and spatial experiments, the latter needs the 'compression of spatial–temporal dimensions' and therefore might well be in a 'fundamental contradiction' with each other. As frames of war open up certain kinds of spaces, they might be closing others. How to negotiate between these two poles is a question of different order from the two-pole imaginary—bourgeoisie versus working class—of the revolution. To make alternatives look viable and in that ordering and prioritising issues can make difference to the way we conceive politics. If Maoists were to begin with some of these complexities, what difference would it make to their politics is a way too complex a question to be taken up here, but suffice to say it might involve a massive shift in the way they might pursue their agenda, including whether or not capture of state power should precede or follow this kind of an experiment. And whether or not prioritising capture of state power enables or disables the space for such experimentation might be well a relevant question to pose.

Where Is the Alternative?

When we then talk of an 'alternative model', to present democracy and development, of the Maoist politics becoming viable, we need to ask: when does the 'alternative' actually begin to become an alternative and also viable? When is the Maoist movement responding to the agenda set by the state, capital and class, and when are they actually setting an agenda for society to respond?[17] How does this alternative emerge? Is it by breaking the system by force, which it might require, or by stretching the limits of the logic of the democratic potential within the existing ideas, institutions and practices? Recent experiment by the Maoist party of taking part in the elections to the local bodies in Odisha is in that sense a welcome move, as was their willingness to be part of peace talks.[18] May be, the democratic potential in each institution needs to be exhausted before we really understand the potential of alternative radical politics. How much alternative politics can ground themselves will depend on what is left after exhausting the potential of representative bodies, current welfare policies and policy against social ills. This will require that they take existing practices and institutions more seriously than those who have thought of them and working through them. Each institution is a site in itself to experiment not merely to de-legitimise it but to grasp the possible limitations of revolutionary ideas in themselves. The challenges to the revolutionary ideas, for all we know, could be very similar to those that current institutions and practices face.[19] For instance, Maoists began by brushing aside Courts, very much as they believed parliament to be a pigsty. But there could have been well a shift in their practice in working through these institutions, to understand how they can be rebuilt into newer institutional structures.

The ideas for the new mostly lie in the old. It is not merely by de-molishing them that one learns but by arduously working through the labyrinthine terrain. Every detail needs attention, care and even respect because the target of revolution is also the site for revolutionary politics. For instance, for the student movement and teachers organisations close to the Maoist party, institutions—universities, colleges, schools—are the targets that they need to transform, but to transform they need to preserve them; merely 'bombarding' institutions and the legitimacy of institutionalised practices might end up destroying the site, and not the target. Essentialised understanding of institutions and contempt for anything stable can produce consequences that could be violently different from those goals the movement begins with. Politics outside in-stitutions could demand a different protocol from pursuing them within the institutional structures. Otherwise they might not understand either. Some ideals, such as human rights or social justice, are championed outside institutions, but once they take an institutional form, they are often pronounced as becoming formal and regressive within the Maoist understanding as it stands today. What needs a change is the way we negotiate these ideals inside institutions, and it is not that these ideals become impure as and when they enter institutional frames. This would, therefore, require a more elaborate and patient dialogue on the nature and place of norms themselves. When do norms facilitate politics and when do they perform for authority? What is the difference between norms and law? Which of the norms can have a longer historical role to play and which need to be disbanded with immediate effect? If the movement does not raise questions of this nature, then it is bound to create norms as authority since it never made this distinction in the first place. The suspicion that Maoist and armed movements of this kind might produce totalitarian regimes is neither merely a bourgeoise propaganda nor the fear of 'enemy class' as 'it shudders with the rise of new classes to power'. It emanates from the lack of eye for details in such movements. Reordering structures does not necessarily involve or 'automatically' result in reordering life, because life in many shades is lived in detail. Glossing over details is glossing over life itself, making life dispensable not only of those from the 'enemy classes' but also of those who are part of the Maoist movement, some of whom belong to the most underprivileged backgrounds. While the Maoist movement has unflinchingly raised issues concerning the 'basic classes' that have remained unattended to as part of formal democracy, and in course of which it has faced unprecedented state violence that has now become integral to the nature of violent democracy in India, it however should not be ignored that the practices and ideas that Maoist movement has generated in course of this mobilisation itself require closer scrutiny if only to understand the nature of the emergent violent democracy better.

Endnotes

1. It is estimated that more than 260 MoUs were signed as per the investors meet in Raipur in 2012. Some of them included MoUs with UK based MNCs such as Vedanta to undertake mining of iron ore and bauxite in resource-rich areas of Central India, which are mostly inhabited by the Tribals. The Maoist movement has stalled the entry of these MNCs through use of counter-violence and has so far succeeded in stopping any mining activity that involves displacement of Tribals to go ahead.

2. Refer to Kutty 2012 for a nuanced argument about democracy and the project of citizenship, in particular the construct of the 'as if' aspect of democratic practices. For instance, 'populations' in modern nation states live 'as if' they exist in homogenous time and social spaces.

3. *Economic and Political Weekly* (July 2008) carried a special issue on the Maoist movement in India, where some of the leading scholars primarily critiqued the movement for the use of violence and some of the excesses that happen in course of their militant action, causing collateral damage.

4. One of the most gruesome incidents in the recent past was the infamous Bijapur Massacre:

> On the night of 28 June 2012 when the adivasi peasants of Sarkeguda, Kottaguda and Rajpenta (Bijapur district of south Chhattisgarh)

gathered to plan the performance of the traditional festival Beej Pandum (seed festival), they were surrounded by hundreds of Police and Para-military forces of the Indian state. The armed forces resorted to indiscriminate firing killing, in which 17 adivasis (including 6 minors) were killed cold-blooded and several others injured seriously. Two other villagers were likewise killed near Jagargunda village of Sukma district in the same night, and predictably, were shown as casualties of an 'encounter' between the Maoists and the armed forces. (http://students4resistance.blogspot.in/2012/08/press-release-on-protest-demo-and-march.html [accessed 14 May 2013])

The response of the armed forces:

After the killing of 17 civilians in Kottaguda, Bijapur, the SP of Bijapur reportedly told a reporter, 'It is difficult to differentiate between Naxals and villagers. They all have voter ID cards and ration cards. On regular days, they take part in farming activities and at other times, they help the Naxals. In effect, they are also Naxals.' The CRPF, the Chief Minister of Chhattisgarh and senior ministers at the Centre also went on to talk of 'human shields' and tried to obfuscate the killing of unarmed children attending a meeting in their own village by bringing in the Maoist recruitment of child soldiers. The latter needs to be condemned but is a different issue altogether.

What is shocking in the Kottaguda case is not just the massacre itself but the cover up that followed and the refusal to observe the basic laws of war, despite evidence that many of those killed were minors, and all were unarmed. Magisterial enquiries and even judicial enquiries ordered by the Chhattisgarh government are designed as eyewashes—the few that have been ordered in response to public protest have been pending for years. As for revising the standard operating procedures to be followed by the CRPF and police—the fruits are already before us. In response to the killing of a constable in Orcha on August 1st, the police have ransacked all the shops in the village. (http://nandinisundar.blogspot.in/ [accessed 15 April 2013])

5. This aspect of subaltern gradually moving from popular street protest politics to powerlessness is analysed in the fourth chapter on 'political society'.
6. 'Salwa Judum' is a violent vigilante group sponsored by the government in the state of Chhattisgarh in Central India. Here young tribal boys have been supplied arms, including sophisticated guns to fight the Maoists. This group, however, the government claims, as we elaborated in the introduction, to be a spontaneous uprising against the Maoists for the atrocities they commit on tribals.
7. Former Home Minister of India P. Chidambaram is known for giving a call to Maoists to abjure violence, as a precondition to invite them for 'peace talks'.

Dialogue by the state and in civil society is only recognised necessarily to supplant militant methods, while the state is prepared for a dialogue precisely because militant politics have mounted pressure through their armed mobilisation of the 'basic classes'. I have analysed this in some detail elsewhere (refer to Gudavarthy 2013a).

8. Secrecy has been the very practice on which the state expands its visible and invisible modes of control. It is against this that acts such as RTI have been demanded by political activists, and experiments such as Wikileaks have been made to expose secret communication and directions given, which is where real and hard 'politics' take place.

9. Maoist movement has produced extensive literature, amongst which is included the creative literary form of Balladeer Gaddar through the organisation he envisaged and launched by the name *Jana Natya Mandali*, which performed cultural shows across the length and breadth of the country. For a detailed account of the nature of literature that came from the rank and file of the Maoist party, refer to Venugopal 2013. However, the Maoist movement produced, in comparison, very little of political analysis and theory.

10. Kobad Gandhy is widely known as the ideologue of the Maoist party and was arrested in 2011, in Delhi.

11. Committee of Concerned Citizens in Andhra Pradesh began concerted efforts to bring the Maoists and the Government of Andhra Pradesh to sit across the table and sort out issues that can bring down the scale of violence (refer to CCC 2006) that in fact fructified into talks in October 2004 (refer to Gudavarthy 2008b). Later another organisation of left-leaning intellectuals and activists in Delhi was formed by the name Citizens Initiative for Peace (CIP) to attempt peace talks at the all-India level, in 2010.

12. This was indeed the history of civil rights movement in Andhra Pradesh. When the activists within the civil rights organisation Andhra Pradesh Civil Liberties Committee (APCLC) began to question some of the modes of its own working, failing to offer a critique when excesses—for instance, killing of innocents not directly related to armed battle—take place, the organisation witnessed a split, with the formation of Human Rights Front (HRF), in 1998. For a more detailed account and analysis of this, refer to Gudavarthy 2013a.

13. K. Balagopal was a leading human rights activist. He began his activism with strong sympathies for the Maoist politics, but differed on the point that human rights organisations need to critique even Maoist violence when it becomes excessive and thereby unjust—not because it is violence but because it is unjust.

14. For a detailed account of the Telangana movement for a separate state, refer to Gudavarthy 2013b.

15. In Vempenta, a village in the state of Andhra Pradesh, the Maoists mobilised along class lines, demarcated by the amount of land individual families owned. However, this ownership pattern overlapped with sub-castes within dalits. Thus Malas owned relatively more land than the Madigas. Maoists ended up

mobilising only Madigas, while the Malas to oppose this switched sides to join the more powerful upper castes.

16. Azad, a spokesperson of the Maoist party, and Kobad Gandhy, a highly educated foreign return graduate, were recently killed and arrested, respectively. The response of the media and the civil society was markedly different from that of their response to the routine killing of Maoist leaders and cadres, who happen to come primarily from the lower echelons—caste and class—of the society.

17. As a way of asking about the alternative that the Maoists present regarding industrialisation, Arundhati Roy wished to ask Maoists: 'Can we leave the bauxite in the mountain?' She was referring to the bauxite in Odisha, which is worth $4 trillion. This was in response to the Maoist's idea of 'humane mining', but Arundhati raised the question as to whether or not we can conceptualise a development paradigm that might not require large-scale mining at all. You can access more details of this talk from http://www.thehindu.com/news/national/can-we-leave-the-bauxite-in-the-mountain/article444987.ece (accessed 7 April 2013).

18. Maoists took part in the Panchayat elections in Malkangiri and Koraput districts in Odisha in 2012, and won more than 50 seats. In fact, there was an inquiry that was instituted after their victory. This was a major shift in their strategy from complete boycott to taking the opportunity at the local level, which will also allow them to take up developmental activities.

19. If the ongoing experiment in Nepal is an indication, then the problems that Maoists will face, in terms of allocation of resources, cultural diversity and conflicts, intra-subaltern conflicts, and caste-based differences, will continue to exist in the post-revolutionary situation. How to negotiate with them in terms of policy formulation is a vexed question, and it will be useful for Maoists to understand the limitations, and to also chart out a course that might be different.

Democracy

2

Middle Classes: Urban Activism and Anna Hazare's Soap Opera

The developmental state during the Nehruvian era was dominated by three proprietary classes that included the industrial bourgeois, the rich farmer and the professionals (Bardhan 1984). The middle class that had already accumulated educational and cultural capital during the colonial period 'came to play an inordinately large and influential role given the functional requirements of extended state management (both in terms of state-directed industrialisation and social reform) and the heightened political–ideological tasks of securing legitimacy in a socially diverse and fragmented liberal electoral democracy' (Fernandes and Heller 2008: 150). The middle class since the time of independence claimed to represent 'national interests', which was carried out in the name of democracy but was pitched at odds with popular-representative politics. It was a contest between the vagaries of popular-representative politics and a calculated exertion of cultural capital to claim hegemony over the policy regime, best represented by the acrimonious debate over affirmative action policies.[1] However, after the liberalisation of the economy in the 1990s,

> the focal point of middle class structural power (especially the dominant fraction) has shifted not only from the state to the market, but also from playing an auxiliary role in the market to playing a leading role. ... With the rapid rise of the information economy and the shift in the valorization process of capital from production to innovation, design, branding, coordination, and other knowledge-intensive functions, a pattern clearly reflected in the service-intensive composition of growth in the Indian economy, the dominant fraction of the middle class occupies a strategic position in India's new economy. (Fernandes and Heller 2008: 152)

It is at the cusp of this transformation that the urban and professional classes, which draw their power not so much from property but cultural and educational capital, and the dynamics of the market, have a 'difficult' relation with the state. They envisage a minimalist yet an interventionist state; they delegitimise public institutions vis-à-vis the professed language of meritocracy and efficiency of the corporate sector and the market, yet continue to attempt to wield hegemonic influence on the policy regime through demands for a more centralised state structures, and decision making by the 'experts'; they have a chequered relation with democracy itself, attempting to occupy the public sphere through democratic forms such as street protest politics, yet express deep cynicism about representative-democratic processes and the avocation of politics itself. It is in the interstices of these changes that the Anna Hazare led urban campaign against graft assumes significance in terms of analysing the politics of middle classes and its equation with democracy, globalisation and the militant protest forms of the subaltern classes.

The demand to institute an ombudsman that can check corruption in the government was a long pending one in India. The Lokpal Bill was first introduced in 1968 and subsequently debated on many occasions in the Parliament but it failed to pass the bill. It was again in August 2011 that Anna Hazare brought the demand back into public discourse by launching and heading India against Corruption (IAC) and announcing his plans to carry out an indefinite fast from 5 April 2011. The fast ended on 9 April, with the government agreeing to constitute a Joint Drafting Committee, to draft the Bill and get it passed in the Parliament. The government introduced the Bill but failed to accept many of the recommendations of Team Anna, and that was when, in August 2011, the second phase of the campaign was launched by Anna Hazare, with a hunger strike that went on for 12 days. The public spectacle was carried out at Jantar Mantar and Ramlila Maidan in Delhi, and relied heavily on the campaign through the Internet and text messages.[2]

> 2011 was a turning point in the fight against corruption. Around the world, protest after protest had one common denominator: outrage at some form of corruption. In the Middle East, people took to the streets to oust political elites who had been building vast personal wealth while depriving citizens of the most basic necessities. Israel, too, saw its first mass middle-class economic protests ever. In India, meanwhile, the social activist Anna Hazare led several hunger strikes in a campaign against graft. And Chinese citizens staged protests against corruption. Following seemingly fraudulent parliamentary elections in December, Russia also saw an unprecedented middle-class movement mobilized against the existing establishment.

Even in the United States and Western Europe, citizens rallied against unemployment, corporate greed, and inequality. (Bonime-Blanc 2012)

It was this middle-class social base of the campaign led by Anna that determined the nature of demands, public discourse and its relation with democracy.

Anna Hazare's movement promised to eradicate corruption, however without a reference to even the elementary aspects of the changing nature of political economy of India, especially post-1990s, yet it had an appeal, even if it was primarily in the metropolitan cities and amongst the urban dwellers and the upwardly mobile middle classes of India. It is this disconnected nature of the campaign that lent it the proportions of what could be referred to as an epic predicament.[3] An epic predicament, like any major epic of India such as the Ramayana or Mahabharata, is a moment where we know the end result but precisely because of that our interest in the phenomenon sustains. We all knew watching Ramayana who would win and why, yet the story keeps us spellbound and of course glued to the television when it was telecast. Not the suspense but its predictability is what endears it and makes it so familiar. In a democracy marked by everyday uncertainty, here was a movement that promised a radical change without any risk, pain or unpredictable overtures, which is what only an epic can do. It promises a drastic change without shocking us, and in fact adhering and confirming to the dominant values in the society. It was, perhaps, self-evident that the Lokpal Bill, even if passed, could not in any significant measure contain corruption, since corruption has always been a lot more structural and has its roots in the nature of the political economy. The proportion and the scope of corruption have grown many fold post-economic reforms and opening up of the economy. It was both due to the manner in which reforms have been introduced and initiated in India best described by Jenkins as 'reforms by stealth' (Jenkins 1999) and also the changes it brought to the economy from being an agrarian economy to the sudden rise of the rent-seeking class that dominates the state.[4] Today the economy and its relatively high growth owe a lot to these newly emergent middle-men-like classes that are neither an industrial class nor the ones that make profits out of manufacturing base. Instead they make big money out of contracts of various kinds. The state is therefore dominated by the rising 'contractor class' including civil, liquor, real estate and more recently the mining contractors best typified by the infamous Reddy Brothers of Karnataka.[5] In fact, a bulk of state revenues is today generated from and by this contractor class (Gudavarthy 2012a). The old distinction between the economic and political class is collapsing, with these classes themselves entering and controlling the state, as part of its executive organ. In fact, it would not perhaps be an exaggeration if one were to mark the shift of the Indian state from being a contractual state to a contractor state (Gudavarthy 2012a).

The nature of the capital is speculative, and that makes this class indifferent to long-term planning and democratic procedures; it instead relies more on quick and speculative modes for making profits, where the growing real-estate economy is a case in point in India. Many state governments such as those in Haryana, Punjab, Andhra Pradesh and Delhi have made policies to sell surplus land to generate additional revenues. For instance, 'a Cabinet note prepared by the finance ministry within days of the Kelkar panel submitting its recommendations says that proceeds from the sale or lease of surplus land, seen as a non-performing asset, would be used only to repay loans or create capital assets that will generate recurring revenue' (Ghildiyal 2012).[6] This mode of economic operations has created new lobbies, since most of these transactions are based on speculative value. It is these changes in the nature of the political economy that are in turn inextricably linked to the growing phenomenon of corruption by private lobbies in nexus with public officials.[7] There was very little that Anna's campaign for Lokpal Bill did about setting this structural limitation right, yet it sustained the collective interest of the civil society, as essentially a simulated exercise. A simulated exercise addresses itself at the level of the symbolic, driven by a culturally constructed idea of 'corruption' that is at the heart of popular democracy. It is therefore pertinent in analysing campaigns such as those led by Anna Hazare, drawing the possible (and perhaps hidden) equivalence and 'conjunction' that they bring to the fore in workings of popular democracy.

Lloyd Rudolph and Susane *Explaining Indian Democracy: A Fifty Year Perspective, 1956–2006, Volume III: The Realm of the Public Sphere: Identity and Policy*, Oxford: Oxford University Press, 2008 make a similar kind of argument when they observe that even in the times when the tele-serial Ramayana was televised such underlying mediation was the reason for the meteoric rise of right-wing politics in India. They argue that

> the 'Hindu' content of the mega-series [Ramayana] has not been explicitly communal. Rather, it has approximated the 'tolerant' ethical stance that

defenders of India's composite culture claim is compatible with India's constitutionally defined secularism, the equal treatment of all religions and the freedom to practice them. But the mega-series, in conjunction with the outlook and practice of the Vishwa Hindu Parishad and other 'national' Hindu Organisations, opens the way contextually to communalise the series. The programmes may be making it possible for Hindu mobilisation and cultural transformation to occur. For example, the celebration of Ram in the *Ramayan* seems likely to have helped fuel the agitation to build a temple near (how near?) the Babri mosque (established in the sixteenth century by the first Mughal emperor Babar) at Ayodhya. (Rudolph and Rudolph 2008: 228–229)

For instance, Advani launched his initial Rath Yatra to Ayodhya meticulously organised with the tele-serial Ramayana as the backdrop and his recent Jan Chetna Yatra with Anna's soap opera in the background. Popular democracy appeals at the level of intention and not merely evidence,[8] and this is so with any epic that cannot be questioned with any amount of archaeological or textual evidence, as witnessed with not just the Ayodhya temple but other controversies such as those around 'Many Ramayanas' in Delhi University.[9] Commentators on democracy only read the impact of principles such as rule of law, for instance, on democracy but rarely do they attempt to understand the impact of popular democracy on rule of law. It is usually assumed that law is beyond the influence of popular dynamics, and that is what in fact makes law unique—law qua law. However, it is evident that in the context of democracy in India, collective understanding of law itself has undergone a transformation wherein it has moved from the realm of evidence to intention. Almost all extraordinary laws such as TADA, POTA and AFSPA allow law to work based on the perceived intent of those who either appear or attempt to violate law. Principles of preventive detention and first strike are justified around preventing harm based on the perceived intention of the perpetrator. As popular practice of law has moved from evidence to intention, simultaneously it has moved from its emphasis on investigation to an emphasis on having a demonstrative effect in order to convince the citizens that law and state machinery is actually effectively working. The manifold rise of encounter killings, extrajudicial killings and strong-arm tactics of the state draw their 'legitimacy' from the idea that they 'create' a demonstrative effect—an idea necessary to create security and confidence, apart from boosting the morale of the state police, army and paramilitary forces. The pull of legal machinery increasingly into the realm of intention and demonstrative effect is the influence of popular democracy on the workings of law.

The demonstrative effect of law is made necessary since in any electoral and representative democracies, creating a real or perceived impact becomes necessary.[10] There are other glaring examples of the Ishrat Jahan encounter in Gujarat and Ansal Plaza encounter in Delhi, which were also in the order of creating both perceived threat and demonstrative action in preventing threats to democracy and effectiveness of legal machinery.[11] In Indian democracy, however, the pulls of representative democracy have, at certain points, coincided with the growing influence of the middle classes and media that has the capacity to convert the event into a spectacle. It is this combination of the pulls of popular democracy and the over-reach of the governmentality of the state, 'mediatisation of politics' and the undue influence of the middle classes that marks the current condition in which a movement against graft essentially led with an appeal to the urban middle classes has an impact well beyond 'merely' highlighting and containing corruption. Coming to grips with such simulated constructions and their equation with popular democracy was at the heart of understanding the Anna Hazare soap opera.

The Left-of-Centre and progressive and radical forces, including the Communist Party of India (Marxist) and to some extent the Maoists, were caught in the dilemma that they have been part of since the days of the death of the 'developmental state'. In the heyday of the developmental state, the Left in India had a safe and a promising posture of critiquing the state itself, and questioning its legitimacy, but once the period of neoliberal reforms began, they were caught unawares as their job—of delegitimising the state—has been taken up more robustly and vigorously by the corporates and their associates, including the media. They are now aware that any excessive critique of the state and public officials only further legitimises and entrenches the global corporate model of development. Commentators on the Left-of-Centre therefore took upon themselves to highlight the issue of the silence of Anna's campaign on the role of the corporate houses. Sumanta Banerjee, for instance, argued that 'Anna Hazare's silence on allegations of corruption against corporate houses may be attracting the latter to lend their voice in support of his campaign against corruption in only the administration' (Banerjee 2011: 14). They were caught with the unenviable position of critiquing the state without delegitimising it to the extent that it lays a red-carpet welcome to the global corporate. On the one hand, they could not wholeheartedly side with Anna since his campaign did not raise the issue of corruption by the corporate, and on the other, they could not either oppose it since they shared his angst and concern for the decaying democracy and the moribund state that is best reflected in the mammoth corruption it's ruling elite was structurally entrenched in. The popular rhetoric that corporate encourages growth and efficiency while state is all about corruption was an argument not agreeable to them.[12] The choice they seem to have had was to extend measured support while attempting a structural analysis, which could not have had an unproblematic equation with imagined constructions in the popular rhetoric. This is where Arundhati Roy was right in drawing a comparison—at the level of popular rhetoric—between the Maoists and popular democracy, as represented by the campaign led by Anna Hazare. Both kinds of politics tend to flatten politics, at a certain level, and also disengage with democratic procedures and institutions and offer an external critique that overlooks, as we pointed out in the previous chapter, details necessary to keep the pores of representative democracy open, accountable and progressively inclusive.

The liberal democrats, on the other hand, were worried that Anna's movement undermined democratic procedures and representative institutions, including and above all the Parliament. Nobody, according to them, was above public representatives, and undercutting procedures and deliberation in a democracy could be dangerous. Thus, they argued that civil society can play a complimentary role and cannot supplant democratic institutions, which amounts to undermining democracy itself. They were therefore unhappy with the so-called 'blackmail' tactics by Team Anna and raised the pertinent question as to who are Team Anna accountable to? And what if those appointed to the proposed Lokpal were themselves corrupt? But here again the story is not so simple. We are today witnessing a strange irony where procedures and the endless delay they entail are used by the ruling elite as a shield against being prosecuted. They escape hiding in the interstices of the time lag that procedure of checks and balances offer in a representative democracy. However, this does not mean democracy can work without elaborate procedures and checks, since even with all of the elaborate procedures and rules in place we routinely are witness to the brazen abuse of organisations that need to maintain their autonomy and anonymity, including the way CBI has come to be used.[13] It is a case of democracy turning against itself. The predominant response of the liberal democratic voices was to reemphasise procedures. For instance, Neera Chandhoke argued that

> yet a word of caution might be in order here. Confronted with the intractable problems that the messy but occasionally creative world of democracy brings with it, some civil society organisations prefer to substitute democracy with administration. Establish a Jan Lokpal, endow it with colossal power, bestow on it the status of a Leviathan, and all our problems will be solved. Sorry, this is not democratic. If democracy on the one hand is about popular sovereignty, freedom and equality, it is also about procedures and principles. One of these principles is the separation of powers. It is of the utmost importance that power should not be concentrated in one institution, and that democratic decisions should be subject to review not only by citizens, but also by other state institutions to ensure conformity with the Constitution. Democracy is the only form of government that is capable of self-correction; this should not be compromised for any reason whatsoever. (Chandhoke, 2011)

Positions such as these, however, failed to explain what kinds of options were left when probity in public life is violated not in spite of but precisely because of the delays incurred in following the procedures.[14] It is in this context that the radical left voices expressed their reservations against making procedures sacrosanct and instead evaluate them only in terms of their outcomes, since they rightly believed that 'procedural justice' was never neutral, and therefore for them,

> procedures are to be respected by the people when they provide good solutions. They are to be tolerated when they provide tolerable solutions. They are resented when they lead to bad solutions. They are jettisoned when they are constantly manipulated to benefit a few in full view of the public' (Bhaduri 2011: 16).[15]

Anna's campaign brought to the fore the moot question in a democracy as to how do social forces negotiate transgressions that occur, not in violation of procedures but precisely because or in the name of procedures.[16]

Perhaps, it was the right-wing parties such as the Bharatiya Janata Party (BJP) that gained, in expressing explicit support to the campaign by Anna and also converting it into an occasion to stall the Parliament, in order to demonstrate the inefficiency of the ruling Congress party.[17] However, more importantly, it also could afford a more wholehearted support to the movement since they could sense that the spectacle of Anna had all the elements that are usually part of the repertoire of right wing's modes of mobilisation in India. The performative aspect of Anna's spectacle included his ascetic living, bachelorhood and use of slogans like 'Vande Mataram' and 'Bharat Mata ki jai', which whether intended or not come a tad too close to the persona of an Rashtriya Swayamsevak Sangh (RSS) *pracharak*, notwithstanding his Gandhian believes. This again is what is dynamic about popular democracy; the symbolic can easily subvert the content, because content without the symbolic can be reduced to the synthetic. It is this gloss alongside the commonsensical propositions and the naivety of Anna that is often confused for simplicity in Indian public discourse, well suited the mobilisational modes of the Right. Anna's soap opera was a Bollywood style hero versus anti-hero narrative that goes well with Hindu versus Muslim or Ram versus Ravan type popular narrative style that has distinct and identifiable symbols of good and bad and thus fit well with the rhetoric of nationalism and patriotism. This indeed is a rich resource, again in the times of neoliberal globalisation, where the targets have become transnational and therefore invisible. To bring alive something that is silent, invisible or dead can be very empowering in the populist mode that democracy works within.[18] This brings to the fore a unique and rather intangible relation between democracy and globalisation.

Anna Hazare's movement brought to the fore the question of the link in popular imagination between the fight against corruption and the tilt towards right-wing mobilisation. Historically, India has been witness to popular anti-corruption movements on two previous occasions, in the 1970s that 'climaxed in the JP movement' and in late 1980s when the VP Singh led campaign managed to oust Congress government.

On each of the previous two occasions, the culmination of the anti-corruption movement did not lead to a decrease in either its spread or intensity. What did happen on each of these junctures was that the electoral fronts of the Rashtriya Swayamsevak Sangh (RSS)—the Bharatiya Jan Sangh in the 1970s and the Bharatiya Janata Party (BJP) later—gained access to state power. (EPW 2011a: 7)

It is in this context that one needs to explore whether or not there is a link between the shift towards the right-wing mobilisation of a movement that was all through essentially a middle-class-based phenomenon, with the active support of the corporate media.

> If one sees the political consequences of anti-corruption movements (the strengthening of the RSS and its affiliates), it is easy to gauge why the middle class supports anti-corruption movements—they lead to a rightward shift in the policy. Anti-corruption movements, by raising an issue which hurts the poor and powerless most, enable those who primarily benefit from corruption to gain crucial political allies from among the masses. (EPW 2011a: 7)

If this is what has been historically demonstrated, it is pertinent to ask not merely how the middle-class base has helped the right wing but also how this kind of mobilisation has brought the middle classes to the centre stage of Indian democracy, wielding influence on both the right-wing parties and the centrist parties such as the Congress, especially post-liberalisation and globalisation of the economy. The conjuncture between the rise of middle classes with the processes of globalisation and the coming of the agenda against corruption to the centre stage of Indian democracy therefore needs further exploration.

The Middle Class and the Politics of Graft

The convergence of interest between middle classes, media and the anti-corruption crusades after globalisation seems to go beyond the rightward shift and the support for the right-wing parties. On the contrary, it has been representative of increasing 'middle-classisation of Indian democracy' itself. We can make better sense of this when we raise the more difficult question: why did the Congress as the ruling dispensation respond with such alacrity to the pressure mounted by Anna Hazare? The argument that it was because of the mass mobilisation and the pressure Anna's campaign could build, or that the moral pressure that fasting can bring seems to be extremely insufficient in explaining the way the Congress looked to have buckled under pressure. If these were the reasons, then how could the Congress so blatantly ignore the struggle for a separate state of Telangana that witnessed unprecedented mobilisation in every nook and cranny of its districts[19]; if hunger strike was effective because it's the land of Gandhi holds any truth, then how do we explain not only the sheer negligence of the suffering by Irom Sharmila for well over a decade, but also attempts to criminalise her protest?[20] The Congress was not even open to a debate, even though the Chief Minister of Jammu and Kashmir, Omar Abdullah, had been bargaining for piecemeal withdrawal of AFSPA.

The answer could well lie in the social base that was attracted to the anti-graft movement. While there was some truth in the fact that people from all walks of life and all classes, including people from rural hinterlands in the north, supported the movement, it was primarily a movement that gained support from the professionals and urban-rich with keen interest avowed by the NRIs. Their interest overlapped with the belief not only that a corruption-free India would directly benefit them but also that India would become a more attractive destination for global investments. Better infrastructure, more efficient work culture and violence-free India with a strong 'law and order', it was believed, would enrich the global image of India and would move a step closer to being a superpower that it can in a foreseeable future. In this frame, a corruption-free India was a cause worth fighting for, notwithstanding the fact that these classes were also the beneficiaries of corruption themselves. As sociologist Dipankar Gupta argued, 'the middle class finds itself in the curious position of being the perpetrator and the victim of the corruption it is fighting' (Gupta 2011). This anomaly could not hold these classes back, and instead it was their firm belief of serving national (read global) interests that motivated these privileged sections of urban India and also propelled them to occupy the streets that have been, for some time now, vacated by the poor who with growing distress levels, it seems, have little time for protest politics at their disposal. With the moving in of the middle classes to the centre stage, they brought in their kind of politics that need to short-circuit the numerical strength of the subaltern classes with the cultural capital they wield, in the name of democracy and a new global India. As Pranab Bardhan rightly argued,

> As it is, our influential middle classes who are often too impatient with the slow and dirty processes through which the numerical majority of the unwashed and the uneducated give their democratic verdict, are always on the lookout for short cuts to cleaner politics, national prestige and super-power status. (Bardhan 2011: 18)

There have been historical roots to this kind of undue influence that middle classes wield in the context of India. Unlike Europe, in India the emergence of middle classes into the political domain preceded introduction of formal democracy; they were a product of an explicit colonial policy to create intermediaries between the British and populations in the colony. The British attempted as part of their educational policy to create a class comparable to their own, so that it might assist them in the administration of the country and help in the development of its internal resources, necessary for the payment of the increasing imports of British manufacturers. In Macaulay's words, this was to be a 'class, Indian in blood and colour, but English in tastes, in opinions, morals and intellect' (Misra 1961: 10–11). While in Europe middle classes became the social base on which autonomous intermediary institutions grew and it was the class that had stakes in open and representative-democratic processes, in India since the middle classes preceded democracy, they always played the role of superimposing their own modalities of functioning on the workings of democracy.[21]

Again, ironically this dream of India going global was initiated by the Congress itself and by, more than anyone else, Prime Minister Manmohan Singh himself.[22] But then this precisely is the reason for the protest. Popular democracy, as it has evolved over a period of time in India, has acquired this strange dimension where, within a fractured polity, parties and governments are being increasingly identified with a particular constructed social base, and are expected to be loyal to that base. Today, while there is enough pressure that governments are supposed to represent all sections of the society, the polity and primarily the electorate seem to be reconciled with the fact that governments rule in the name of certain sections, which in turn, it is expected, benefits everyone. This could well be the consequence of the economic reforms and the political side of the trickle-down theory, representing what we earlier referred to as the 'neoliberalisation of politics'—trickle-down of democracy. As is argued, achieving growth by giving concessions to the corporate would eventually become inclusive and benefit all sections of the society; similarly, governments in supporting and nurturing specific social base would actually make democracy more inclusive. This new discourse reflects the new kinds of welfare policies that are put in place without a welfare state. In such a mode, welfare can be pursued without an explicit welfare-policy regime but through a few welfare schemes that are pronounced to be explicitly dependent or contingent on growth and are not in any way a commitment that state is obliged to make to its citizens. It would therefore not be, perhaps, inappropriate to argue that this kind of neo-welfarism was intended to justify and seek legitimacy to neoliberal reforms.[23] It is growth that is making welfare possible, and therefore neoliberal reforms and welfare are not inimical but the latter is squarely dependent on the former, and any policy favouring growth eventually is inclusive and democratic.

Therefore, in contemporary Indian democracy, it is not so much of an issue if governments fail to keep the promise of universal representation, since conflict of interest looks like an irreducible fact of modern democracies; however, it does assume eruptive proportions when governments fail to serve the agenda of the class and sections of the society they actually promised to work on behalf of. The Congress under Manmohan Singh, notwithstanding its elaborate welfare regime, projected itself as a government in favour of the private and global corporate capital, and professionals working for it. When corruption, as they perceive, hurts their interests and the Congress looks reluctant to act, then it is construed as not only an inefficient government in power but also a party that is betraying and disloyal to its own stated ideals and social base. It now seems to be a more important criterion in popular democracy that political parties stand up to their stated ideals and represent their distinct social base, however partisan they might be, more than enacting their universalist aspirations. We might be actually, as a society, getting reconciled to this partisan nature of democracy rather than expecting it to be close to its ideal-type functioning.[24]

It therefore makes for dramatic change in the democratic current today whenever parties or individuals representing them overstep the brief of representing only a particularistic social base that they have themselves constructed as part of the inherent dynamics of contemporary polity. Therefore, there is more uproar when Advani, for instance, makes what were considered as pro-Jinnah comments, without much interest shown in the veracity of the historical truth or accuracy of these observations. Even if what Advani observed about Jinnah were to be historically true, coming from him makes them 'false'. He could never perhaps recover the stature he enjoyed before those comments, however well meaning they might be or however desperate he might be to switch to a more moderate image in the interest of the future prospects of his party. Similarly, the Communist Party of India (CPM) could never recover from the damage it inflicted upon itself after it ostensibly betrayed the very peasants it had once mobilised. This betrayal, even if it involves a move in the positive direction, is seen as graft in popular democracy. Similar is the case of Chandrababu Naidu in Andhra Pradesh. After he shifted his political discourse centred on the corporate/IT sector and began to raise the issues of the farmers and agrarian crisis (after his defeat in the 2009 Assembly elections in Andhra Pradesh), he came to be looked upon as a more 'cunning and opportunistic politician' in the popular imagination, more than when he proudly projected himself as a CEO of the state and pronounced the irrelevance of agriculture to the economy. It is therefore not surprising as to why Narendra Modi emerged as a frontrunner in the BJP for the prime ministerial candidate. He never destabilised his majoritarian image, and yet took recourse to the rhetoric of inclusive polity through his development agenda. The argument that was often extended by his colleagues in the BJP was that growth and development in Gujarat has benefitted the minority community, and thereby it is implicitly sought to be argued that his role in riots and a social agenda of treating Muslims as second-class citizens remains effectively countered, while providing the continued assurance to the majority Hindu community that his government is not apologetic about its role during the riots in 2002.[25] The model of Narendra Modi is almost the ideal-type representation of 'neoliberalisation of politics'.

What the Congress therefore faced, in course of the Anna Hazare movement, was a crisis from 'within' its own social base, and it is this anxiety of loss of an image—as having ushered a global India—it constructed and stood by that propelled it to take Anna's movement so seriously and begin to work towards a possible resolution. The same Prime Minister who had worked overtime not to respond to a popular movement like Telangana went to the extent of dissolving his government over the nuclear deal. This is not the pressure of democratic mobilisation, even if it is a part of the logic, but more an implosion from within that politics seems to be succumbing to. Anna's movement appealed to the 'dominant' social base of the ruling party and it could ill-afford to ignore, lest it looks inefficient and 'corrupt' in popular imagination.

It is this explicit shift in the logic of the representative-democratic politics that allows for a fractured and a fragmented legitimacy to the system. 'Strategic legitimacy' functions on a quid-pro-quo logic of fulfilling specific interest in exchange for contextual legitimacy to the system (Held and McGrew 2002). The shift from 'democratic legitimacy' to 'strategic legitimacy' is also then the terrain for a more expanded role for the affluent middle classes. Further, this allows for a new kind of role to the media. The media becomes part of this logic of a fractured polity and shift to a selective or strategic legitimacy, wherein it is less apologetic about its political preferences and lending its support to causes that it feels are worthy. It shifts from reporting to supporting, as it became more corporate with a convenient focus on the urban India and its affluent middle classes. Soon after his arrest in April 2011, Anna's campaign got unprecedented and uncritical coverage.

> One reason could be that the response in April to the fast had alerted news media that this was a story their largely middle class urban viewers would follow. Television revenue is based on viewership. Over the two weeks in August that all news channels, with the exception of Doordarshan, focussed exclusively on Ramlila Maidan, news viewership increased while that of sports as well as Hindi movies dropped. A second factor could be that the people who staff our media come from the same class as those leading the anti-corruption protests. The Anna Hazare group included journalists and technology savvy young people. They knew how to talk to journalists; journalists knew how to relate to them. (EPW 2011b: 7)

Unlike the debate on economic reforms, this was a clear case where bereft of good or bad politics, it was good economics. The medium and its capacity and compulsion to create spectacles determined the nature of the coverage. The spectacle of this mammoth proportion could only be construed and constructed when protests are urban, interest the middle-class viewership and confine to 'logistically convenient locations'. Thus, middle-classisation of politics reflected in the growing influence of the middle class in controlling the levers of democracy had a symbiotic relation with the growing 'mediatisation of politics', along with 'neoliberalisation of politics'.

Anna's soap opera entered a new phase in 2012 with the debate on its possible conversion into a political party, and contesting elections on the issue of corruption. After a series of flip–flops, Anna Hazare decided in September 2012 to withdraw and dissolve Team Anna, and move back to his village, Ralegaon Siddhi in Maharashtra, and the reigns were taken over by his onetime ardent follower Arvind Kejriwal, who launched his political party, Aam Aadmi Party (AAP), on 26 November 2012. This shift from social activism to politics, split between Anna Hazare and Arvind Kejriwal, inaugurated a new set of dynamics into the campaign against graft, the moot question being whether the consent and unproblematic consensus that was generated in the social domain could be replicated in the political terrain. Whether or not the consensus in the social domain had anything to do with the campaign that was primarily a middle-class-backed one. What then was the response of the middle class to this shift from the social to the political, as against other social groups such as the urban poor, Muslims, women, and the youth? Finally, does the response of the middle class reinforce its attempts to undermine popular-representative democracy, and put in place a set of mechanisms—centralisation, emphasis on the role of experts and law, among others—that allows it to retain its disproportionately hegemonic role in comparison with other subaltern classes? The analysis of the question of the equation or equivalence between middle class and democracy will be explored based on a survey, around the possible responses of different social groups to the electoral prospects of the kind of campaign that Anna Hazare leads.[26]

Democracy and Electoral Prospects of Anna's Campaign

Based on a purposive survey in seven constituencies of Delhi, among five social groups that included the poor residing in the slums, affluent middle class in the residential colonies, youth/first-time voters in the colleges, Muslims and women, this study through an open-ended questionnaire attempted a qualitative opinion survey of Anna Hazare and his teams' electoral prospects.[27] The purpose was not merely to arrive at whether or not these social groups were willing to vote if Anna is to launch or support a new political party but also to get close to the reasons as to why they were willing or unwilling, and how people have come to see the interface between corruption and electoral politics and the shift from the social to the political arena.

The survey threw up very intriguing differences between the opinions of these five social groups and it also showed a trend in how social groups perceive electoral politics and the new experiments that promise to change the rules of the game. The survey clearly reflected that on the one hand the rhetoric of honesty looms large, and there is a will among the electorate to vote for that agenda, while on the other hand there was a wide-scale scepticism about how that agenda would translate into reality and more importantly connect with the everyday problems specific to these different social groups. It seems that the gap between the social and the political is too large to be easily breached or bridged. Movements that are attractive as a social phenomenon are not necessarily considered effective in political or electoral terms. In fact, much of the legitimacy of a movement such as Anna's has drawn it from its avowed distance from electoral politics and pursuit of political power.

What can bring people together on a social plain can be divisive when it comes to the political domain, since the latter is not merely about normativity, or right and wrong sort of distinctions, but it is also about getting concrete benefits that are indispensable for the everyday life. It is the hard pursuit of interests that are tangible that makes politics enormously complex and distinct from all other activities. What can draw a relatively easy consensus in the social domain does not necessarily or neatly translate when it comes to the domain of politics. Each of the social groups had distinct reasoning(s) as to how it relates to this new anti-graft movement, what would be its prospects in electoral politics and what would be its own position in supporting the movement in terms of casting its vote. It is important to observe that the reasoning to each of these queries itself need not match or complement the other, and can in fact present us with a picture as to what goes on in the minds of people from different social backgrounds before they decide whom to cast their vote.

The urban poor when asked to identify the most pressing problems they were facing, they pointed towards price rise, unemployment, lack of sewage, health and educational facilities, along with lack of savings, public transport, ration cards and finally the irony of lack of drinking water supply and water logging. Regarding Anna they seem to have had the dilemma that while he himself is poor and honest, and would stand by them, but this in itself raises the doubt whether he will be effective enough in a system that is marred by power, money and manipulation. His goodness can also be his weakness in a system that is corrupt. They therefore, for instance, had a doubt if his campaign will be able to bring relief from the routine harassment for bribes that they, for instance, face from the police. Similarly, many of them doubted if he can win elections without money; therefore, the capacity to win elections became important in their final decision whom to vote for. They also agreed that during elections they are offered money and liquor and this looks like an attraction as much as a welcome relief in lives that gain very little otherwise from whichever party comes to power. Majority of respondents however drew a direct link between inflation, price rise and corruption, and they felt that if corruption could be rooted out, prices will come down and that would be a very big relief. This seems to be the strongest point of the campaign against graft.[28]

If the poor increasingly get convinced that in arresting corruption price rise could be controlled, there would be a possibility of the poor voting for the initiative by Anna Hazare, as Table 2.2 reflects.[29] The response from women among the poor seems to tilt more towards Anna since many of them saw a link between corruption, liquor and domestic violence. Many of the women among the poor felt that if Anna is at the helm of the affairs, then they would get relief from domestic violence, and they strongly supported his campaign for prohibition of liquor. Women were of the opinion that last minute distribution of money and liquor plays a way too important a role in how men decide to vote. Here corruption is not merely about bribes but also about how it translates into other cultural practices within their homes. If Anna could widen the scope of corruption to include such issues, there would be a strong possibility of it appealing to the women among the poor. Finally, many among the poor, both men and women did not perceive Baba Ramdev to be pro-poor. Instead they seemed to see him more as a businessman, as against Anna being a common man. Some even raised the issue as to why Baba cannot sell his medicines at a cheaper price for the poor.[30]

Much in contrast to the poor, the affluent middle classes identified theft, law and order, taxes, growth, lack of implementation of developmental projects, illegal encroachments, petrol prices, condition of the roads and traffic, power cuts, growing population, and above all problems of parking as the most pressing problems they face. The majority of respondents seemed to sympathise with the BJP and suggested the need for leaders such as Narendra Modi, and even T.N. Seshan to bring order and fast paced growth.[31] Regarding Anna, they seemed to have a rather caviar attitude of being too simplistic to handle a complex political system and issues of governance. By and large they felt that he would be ineffective, and will make no difference to the electoral results in 2014, and they were explicit in their decision not to vote for candidates supported by him. In fact, many felt that he is better off as a social activist rather than a politician. He should campaign against corruption but not by entering electoral politics. They pointed out that in fact corruption perpetuates in the system because not merely those who receive bribes but even those who offer them benefit, and therefore in spite of the rhetorical support of many for a campaign against corruption the picture will be very different when it comes to everyday reality. The only merit, if any, in Anna launching or supporting a political party will be, according to many, in damaging the vote share of the Congress, which augments well for the BJP; however, majority of them felt that they will have a coalition government at the Centre. Finally, this was the only social group that was, in comparison with others, less critical of Baba Ramdev and they drew the analogy that he is serving the nation to produce healthy people and healthy individuals are a precondition for a healthy society.

The overwhelming majority of Muslims interviewed in the seven constituencies of Delhi were the most sceptical of all the five social groups regarding the campaign by Anna Hazare. They seemed to suspect a close link between him and the BJP. In fact, many were convinced that this was a BJP- and RSS-backed campaign. The poor among the Muslims seemed to be politically astute in their responses and in identifying where their interests lie. They were very conscious of the fact that if Anna launches or supports any political party, that will cut into the vote share of the Congress, and that was all the more reason for them to vote for the Congress. Their suspicion, they pointed out, was further strengthened both by the refusal by Kiran Bedi to join the protests against the BJP and the proximity of Anna with Ram Dev Baba, and by the fact that there was no Muslim leader who was part of their campaign.[32] Many of them pointed out that the lack of unity in the team was due the fact that the intentions of many of those involved were not very clear.[33] For the poor among the Muslims what seemed to matter the most is the approachability of the local MLA and the assurance for their physical protection including the assurance to not to demolish the slums they reside in. With regard to the question as to whether Muslims would benefit from the campaign against corruption, many struggled to identify any specific benefits, while others took objection to such a question and retorted why it should be asked singling out the Muslims. While all other social groups found specific advantages that they might get with the anti-graft campaign, Muslims took serious objection. Their response about the Congress was also therefore very contextual. While they felt that the Congress did very little to improve the law and order situation, especially in relation to the vilification of the Muslims, they felt that specific leaders such as Sheila Dixit in Delhi were strong and worked in the interest of the minorities. Many of the more affluent Muslims shared the suspicion about the campaign by Anna and pointed to the fact that it had a single agenda against corruption, and wondered where would other burning issues figure in? They argued that Team Anna had no public position regarding the recent spate of attacks on Muslims in Assam, had never pressed for the implementation of the recommendations of Sachar Committee, never pointed to the dire needs to better educational facilities for the minorities and never discussed about the witch-hunt by the police in the name of 'war against terror'. It is intriguing to see that on the one hand Muslims scourge at the possibility of separately benefitting from a campaign against corruption, while on the other hand they had a list of demands that they felt were not part of the anti-graft movement. They could draw no immediate link between their interests as a religious minority in a polity and a more generic campaign against corruption and the perception of having no 'secular credentials' definitely made Team Anna least popular among the Muslims.

Women pointed out, across class and religion, that safety and law and order are their top priority, along with admissions to schools for their children. They pointed out that as they draw strength from having Sheila Dixit at the helm of the affairs, they also draw strength from someone like Kiran Bedi being associated with a campaign against corruption. In addition, women felt that her being a former police officer was reassuring. Many pointed out those campaigns against corruption will eventually also translate into a campaign against eve teasing and sexual violence against women in the city. It is according to them essentially a movement for ethics, and it will benefit women in terms of getting better employment facilities, being treated as equals, and above all in gaining access to public spaces. As pointed out earlier, this seems to corroborate with women among the poor who expressed a similar link between corruption, consumption of liquor and relief from domestic violence. Though many women expressed the desire to vote along with and in consultation with other members of their family, individually they seemed to both admire Anna and his ideas against corruption. Finally, it was women who most strongly supported the idea of Anna entering the electoral politics, but they also expressed the doubt whether Anna will be allowed by other mainstream political parties to either launch a political outfit and even if he manages whether it will be allowed to survive.

The last of the social groups that was interviewed was the youth/first-time voters in various colleges of Delhi. By and large the young seemed to sympathise with the cause that Anna had taken up. However, they were also the most cynical about politics itself. They expressed the least confidence in bringing change through politics and more so electoral politics. They expressed a series of doubts about the move by Team Anna to enter the electoral arena. They questioned if it is feasible for Team Anna to win elections without an organisation and by the efforts of a few individuals; if they could be a political party with a single issue of fighting corruption; and if they have made a hurried entry into politics more as a face-saving device rather than as a well-thought-out decision. Some even asked where the funding for the campaign by Team Anna is coming from and had a doubt that they have never been transparent about this. They believed that age matters in carrying a political programme and Anna is already very old to carry on for too long. They were doubtful whether the campaign will only be restricted to urban areas and metropolitan cities, and sceptical about its reach to rural hinterlands. Some thought that even if Anna's party wins a few seats, they cannot enter into post-poll alliance with any other party since they consider all others to be corrupt, and in this age of coalition politics whether they have any chance to form a government; they have already overstretched the anti-Congress rhetoric. Finally, some believed that strategies such as holding fasts have a limited impact, and since they could not devise any effective alternative strategy of mobilisation, under compulsion, they have to declare that they would enter electoral politics. Along with the Muslims, the young were the next most sceptical social group to question the proximity of Anna with Baba Ramdev. Some of them made an interesting observation that while Anna is with the masses, it is important to see if he can carry the elites and the middle classes with him, and while Baba Ramdev is with the elites and the middle class, it is pertinent to see if he can gain credibility among the masses. It is in symbolic terms for some a battle between *khadi* and *saffron*. While the young undoubtedly seemed to have been disillusioned with both the Congress and the BJP, it was important to note that they were disillusioned with politics itself as a way of bringing about change. This seems to be the single most palpable effect of media, especially the television and news channels that have held a high moral ground against politicians without ever seriously questioning the corporate houses or corruption in all other walks of life.[34]

Tables 2.1–2.4 give us the trends with regard to the interrelation between political parties, social issues and social groups.

Table 2.1:
Performance of the Sitting MLA (in %)

Constituency	Satisfactory	Not Satisfactory	Don't Know
New Delhi	22	43	35
South Delhi	50	39	11
Chandni Chowk	42	47	11
East Delhi	34	60	6
West Delhi	31	60	9
Northeast Delhi	37	50	13
Northwest Delhi	40	51	9

Table 2.2:
Social Group-wise Support for Team Anna (in %)

Social Groups	Yes	No	Don't Know
Youth	67	31	2
Affluent	49	43	8
Women	64	30	6
Muslim	33	63	4
Poor	74	17	9

Table 2.3:
Impact of Team Anna (in %)

Damages Congress	36
Damages BJP	4
Damages Both	23
No Impact	21
Anna Will Win	11
Don't Know	5

Table 2.4:
Weakness of Team Anna (in %)

Financial	6
Internal Disturbances	15
Political	34
No Weakness	17
Don't Know	15
Others	13

Note: Political weakness includes lack of experience in electoral politics, dominance of existing political parties, lack of clear-cut political agenda, manipulation of votes, etc.

To conclude, in terms of converting the campaign into electoral prospects, it needed to work out the links between corruption and local factors, and issues specific to different social constituencies, beyond the confines of the modalities of middle classes in urban areas. The campaign, it looked, would have stood much better electoral prospects had it come as a social upheaval or a wave questioning power, money and muscle power in politics, but to sustain it as a political party will raise the questions that many of the respondents have alluded to in course of this study. The Anna campaign brings into relief the new dynamics in Indian democracy marked by the growing fit between the rise of middle class, 'mediatisation of politics' and the shift to fragmented and strategic legitimacy. This in turn demonstrated the top-down nature of change that is being sought, where consensus is generated in the social domain and superimposed on the political terrain that is marked by contested and conflicting interests. I argued elsewhere that

> imagining a simplistic consensus "for the people" has always given rise to authoritarian regimes, which is what partially explains why all campaigns against graft, even in the past, have tilted towards right-wing modes of mobilisation, including that led by Jayaprakash Narayan. Politicians of the day need to be critiqued and held accountable but the avocation of politics and the creative image and role of a politician in a democracy need to be avowedly defended. (Gudavarthy 2012b)

The response of the middle class was distinct in the separation they drew between the social and the political domains. The anti-graft campaign, it looked, was more of a mechanism to discipline democracy, against the new transgressions that were being made with the proliferation of the political domain by the new actors, including the Dalits, Muslims and OBCs. It could therefore also be argued that the other major movement that the middle class took up during this period against sexual violence, more specifically against a gang rape that took place in Delhi in December 2012, was a way of framing a class anxiety through the discourse of sexual violence, against urban/professional women. This issue becomes pertinent in light of the fact that routine rapes of Dalit and adivasi women, even by state and paramilitary forces, do not evoke the same kind of response from the urban/professional middle class. It becomes even more intriguing that not many from the rank and file of this class are critical of what happened in Gujarat in 2002, where many Muslim women were gang raped under the watchful eyes of the government headed by Narendra Modi. It could be asked how then the class that protests against rape also chooses Modi as the most popular leader in the post-Emergency period of Indian politics.

How do these dynamics fare when comprehended from the point of view of other social classes differentially positioned, in terms of their influence on the Indian state and democracy, then becomes a pertinent question. It is to understand this that we turn to the new rise of the backward classes that has been referred to as the 'second democratic upsurge' in the next chapter. The same query regarding the equation between the social and the political is represented as the emergent binary opposition between the civil and the political in the context of subaltern politics through the formulation of the concept of 'political society', which will be the focus of discussion in Chapter 4 in this section on democracy.

Endnotes

1. We would be analysing the issue of politics of reservations in the next chapter.
2. Anna Hazare claimed to have received over 60 million text messages from across the country in support of his campaign. A recent study claims that 160 out of 543 seats Lok Sabha are likely to influenced and impacted by social media, including facebook and Twitter. India's Internet user base is likely to go up to 800 million by next general elections in 2014 (refer to the study by IRIS Knowledge Foundation and the Internet and Mobile Association of India).
3. The use of epic predicament here is different from Ashis Nandy's use of epic culture, wherein he believes that 'It is in this chaos and plurality of spiritual belief that the binding cement of this civilisation existed'. Here the emphasis is not merely on the plurality but the cultural aspect of developing an affinity with the predictable, as against the overwhelming discomfort with the vagaries of politics that draws its animus from the unpredictable dynamics of the everyday.

4   Rent-seeking is an attempt to derive economic rent by manipulating the social or political environment in which economic activities occur, rather than by adding value. An example of rent-seeking is to create and sustain artificial monopolies in an economy. Rent-seeking may be initiated by government agents soliciting bribes or other favors from the individuals or firms. (HolgerSieg 2012)

5. The grip of the mining lobby in Bellary district of Karnataka is so strong that as Reddy brothers were framed by the CBI and were suspended from the BJP, in the recent Assembly elections in Karnataka in May 2013, the Congress gave ticket from Bellary to Mr Anil Lad, a mining businessman, and a close confidant of the Reddy brothers, who had won earlier as an MLA on BJP ticket from Kudligi district. He has assets worth 288 crores as per his affidavit.
6. Similarly, it was widely reported that 'Punjab Government has initiated a major drive to enlist vacant and under-utilised government lands and to put them to better use and generate revenues for the government'. http://news.oneindia.in/2008/02/19/punjab-to-use-vacant-land-to-generate-revenues-1203420884.html (accessed 30 July 2013).
7. For instance, In China,

cross-sectional research finds that corporate financing choices are not only affected by firm and industry factors, but also by country institutional factors. This study focuses on the roles of public governance in firm financing patterns. To conduct a natural experiment that avoids endogeneity, we identify 23 corruption scandals involving high-level government bureaucrats in China and a set of publicly traded companies whose senior managers bribed bureaucrats or were connected with bureaucrats through previous job affiliations. We report a significant decline in the leverage and debt maturity ratios of these firms relative to those of other unconnected firms after the arrest of the corrupt bureaucrat in question. These relations persist even if we only focus on the connected firms that were not directly involved in the corruption cases. (Joseph Fan et al. 2008)

This is also the case with corruption in India, where the institutional context also determines the nature of the economic transactions. This includes the powers of bureaucrats, lack of transparency, diversity in procedural set ups, among others.

8. We had alluded to this point in the Introduction, and later in Chapter 1 on the Maoists, arguing for a convergence between the Maoists' use of intention and the place of intention in the emerging exceptionalism of the state.

9. 'The essay, "Three Hundred Ramayanas: Five examples and three thoughts on translations," which forms part of the B.A. History (Honours) course, had attracted the ire of Hindutva activists because it talks about 300 different versions of the Ramayana that abound in our country and beyond. And when the decision to scrap the course was put to vote at the Academic Council meeting ... only nine of the 120 members present dissented' (*The Hindu*, 15 October 2011).

10. To cite only a few examples of this one could recollect the infamous Batla House Encounter in Jamia Nagar in Delhi. This encounter coincided closely with the attacks on Mumbai. There was a general perception that the then Home Minister Shivraj Patil was proving to be ineffective, and then you have an encounter which raised more doubts in terms of the veracity of the claims of victims' background being linked to Indian Mujahideen. Jamia Teachers Solidarity Association (JTSA) closely followed up this case and carried out a campaign demanding the central government and Delhi Police come clean on the veracity of the encounter. There were many acquittals in relation to this case. For details on this case refer to the JTSA website www. teacherssolidarity.org.

11. The CBI in July 2013 declared that there is conclusive evidence that the encounter in which Ishrat Jahan and three others were killed was a fake one. It was created, as is reported, to enhance the image of Gujarat Chief Minister Narendra Modi, in claiming that there was threat to his life, in spite of which he is working towards protecting the interests of the Hindus. For a more detailed analysis of the spread of exceptionalism through such constructed/demonstrative effects, refer to Gudavarthy 2013d.

12. Left parties and activists had the same dilemma while supporting the RTI against public officials, leaving aside the corporate sector.

13. This has often prompted some in the BJP to refer to the CBI as Congress Bureau of India.

14. Many of us have often experienced being mute spectators when political leaders in the executive announce, soon after a scam or a public offence by those in the ruling elite, that 'law will take its own course', tongue-in-cheek. In course of Anna's campaign the liberal voices struggled to distance themselves from those in the ruling party, especially the likes of Digvijay Singh (General Secretary of the Congress party), who kept reminding about the importance of procedures and rules in a democracy. It is relevant in this context to raise the question of radical provisions such as the Public Interest Litigation (PIL) made by the judiciary in India. Provisions such as these have made judiciary accessible to common people but at the cost of cutting down due procedures. Here the arguments of those who championed PIL were that outcomes are more important than procedures, since 'procedural justice' is never neutral.

15. Amit Bhaduri pointed out the fact that

> the number of cases registered during 1991–93 was an average of 1231, and then 892 (1994–96), 885 (1997–98), 845 (2000–02), 763 (2003–05), and 694 (2006–08) and thereafter increased slightly as scams began to draw the Supreme Court's attention ... procedural wrangles hardly hide what this government and more generally the political class wants. (Bhaduri 2011: 17)

16. It was in this context that the MPs were keen to invoke the 'breach of privilege' motion against social activists who were critiquing the parliamentarians and bringing down the respect for the Parliament as a democratic institution. 'Notices for moving a privilege motion were sent by 10 Mps from various parties to lawyers Prashant Bhushan, Shanti Bhushan, former bureaucrat Arvind Kejriwal, retired police officer Kiran Bedi, and actor Om Puri for their utterances at the Ramlila Maidan during the course of the hunger strike by Anna Hazare' (EPW 2011c: 9). This editorial in the EPW observed that while the constitution made a provision via Article 105 to provide immunity to parliamentarians, it however concluded asking of representative democracy whether 'in the ultimate analysis ... privilege motions for criticising MPs in Parliament have any place at all in a representative democracy' (EPW 2011c: 9), foregrounding the nature of the debate on the place of procedures in parliamentary democracy.

17. Here again the debate between democracy and procedures became relevant. While the BJP was throwing its support to highlight the issue of series of scams by the ruling Congress party including the 2G spectrum scam, and later the 'coalgate', worth thousands of crores, it was violating the basic norm of parliamentary democracy by stalling the proceedings of the Parliament. Following, 2G and the findings of CAG, and 'coalgate', the BJP stalled the Parliament with regard to the alleged land deals involving Robert Vadra and Home Minister Shinde's comments on 'Hindu Terror'.

18. Anna made populist statements that those found drinking liquor should be tied to a tree and slapped; he impishly congratulated an anonymous person who

attempted to slap Agriculture Minister Sharad Pawar. These modalities have a reach and strong appeal at the level popular-symbolic in Indian democracy.

19. For a detailed account of this, refer to Gudavarthy 2011. Though the Congress finally relented after the Congress Working Committee (CWC) accepted to grant separate statehood to Telangana, after a long delay that can only be explained with a neologism—*Con-Crastination* (Congress way of procrastination) in July 2013.

20. For a detailed account of this, refer to Teltumbde 2013.

21. However, what is necessary to understand is that the role of middle classes and their relation with democracy always requires a political analysis; however, often in the context of political dynamics including that of the political movements they have offered a moral critique of the middle classes.

22. It is in this context of the growing rhetoric of India becoming a superpower that Arundhati Roy demystified this image in her article suitably titled as 'Emerging Power? Ha' in the weekly magazine *Outlook* 2010.

23. This kind of neo-welfarism could be attributed to the logic of 'difference principle' that John Rawls formulated. He built a defence for welfare states through the 'difference principle' that argued that inequalities are justifiable so long as least well off was relatively better off when the affluent accumulated wealth. It was not the question of absolute equality between the rich and the poor but relative equality where everyone progressively was ameliorated. While there is truth in the fact that inequalities were perceived more in relative terms, it is arguable if a system based on neoliberal logic could ever not be mutually exclusive with regard to the interests of the basic classes. The Maoist movement that we examined in the first chapter is an explicit example of the fact that without dispossession of the basic classes, accumulation on the scale the newly globalised economy aspires is not possible. This is the new phenomenon captured by David Harvey's formulation, 'Accumulation by Dispossession'.

24. It is interesting to see how one can conceptualise this shift in popular democracy. Would it be a more regressive move in the polity getting reconciled and giving up aspiring for a more universalist government/state, or would it prove to be more effective for the subaltern classes to have a more pragmatic understanding of the political regime? More analysis on this is attempted in the Chapter 4 on subaltern classes and their changing role in Indian democracy.

25. It is interesting to observe that Modi continues to adopt this two-pronged strategy, while many other politicians have wavered in taking different images that make them look inconsistent and opportunistic. During the *Sadbhavana Divas* that Modi organised in 2012, he refused to wear the skull cap offered by the Muslim leaders on an occasion that was meant to bring all communities together. In an interview, he referred to himself as a 'Hindu Nationalist' and compared Gujarat riots to a 'puppy' coming under the wheels, leading to outrage from the minority Muslim community in India.

26. This survey was conducted before the split between Anna Hazare and Arvind Kejriwal and dissolution of Team Anna. The idea was to ascertain whether what was unproblematically possible on the social plain in building a consensus against graft and popular support base would be possible at the political level, even with a strong socio-spiritual symbol like Anna Hazare. This could be repeated after the split but the results would not be, I guess, very different. In fact to get the nuances of the relation between the social and the political, it was more prudent to test the response of the electorate with Anna supposedly at the helm of the affairs.

27. This survey was carried out in August 2012. It was carried out with the assistance of Hyderabad based research organisation People's Pulse and students from the Jawaharlal Nehru University, which included Sajjan, Ekta, Manas, Krishna, Richa and Ankita. The sample size of the survey was 100 questionnaires for every constituency. I am thankful to both People's Pulse and the students for their assistance.

28. It was therefore picked up by Arvind Kejriwal after he launched his party Aam Aadmi Party, his strongest campaign after making disclosures regarding graft, including the illegal land deals of Mr Robert Vadra (son-in-law of Mrs Sonia Gandhi), was against electricity charges that went up threefolds after the privatisation of the distribution system of power in Delhi. Kejriwal initially appealed to the electorate of Delhi not to pay their power bills, and then went on a 15-day hunger strike in the month of March/April, against the nexus between the Delhi government and corporations supplying power. Perhaps, Kejriwal saw in this campaign the possibility of bridging the gap between the demands of the middle class, who constitute a large section of the electorate in Delhi, and the urban poor.

29. Kejriwal drawing a direct link between corruption and inflation was termed as 'economic illiteracy' by many economists. For more on this, refer to http://www.livemint.com/Opinion/xlDkKDre1EI4JKKTm5pFgP/Arvind-Kejriwal-and-the-economic-illiteracy-in-public-life.html (accessed 9 April 2013).

30. Baba Ramdev was another important symbol against corruption that emerged alongside Anna Hazare. He highlighted the issue of black money stashed away in Swiss banks. On 27 February 2011, Baba Ramdev held a large rally of over 1 lakh people at the Ramlila Maidan, New Delhi to protest against corruption.

31. Refer to two recent biographies of Narendra Modi—*The Namo Story by Kingshuk Nag* (Roli Books, Delhi, 2013) and *Narendra Modi: The Man, The Times* (Tranquebar, Delhi, 2013)—to get a close glimpse at the making of his persona, how it was carefully built through publicity, and his climb from being a son of a teashop owner in Vadnagar and belonging to the Ghanchi (oil-presser) caste to being the image of the growth story in Gujarat and winning three Assembly elections on the trot.

32. Mufti Shameem Kazmi, who was the lone Muslim in Team Anna, was suspended after he was found to be secretly recording the proceedings of the discussions among the members of Team Anna. Kazmi responded by arguing,

'I was a Muslim member in Team Anna Core Committee and I am out of it now. They don't want Muslims in it. I tried to bring more Muslims into it' (refer to http://news.outlookindia.com/items.aspx?artid=760386 [accessed 9 April 2013]). Further, the alienation of Muslims from the campaign against graft was strengthened after Kiran Bedi refused to join the protests against the then BJP president Mr Nitin Gadkari. Bedi did not join the IAC agitation as she felt that the target of the protesters should be only the ruling Congress. She said that she was 'only for focus of the movement to hold the party in power accountable. They alone have the power to replace the rotten system' (http://www.mid-day.com/news/2012/aug/280812-Former-top-cop-wont-protest-against-BJP.htm [accessed 9 April 2013]).

33. Earlier social activist Swami Agnivesh, Justice Rajinder Sachar and activist P.V. Rajagopal quit Team Anna for reasons of undemocratic mode of functioning of the Team lead by Anna Hazare.

34. The routine humiliation of politicians, who are made answerable on news channels but rarely have we witnessed this attitude of media towards the private big corporate houses that have been hand in glove in all the major scams that we have been witness to during the current dispensation.

3

Backward Classes: Reservations, Recognition and the Republic

Since 1990s, India's democracy has been witness to what has been referred to as the 'second democratic upsurge' (Yadav 1999) marking a phenomenon of 'deepening democracy' to include new social groups, especially in the rural hinterland. However, this process happened alongside another phenomenon of 'secularisation of caste', which included de-ritualisation and politicisation of caste. The consequence of this was to aspire not for higher ritual status but for an entry into the 'new middle class'.

> However, the 'new middle class' cannot be seen as constituting a pure class category—a construct which is in fact a theoretical fiction. It carries some elements of caste within it, insofar as the entry of an individual in the middle class is facilitated by the collective political and economic resources of his/her caste. For example, upper-caste individuals entering the middle class have at their disposal the resources that were attached to the status of their caste in traditional hierarchy. Similarly, for lower-caste members lacking in traditional status resources, entry into the 'middle class' is facilitated by modern-legal provisions like affirmative action to which they are entitled by virtue of their low traditional status. It seems the Indian 'middle class' will continue to carry caste elements within it, to the extent that modern status aspirations are pursued, and the possibility of their realisation is seen by individuals in terms of the castes to which they belong. (Seth 2000: 258)

While we discussed the mode of urban/upper-caste middle-class activism in the previous chapter and its consequences for popular democracy, here we would attempt to discuss the impact of this emergent 'new middle class' that carries with it the traces of 'kinship-based cultural community'. The interface between kinship, class mobility, urbanisation and political power has initiated a new kind of 'politics of recognition' that is shrugging off stigma attached not only to caste, but also to the discourse of reservations, which has been at the heart of making this new kind of mobility—beyond ritual hierarchy—a possibility. The 'new' mode of discriminating the emergent 'new middle class', has been not so much on the basis of Louis Dumont's emphasis on ritual hierarchy but by stigmatising the policy of reservations that has allowed for such a mobility.

The singularly debilitating limitation of the system of reservations in India has been to increasingly produce a large number of social groups that suffer various forms of public humiliation, resentment and insult. The purpose of reservations to provide the disadvantaged social groups a head start in realising their potential remains arrested and minimal, due to their inability to overcome the stigma that is attached to such policies. Amartya Sen argues that 'substantive freedoms' include the idea of 'human dignity' that refers, along with access to resources, health, education and equity of opportunities, also to the participation in the life of the community and the freedom to speak without fear. They should all finally contribute towards 'giving individuals greater control over his/her environment and thereby increase their freedom'. Sen considers both a 'sense of self' and the capacity 'to appear in public without shame' as relevant to the 'capability to function', and hence as falling within the scope of an account of justice and development (Sen 1998).[1]

The processes of stigmatisation that are socially and politically con-structed replace the 'sense of self' with a stigmatised self and public shame. For instance, scheduled castes have often been referred to as '*schaddu*' or as '*sarkar ke damad*' (sons-in-law of the government) to both demean them and to remind them that what they are getting is a 'charity and not parity' (Guru 2009: 18).[2] The other form that is often used by the upper-caste students in protesting against reservation is sweeping the streets, polishing shoes in the streets and holding placards that read 'murder of merit'. Polishing shoes and sweeping the streets signify as a reminder that earlier Dalits (scheduled castes) pursued these for their livelihood and therefore socially belonged to lower social status and to convey to the fellow upper-caste students that government policy of reservation will eventually push them towards these menial jobs. Thus, scholars reflecting on caste have often argued that 'social stigma and a variety of disabilities were based on caste; these were and to a significant degree still are the defining character of a Dalit, even if a Dalit moves up in social class or changes religion' (Michael 1999: 19).

The policies of affirmative action seem to create an inherent conflict between the processes of redistribution and the demands for recog-nition. While it is a fact that the policies of reservation have created new opportunities for the specific disadvantaged social groups, these however have come at a cost of causing the more intangible injury of mis-recognition.

> The result is to mark the most disadvantaged class as inherently deficient and insatiable, as always needing more and more. In time such a class can come to appear privileged, the receipt of special treatment and underserved largesse. Thus, an approach aimed at redressing injustices of distribution can end up creating injustices of recognition. (Fraser 2008: 31)

As Fraser puts it, stigmatisation is a mode of 'adding the insult of mis-recognition to the injury of deprivation'. We could rephrase this, in the context of the Brahaminical social order in India, as mobility without dignity. The very practices and policies that entail economic and material mobility rob such social groups of basic dignity or, as Axel Honneth identifies, self-confidence, self-respect and self-esteem (Honneth 2001).

It was precisely to overcome this kind of a deadlock or negation that Ambedkar while tirelessly struggling for the material amelioration of the scheduled castes also cautioned them against reducing it 'merely' to those as the larger agenda was that of regaining 'honour' and 'dignity' and reclaim the 'title deeds' of their humanity that had been taken away by their masters. He argued:

> You should realize what our objective is. It is not fighting for a few jobs here and there or for a few concessions. It is the highest cause that we have cherished in our heart, that is, to see that we are recognized as the governing community. (quoted from Parekh 2009: 10)[3]

It was in order to regain or reclaim dignity that Ambedkar made a series of experiments that not only looked, at times, mutually exclusive, but also failed to realise the objective they set themselves. Ambedkar on the one hand wished to use the power of caste as community to overcome the caste system, and on the other argued for its 'annihilation' by abandoning the caste status through conversion. By way of using the caste identity, Ambedkar argued that the 'depressed classes' need to realise that they are the majority and can easily get political power, provided they succeed in forging political unity.[4] He argued:

> [T]he scheduled castes and the backward classes form the majority of the population of the country. There is no reason why they should not rule the

country. All that is necessary is to organize for the purpose of capturing political power which is your own. (cited from Rodrigues 1990)

With this in mind, he argued, as part of the Poona Pact in 1928, for separate representation 'either through separate electorates (in the absence of adult suffrage) or through joint electorates by adult suffrage' (Pantham 2009: 189).[5] Finally, it was decided that reserved seats were a better option in order to empower the 'depressed classes' without making them 'politically untouchable'. It was also in this spirit that Ambedkar later argued for reservation, for those coming from the scheduled castes, in jobs (especially bureaucracy) and institutions of higher education. He believed that the new elites (born out of reservation in both representative bodies and jobs) from the scheduled castes would represent and play a positive role by way of both lending confidence to their fellow downtrodden and struggling on their behalf to extend all the benefits that they themselves managed to get.[6] Through such a strategy Ambedkar felt both a sense of agency through struggle and thereby dignity, and that economic benefits can be assured to the Dalits. He believed that the newborn elite would be the social force that would be representative of his belief that 'out of hard and relentless struggle that one derives strength, self-respect, self-confidence and recognition'.

However, Ambedkar was also amongst the first to realise the failure and criticise the limits of such 'politics of presence' when he expressed his disappointment that 'the educated few have proved to be a worthless lot, with no sympathies for their downtrodden brethren'; they were busy 'fighting among themselves for leadership and power' (cited from Parekh 2009: 28). Further, the new elites themselves remained stigmatised and failed to move beyond the socially imposed frames, as they were perceived to be enjoying undue benefits, and lacked the merit and efficiency to handle the positions they occupied.[7] In fact, Bhikhu Parekh alluding to this is critical of Ambedkar for his insistence and emphasis on the role of the elites. He believes that 'Ambedkar's approach suffered from a strong statist and elitist bias' and the state could not play a transformative role 'unless it was led by a Westernised elite, of whom Ambedkar saw himself as one' (Parekh 2009: 22)

The alternative strategy of Ambedkar to regain recognition and self-confidence was by way of abandoning Hindu religion when he famously said: 'I will certainly not die as a Hindu' and therefore sought 'liberation from Hinduism and not reform of Hinduism'.[8] On 14 October 1956, Ambedkar converted to Buddhism in a ceremony in Nagpur. One of reasons why he preferred Buddhism over other religions was that it provided a 'theory of social action' through a cultural template. It was, in a sense, transference of his earlier conviction of building recognition and dignity through struggles, as 'the fundamental purpose of *dhamma* is the recognition and removal of suffering through human action' (Verma 2010b: 60). However, even conversion did not help realise the kind of recognition that Ambedkar was looking for. Ambedkarite Buddhists are associated primarily with the Mahar sub-caste, and it has therefore failed to eradicate caste identities and varied forms of humiliation associated with it.[9] Further, the conversion strategy was inextricably interlinked with the debate on reservations. Both neo-Buddhists and Dalit Christians have been demanding the extension of reservations to them as they belong to the SC and ST communities, which has made them further susceptible to the popular prejudice that though they are 'liberated' from caste, they continue to seek benefits accrued due to caste identities.[10] In fact, in a strange but pertinent case, Dalit Buddhists registered as Buddhist Society of India, complaining of social stigma, filed a case seeking scrapping of reservation benefits to Dalit Buddhists under the Constitution, with specific reference to the Presidential Order of 1990 extending reservation to Dalit Buddhists. The Supreme Court of India however struck down and dismissed the petition (*Hindustan Times,* 7 January 2010).

The other kind of failure of the strategy of conversion as 'politics of recognition' has been the objection raised by some of the Dalit leaders more recently, such as Thirumavalavan in Tamil Nadu, that conversion is in fact converting Dalits into a numerical minority. He argues that numerical majority is an absolute necessity if Dalits have to get political power, which is in turn indispensable to their emancipation. Conversion, therefore, negates the other significant strategy of getting—representation—political power as stressed by Ambedkar and needs to be abandoned as a useful strategy in contemporary electoral-representative democracies. Without political power and the 'strategic use' of numerical strength, Dalits once again will become dependent on caste Hindus without agency and capacity for decision-making, entailing and enabling practices of mis-recognition.[11] Thus, they believe that certain strategies, in this case, of overcoming mis-recognition have an adverse impact on representation, spinning off complex and conflicting dynamics between recognition, redistribution and representation.

It is imperative to note that both the strategies suggested by Ambedkar get negated as they get inextricably entangled with the processes of legal codification, and thereby become susceptible and subjected to vulgar objectification. While the former strategy of reservation settles to produce self-enclosed elite that plays an insignificant role in dignifying the rest, the latter idea of conversion gets inflected into producing caste identities even outside of Hinduism. In other words, the modern state discourse of reservations based on codification—transition from fuzzy to enumerated communities—arrests the mobility necessary for transformation (refer to Kaviraj 1999; Dirks 2001).[12] Patchen Markell suggests that the 'grammar of recognition' itself becomes a handmaiden of classifying procedures of states, 'rendering their populations cognizable and manageable' (cited from Feldman 2002: 418). 'Politics of recognition' that are toned through the prism of classifying procedures of the state entail the classical 'recognition-redistribution dilemma' entailing either 'displacing' demands of redistribution or 'reifying' cultural identities and reinforcing dominant modes of mis-recognition (Fraser 2000). The politics of reservations, therefore, needs a new methodology as much as a new social force that can successfully avoid both the problem of 'displacement' and the problem of 'reification' in order to overcome stigma.

It is in this context that we need to explore the impact and the possibility of de-stigmatising the discourse on reservations, with the inclusion of the 'other backward classes' (OBCs) within its ambit. It is no longer sufficient to attempt to liberate groups through reservation without liberating the discourse of reservation itself. For this, it is imperative to have new social forces that can substantially 'resignify' (Butler 1994) the meanings and practice of pursuing protective discrimination through self-perception and self-confidence that is not a result of reservations but is pre-ordained or prior to availing such benefits. This pre-given self-confidence can then change the terms of discourse through an assertion against externally imposed unjust reading of reservation as a charity, or an undue privilege. This chapter will argue that the 'second democratic upsurge' that India is witnessing with OBCs as the new democratic social force will construct a new social/political space, by way of liberating all social groups that have been the beneficiaries of affirmative action from suffering humiliation and public shame, by de-stigmatising the discourse of reservations itself. In other words, the discourse will no longer be unproblematically available to the caste Hindus to either hegemonise the public sphere or construct self-contempt amongst those availing the benefits of reservations.

OBCs as the New Democratic Force

OBCs, in comparison with the scheduled castes, are sociologically distinct in terms of being internally heterogeneous and differentiated both culturally and also socially and economically. Unlike the Dalits, the mobilisation of the OBCs was always self-conscious of internal differentiation.[13] Dalit movement, in contrast, began as a cohesive movement of various subcastes that were, though culturally different and hierarchised, economically similar, and Ambedkar could successfully unite them without sub-caste conflicts ever taking precedence over the 'larger' conflict with caste Hindus and Hinduism itself. It was only in the 1990s that India began to witness political movements of the sub-caste within the scheduled castes. For instance, the state of Andhra Pradesh is witnessing the growing conflict between the Malas and Madigas (Rao 2009). While the OBCs constitute 50 per cent of the population, they are not a cohesive social group either through objective criterion or in terms of subjective perceptions. Internally differentiated and heterogeneous groups can neither be socially mapped around stable cultural practices nor can they be attributed with certain economic status that will in turn make it possible to value their 'moral worth' (Sayers 2005). This difficulty in not being able to culturally codify and socially enumerate disallows both the process of being externally (objectively) objectified and internally (subjectively) reified. An escape from these processes makes social groups too opaque to be stigmatised, even if they are availing the benefits of reservations. Instead the public domain is gradually witnessing an assertion, without an accompanying sense of shame, by those demanding and enjoying the benefits of reservations.

OBCs can be mapped into three different categories around the axis of social status, income and educational qualifications. The upwardly mobile backward classes have both economic (land and property) and political power. The middle-level backward classes are the 'dominant castes'—the peasant castes—in the rural areas that are slowly and gradually improving their educational status. Finally, the 'most backward classes' (MBCs) or 'extremely backward classes' are the 'service castes' that are largely landless, belong to low-income groups and are precariously perched between the other OBCs and the Dalits (Pai unpublished).[14] Within this tripartite division these castes/classes can be further differentiated around varied axis including that of region, for instance, between the north and the south. For instance, with regard to the MBCs, while in the north they are mostly poor and landless, in the southern state of Tamil Nadu,

> the Vanniyars for example, designated as MBCs are an assertive, economically better-off and upwardly mobile caste who have formed their own political party, the Pattali Makal Katchi (PMK). The Karunanidhi government designated them the Vanniyars as MBCs in 1989 and provided them 20 per cent of the total 49 per cent reservations in educational institutions and government employment.... (Pai unpublished)[15]

The backward classes in the south due to the anti-Brahmin movements in the early twentieth century gained reservations from the colonial government in both higher education and employment. The bulk of them therefore not only hold professional jobs but are also well versed in English and have urban lifestyle (refer to Pandian 2007).

Similarly, in the north the debate is increasingly shifting from inter-caste discrimination to intra-caste differentiation and discrimination. The Hukum Singh Committee report in Uttar Pradesh, constituted in 2001, pointed that there are 79 sub-castes within the backward castes/classes. Backward-caste category consisted of just one caste—Yadav (also called Ahir/Gwala/Yaduvashiya); more backward castes (MRBCs) included eight sub-castes—Sonar/Sunar/Swarnkar, Jat, Kurmi/Chanau/Patel/Patanwar/Kurmi-Mali/Kurmi-Sainthwar, Giri, Gujjar, Gosain, Lodh/Lodha/Lodhi/Lot/Lodh-Rajput, Kamboj; and finally the most backward castes (MBCs) included 70 sub-castes (Verma 2010a: 12).[16] On the one hand, across economic status the sub-castes got differentiated, while on the other the various *jatis* have emerged as 'large conglomerates of what were earlier small and varied sub-castes'. 'These two contrary trends, one, the differentiation and undermining of the inherited forms of constitution of castes and, the other, that of the process of internal unification have had a simultaneous run' (Alam 2008: 9). This simultaneous move towards fusion and fission between various caste groups makes it difficult to either map or identify them with certain essentialised traits; instead it takes a more pragmatic turn. In course of my interviews with a cross-section of students and professionals coming from the various sub-castes identified as the OBCs, one of the key features was the pragmatic and 'purely' legal approach to the issue of reservations.[17] Backwardness, unlike untouchability, does not produce a victim subject and whose subjective perception is not constructed either with self-contempt or a stigmatised victimhood. It seems to instead produce a citizen capable of speaking and asserting the language of rights, legal and constitutional entitlements, and pointing towards the limitations of planning and public policy in the past. In other words, a pragmatic political language has replaced an essentially cultural moral idiom, in which Dalit movement continues to locate itself for asserting the need for reservations. The pragmatic approach, in this case, represents both a certain distance from the identity standpoint one is speaking from and a self-conscious understanding of one's caste identity and the forced backwardness without any accompanying anxiety about being stigmatised.

For instance, Ravi Kiran is a *Yadava* from a village near Visakhapatnam in Andhra Pradesh. His father is barely literate and sells clothes on a bicycle. He himself received his education from a municipal school till 5th standard and then shifted to an English medium public school. He recollected that education in a public school was expensive. He used to wear torn shoes and vividly remembered being punished for not paying fees in time. It is interesting to observe that suffering poverty of this nature has resulted in a resolve to achieve social and economic mobility, and not in self-contempt and victimhood. These traits of the victim subject, in contrast, distinctly frame the making of Dalit subjectivity. When asked about availing the provision for reservation in education and jobs he clearly articulated that: 'I will claim. It's given constitutionally. I do not have the fear that if everyone knows I am an OBC. I cannot be discriminated. ... It's a right. I should not be discriminated on caste grounds. ... It's illegal.

To carry the argument further, another distinct dimension that is impacting (read dignifying) the discourse of reservation is the fact that groups that are dominant and enjoy political and economic power want themselves to be part of the 'reserved category'. The upwardly mobile Jats argued: 'If Khatis, Charans, Sunars, and Darzis are declared as backward, why not us' (Datta 1999: 2630). Similarly in Andhra Pradesh, there are four different communities that are identified as Kapus. In the north coastal districts of Srikakulam, Vizianagaram and Visakhapatnam, they are called Toorpu (eastern) Kapus; in the prosperous coastal Andhra districts of Godavari, Krishna and Gunjur, they are called just Kapus; in the Rayalaseema districts, they are referred to as Balijas; and in the Telangana region, they are called Munnuru Kapus. While Toorpu Kapus and Munnuru Kapus have already been listed as backward castes/classes, the other two dominant castes in spite of being landed and fairly prosperous have been demanding inclusion into the list of backward castes. Rajputs are mostly organised in Delhi to confirm their status as backward. It is a telling fact that backward-class movement

> clamoured for the 'Kshatriya' status which was denied to them by forward castes…Today, it is no longer interested in assessing the 'Khastriya' status rather the All-India Federation for Backward Classes as well as its varied local forms, have as their chief concerns: access to state resources, representation in decision-making spheres of the government…. (Yadav 2002: 4500)

Demands from such dominant groups are gradually making reservations a more generalised feature of the Indian polity, rather than being identified with any specific caste, community or classes. This in turn makes it very difficult for the so-called forward or upper castes to denounce or stigmatise the discourse of reservations. Instead, this debate has headed in the direction of 'reverse social osmosis' seeking reservation for the poor among the upper castes (Verma 2010a: 13).[18] It has also enabled to seek a renewed justification for the reservations to the scheduled castes and tribes. In course of my interviews, all the respondents argued that it is justified to give reservations to the Dalits, and some of them expressed the view that though for OBCs reservations should be time bound and follow the criterion of 'creamy layer', but for the Dalits at least for some time more it should be given unconditionally. More than altruism what these views reflect is the realisation that without fully justifying the reservations for the Dalits, OBCs cannot demand reservations for themselves.

This pragmatic approach has reinforced, and will further entrench, the idea that reservations are a justified means of achieving social justice, and not a sop for a few.

While on the other hand we could justifiably argue that it is the elites who make such demands and therefore—'reservation is the weapon of the strong'—want to siphon off the public funds, it cannot be still undermined that this in itself augments well for 'politics of recognition' and in overcoming shame and stigma attached to the discourse of reservation. After over two decades of reservations for the OBCs in employment in the central government and in higher education for the last couple of years, we are witnessing for the first time groups who can access and 'appear in public without a sense of shame', and in fact publicly claim that they have 'won'—using their political clout and economic power—what is legitimately due to them. They are uncluttered in who they are and of what practical use caste is to them, and proud that they actually know how to get what is due to them. They are reclaiming the public space and public policy by opening and forging new links between the two.

For instance, Dr Sailesh Suman, who is a *Kurmi,* a doctor by profession and a son of a medical officer with the Government of Bihar, stated that 'I am proud of being a Kurmi' since there are such learned and educated people such as Nitish Kumar, who have because of his intelligence changed the face of Bihar. He further added, with a sense of pride for holding the 'system to ransom', that 'I am not actually backward', but he felt that there are many more in his caste, and other backward castes such as the *Malhar,* who require reservations and he is ready to fight for them. This capacity and confidence to resist mis-recognition by distancing one's self from the societal tag of being 'backward' and to disallow it from influencing the self-perception would have a tremendous impact of dignifying the discourse of reservations. Self-confidence of such groups precedes availing of reservations and not typically dependent on them. While with Dalits the elites were born out of pursuing reservations, with the OBCs the elites laid claim to reservations. It is simply not sufficient, at least in the context of India, to argue that recognition only emerges and is dependent on mutuality and inter-subjective interaction, but it is also necessary to realise the need to be recognition-resistant to generate one's own sense of self from within (refer to Taylor 1994; Honneth 2001).[19]

In the case of the OBCs, for instance like that of Yadavs, it is interesting to observe that there are various internal mechanisms to generate their own sense of self-confidence.[20] Lucia Michelutti argues that in course of her fieldwork she discovered that even rich Yadav businessmen in Delhi kept buffaloes and cows in their farmhouses and they proudly declared that in spite of being rich they cannot forget their 'origins and traditional skills'.

> The Yadavs are proud not only of their genealogical link with Krishna the cowherder but also of the animals that they rear. In India the species of animal a caste domesticates has a bearing on its social status, and since the cow is at the top of the animal hierarchy, the Yadavs consequently think that they must have a high ritual status. (Michelutti 2007: 651)

Yadav political organisations such as the All India Yadav Mahasabha (AIYM) portray Krishna as the 'leader of social justice' and construct a distinct 'ethno-historical imaginary' that also emphasises the need for a 'muscular ideology' that reminds the state that they are no pushovers. The physicality of their politics working like 'gang solidarity' is the performative dimension of their own version of self-respect. Many in course of my interviews expressed the views that Yadavs have 'low intellect', are 'violent' and 'not good in studies but fit for physical activities'. These perceptions might influence the Yadavs to realise the importance of education but fails to dislodge their self-confidence of who they are.

Michelutti argues that Yadav caste rhetoric constructs 'Yadav essences' that include the idea that every Yadav has 'a predisposition for politics' and 'they say that in every Yadav there is a Mulayam' (Michelutti 2007: 647).[21] It is this 'predisposed' self-confidence that they induce into the discourse on reservations. Reservations are merely a tool to achieve what is the 'predisposed' talent of the community, and does not define their 'essence'. The discourse on reservations becomes 'vernacularised'—'the process through which ideas and practices of democracy become embedded in particular cultural and social practices and in turn become entrenched in the consciousness of ordinary people' (Michelutti 2007: 653). It is the internal practices that define and inform the spirit of reservations rather than other way round. The internal resources born out of kinship ties also make this social group mark its distinctness as the 'new middle class', as against the traditional urban/upper-caste middle classes.

Resignifying Reservations

Reservations for the OBCs in spite of following the quota system are fast transforming the way reservations are perceived in the popular imagination in the public domain. This, in part, is also due to the new modalities through which it is being implemented.

The Constitution under Article 340 merely provided a provision to set up a commission to look into the issue of backward classes. Until the First Backward Classes Commission was set up in 1953, there was no definite meaning or method of identifying which social groups constituted these classes, and what role will caste have in it (Galanter 1984). It was Kaka Kalelkar Commission that identified a list of 2399 backward groups on the basis of the various criteria including place in trade and occupation, security of employment, educational attainment, representation in government service and position in social hierarchy. It, however, used caste groups as units to identify backward classes. The use of caste created both confusion and constraints in implementing the recommendations.[22] Janata Government in 1977 set up the next Commission—Mandal Commission— to again look into the feasibility of providing reservations to deserving backward classes/castes. The Commission again emphasised the role of caste in structuring opportunities and backwardness; though it applied 11 different indicators to identify backward groups, they overlapped with specific caste groups. Finally, the Commission identified 3,743 caste groups as OBCs comprising 52 per cent of the total population. Since the Supreme Court put a cap of 50 per cent reservation in the Balaji case in 1963, Mandal Commission recommended 27 per cent reservations in the public services, and scientific, technical, and professional institutions under the central government (Sahoo 2009: 35).[23] Mandal Commission report faced resistance, and Janata Government failed to implement it as it lost power to Congress by the time the report was submitted. It was only in 1990 that the V.P. Singh government took up the recommendations and announced its implementation.

Since caste was not the only criterion and overcoming backwardness was the purpose, the debate and the accompanying clauses in implementing the OBC reservations were different from that of the Dalits. These criteria in themselves have had an impact in de-stigmatising the provision of reservations. One of the central issues was the inclusion of the 'creamy layer' criterion in implementing the OBC reservations. The Justice R.N. Prasad Committee set up in 1993 to decide on creamy layer defined it as 'when a person was able to shed off the attributes of educational and social backwardness and has secured employment or has engaged himself in some high status profession or trade' (R.N. Committee Report, 1993).[24] Apart from the balancing act of making sure that most deserving individuals within the OBCs benefitted from reservations, the criterion of creamy layer had its own positive impact in overcoming mis-recognition due to reservations.

The conventional argument against the creamy layer criterion in reservations has been that 'by disqualifying those most likely to succeed in elite institutions, creamy layer exclusion undermines the very purpose of the proposed law' (Deshpande 2008). The other more culture-centric critique of creamy layer was that the elites in each community have 'given confidence to the others to aspire for higher positions in life rather then come in the way of their advancement, were matters of no relevance to this process of deductive reasoning' (Balagopal 2009: 17). This line of reasoning however does not sufficiently interrogate whether and how the criterion of creamy layer itself will add to the confidence of those availing reservations, and in a manner distinct from the way elite-induced confidence works. Ambedkar himself realised the need for the role of elites in providing others in their community with the confidence to move upwards; however, this dependence on elites has led to both new classes within each community and in turn to a process where the distance between the elites and non-elites was so marked that they were identified more with the affluent classes/castes rather than with their own communities. It is due to these reasons that states such as Andhra Pradesh and Maharashtra have witnessed bitter sub-caste conflicts within the Dalits. The Madigas in Andhra Pradesh, under the leadership of the Madiga Reservation Porata Samiti (MRPS), at one stage even argued that Malas were more ruthless oppressors than even the Brahmins. In a sense, reservations almost had a counter-productive effect in overcoming caste hierarchies and accompanying prejudices.[25] Even those who moved ahead within their castes did not wish to be identified with their communities. This process far from adding to confidence has in fact enabled a process of stigmatisation where the popular belief was that the elites of these communities were rank opportunists and abandoned their fellow sufferers once they benefitted from reservations. The upper caste often used this to delegitimise the very idea of reservations being useful to no one except those few who directly benefitted from it. In other words, it was argued that there was no rub-off effect socially that was often offered as a justification for reservations.

It is in this context that the criterion of creamy layer in a subtle way resignifies reservations as not meant to either create self-enclosed elites or be dependent on elites to induce confidence in others. From elite-induced confidence it makes it possible that the very modality of pursuing reservations is based only on a 'need-based approach' and therefore is a temporary measure to correct an imbalance rather than a permanent feature. Even Ambedkar argued that the reservations for the SCs and STs need to be time bound and restricted to a period of 10 years, though he restricted this criterion to the case of reservations in political representation. Time-bound reservations seem to be necessary to achieve both redistribution and recognition. The Supreme Court, in fact, was of the opinion that reservations should not be in perpetuity but should be periodically revised. The earlier anxiety, in the case of Dalits, was that this was the only instrument available to them to provide opportunities, given both their economic plight and the overwhelming prejudice against them. However, in the case of the OBCs, it seems that given the ability of these groups to articulate their grievances openly, the time-bound criterion will offer them the opportunity to counter and negate either those who use it to discredit reservations as such or those who stigmatise groups that benefit from such advantages.

It is interesting to observe that all the interviewees from both the lower—MBCs—and the upwardly mobile OBCs supported the idea of creamy layer. Amit Yadav, whose father is a class IV railway employee in Aasansol (Bihar), was of the opinion that 'reservations are only to get jobs ... what is important is education'; therefore, once you have the required income, there is very little need for reservations and the creamy layer criterion should be applied. Similarly, Rajesh, who belongs to the Pasi (Fishermen) community and hails from Sahibgunj, a small town in Jharkhand, supported the creamy layer criterion, in spite of belonging to the economically backward caste (EBC). He also observed that 'more in-formation about state policies and proper implementation will lead to less conflict ... and more will agree with the creamy layer criterion'. It could be observed that in order to get state benefits, these young students did not wish to compromise on their dignity, and realised the importance of being equal to the rest, and in order to get a sense of equal 'moral worth' and also convince those not availing of the benefits of reservations, the creamy layer criterion was very important.

The final point on the way the debate on reservations is being substantively transformed is also linked with the manner in which the idea of merit is being appropriated by these new claimants of reservations, in somewhat contrast to the Dalits. In the case of the Dalits, for various reasons, reservations and merit were dichotomised into two watertight compartments. They mostly argued that the very idea of merit is bogus and a fraudulent construct of the upper castes; it does not provide any alternative basis for the working of public institutions. Similarly, Courts that pronounced judgements in support of reservations always believed that though this is a drain on the resources and efficiency of the system, it was necessary to provide special provisions for certain social groups that have failed to adequately avail the opportunities provided by the state and society alike. This has provided a public reasoning for reservations but in a subtle manner reinforced the dominant prejudice against groups availing of reservations. This is very similar to the way Courts pronounced judgements on rape—punishing the accused for violating the 'chastity' and 'virginity' of the victim; in the process they further reinforced the dominant notions of sexuality and lack of control and agency of women on their body and glorifying a 'victim subject' in need of 'protection'. In fact, with regard to caste, this mode of reasoning that Courts furthered was borrowed from the debates in the Constituent Assembly, while making provisions for quotas.

> It was argued that departures from merit selection in the form of group quotas would harm public interest in an efficient administration and good government...the Constituent Assembly made it clear that such special provisions shall be subjected to the 'maintenance of merit and efficiency' of the administration. (Sahoo 2009: 27)

One such caveat was to exclude those professions that require higher skills and specialisation in the name of 'public interests'. For instance, Anathasayanam Ayyangar argued in the Constituent Assembly that 'with regards to appointments which require enormous skill and capacity, certainly these rules cannot be relaxed, because public interests demand otherwise' (CAD, Vol. ix). It was never debated as to what will be the impact of this on groups availing reservations nor was it deliberated, even by present-day

Courts, as to how we could impart these 'high skills' to individuals coming from disadvantaged backgrounds. It was almost assumed that it was not possible to impart such specialisation, for what apparent reason remained largely unelaborated and unknown. The Courts in a convoluted manner reinforced the idea of merit and efficiency of the dominant-caste groups, and Dalits themselves rejected any viable or alternative notion of merit; both these factors entrenched the hegemony of the dominant castes and Dalits effectively remained 'outsiders' to public institutions, and thereby silently suffered humiliation, rejection and indignation.[26]

As against the Dalit discourse, the OBCs seem to re-appropriate merit. They have a pragmatic approach to the idea of merit. Most of the interviewees accepted that merit is essentially linked to the opportunities and there is no community or caste that is intrinsically meritorious or disabled. Along with this, however, they argued that there are many examinations in which OBCs are the toppers and qualify in open competitions. Santosh Kumar, from Madhubani district in Bihar, who is a Gupta and from the *Baniya* community, argued that even within OBCs there is stiff competition and in spite of reservations it is not easy to get through. He took pride that those who qualify through reservations are also therefore meritorious. Amit Yadav argued that if you take a head count, you will find that 'maximum number of intelligent people come from the OBC communities'.[27] This kind of appropriation and linking of merit, competition and reservations goes beyond a dichtomised approach that allows for public shaming of those belonging to the reserved categories. Along with this, the Central Educational Institutions (Reservations and Admissions) Bill 2006, that introduces reservations for the OBCs in Central Universities, provides for a unique provision of increasing seats for the general category students. The earlier argument of illegitimately cutting into the seats does not hold well, and it also proves the point that groups other than the upper castes have a legitimate claim on the resources of the nation.[28]

OBCs and Politics

Along with the new modalities, OBC politics are, unlike Dalits, not exclusively caste-centric. Along with caste they are articulating their demands and politics along the lines of region, religion and language. This mode of pursuing politics across multiple axis and not just caste alone also makes it difficult to essentialise and objectify them. They are active in articulating various issues that are of significance in 'high politics' of the centre and the state, which in turn has a moderating impact on their caste politics in general and the demand for reservations in particular.

Rajini Kothari argued that extending reservations to the OBCs is part of 'a great secular upsurge', as it brings together 'not only all the lower castes but also the poor or "backward" of other religions, while at the same time it prevents Hindus from acting as a solid bloc' (Kumar 1992: 299). As Kothari argues, 'Caste, indeed, is the great secularizer in a society being pulled apart by convoluted religions bent upon tearing apart the social fabric' (Kothari 1990). The fact that there are OBCs in Hindus as well as the Muslims bringing them together within the ambit of the same state policy has its positive impact of foregrounding backwardness and economic or class-centric issues. However, along with this, some scholars also argued to the contrary that this lumping together of backward castes and religious minorities has resulted in the growth of communalism and Hindu identity.[29] For instance, Ornit Shani argued, in the context of Gujarat, that

> In spite of an inter-Hindu caste reservations conflict and prevailing class tensions among them, an all-Hindu consolidation against Muslims emerged. Their general impoverishment in the city [of Ahmedabad] made it difficult to explain why and how the rhetoric about their peril to the Hindu majority became persuasive. Moreover, upper-caste groups who led the anti-reservation struggle and the communal instigation started gaining support from some groups among the Dalits who did not obviously benefit from their agenda. (Shani 2007: 132; also refer to Teltumbde 2005)[30]

Pride of the OBC communities that is, in a sense, a source of a positive impact on diluting the stigma of reservation seems to be also the basis for communal mobilisation.[31]

OBC communities have also gained access to political and economic power, not merely through caste-centric politics but also through the politics of region. OBCs have been a strong force behind the phenomenon of formation of regional parties across the country. They were strongly behind the phenomenon of regional parties and spearheaded the collapse of the 'Congress System'. For instance, in Andhra Pradesh, the BCs were the mainstay of regional parties such as the Telugu Desam Party (TDP).

In January 1983, the state saw the eclipse of the Congress(I) government headed by Kotla Vijaya Bhaskar Reddy and coming into power of TDP. .... In the political charade NTR proved to be cleverer. He established himself as the unchallenged champion of the BCs by enhancing BC reservations to 40 per cent. (Shatrugna 1994: 2398)

In 1988, under the Ninth Finance Commission, 'additionally special care was to highlight the problem of the BCs and out of the ₹72.04 crore pleaded on behalf of the STs and BCs, a whopping ₹56.00 crore was earmarked for the BC welfare alone' (Shatrugna 1988: 1939). More recently in Andhra Pradesh, the struggle for a separate state of Telangana had its roots, along with other issues, in the loss of livelihood of traditional 'service castes'. In various districts, the Joint Action Committees (JAC) formed to mobilise people and organise protest rallies were represented by various caste groups. In some districts, as scholars have observed, 'seventy per cent of these groups are backward castes...' (Kannabiran et al. 2010: 79). The OBCs have been in the forefront to not only demand share in the resources but also to legitimise social recognition of their culture in the struggle for a new state.

> The movement for Telangana ... has become a movement with unique characteristics. Masses belonging to all walks of life have come out to the streets with their cultural symbols. We can see dalit-Bahujans beating drums and dholaks, the Other Backward Classes (OBCs) with their ploughshares and bullock carts, shepherds with their flock, toddy tappers with their moku (rope assembly used to climb palm trees) and muttadu (the belt they wear to keep their hatchet) and stone-breakers with their own iron artefacts. (Kannabiran et al. 2010: 79)

In the north, the Bahujan Samaj Party (BSP) in Uttar Pradesh came to power by experimenting with a new—*Bahujan*—alliance between the SCs, STs and OBCs, defeating both the national parties the Congress and the BJP, before it shifted to the more inclusive—*Sarvajan*—policy in the recent past (refer to Gudavarthy 2008c). Similarly, in Bihar the Rashtriya Janata Dal (RJD) was led by the Yadavs, and the more recent ascendance of Nitish Kumar of the JD (U) was possible with the subdivision of the OBCs into MBCs and MRBCs. Similarly, the OBCs are active in the demand for smaller states such as Bundelkhand that includes six districts in Uttar Pradesh and seven districts in Madhya Pradesh. It is an

OBC dominant region with OBCs constituting more than 50 per cent of the population and the issues of backwardness are being articulated along the lines of region by the OBC organisations and not caste alone, with unusually active support from the government of Uttar Pradesh itself headed by Mayawati. Since it is a *Bahujan* dominant region, she expects to form the government as she enjoys the popular support of Dalit and OBC communities.[32] Thus, OBCs moving beyond merely caste align their caste-based interests with both formation of new regional parties and the demand for new and smaller states.

OBCs have also been foregrounding the question of language that was in the backburner for some time now in Indian politics. After independence the question of official language included primarily the status of English, which was diabolical since it was a foreign language and yet necessary as a 'window to the world'. Similarly, 'the second major issue then arose concerning which one or more of the major languages of India should be adopted as the official language of the country' (Brass 1990: 162). Hindi was considered as a possible option since it was spoken by the largest number of people in the country; however, the non-Hindi speaking states objected as they thought that it would give the states in the north an undue advantage as it would be the language for holding exams for employment in public services, and also that non-Hindi languages are equally national. Revisiting this issue as part of the Official Language Act 1963, on the material issue of entry into the Union public services, it was agreed that all the languages listed in the Eighth Schedule of the Constitution of India, that is, all the major regional languages as well as Hindi and English, could be used as a medium of examination (Brass 1990: 166). Coming into public institutions in a big number following the new reservation of 27 per cent, the OBCs are rearticulating the issue of use of Hindi for the purposes of employment and also education.

The bulk of the interviewees were not only from small towns but also first-generation graduates mostly educated in Hindi medium. Again, somewhat in contrast to the Dalit politics, they have a more pragmatic approach to the issue of language. On the one hand, they refuse to attach any stigma for having studied in the Hindi medium and on the other recognise the need to know English for the purpose of job and being in tune with global communications. Here again the Dalit movement argued that English is a mode of 'emancipation' for the Dalits and the only secular language. Dalit activists such as Chandra Bhan Prasad in fact went to the extent of building a temple for the 'Goddess of English' in Uttar Pradesh, as a mark of gratitude and celebration of Lord Babington Macaulay's birthday (Lahiri 2010). Others, such as Kancha Illiah (Illiah 2011), have argued that

> English education is the key for adopting the modernist approach suitable to the globalised India. The upper castes have handled the contradiction between English and their native quite carefully. But when it comes to teaching English to the lower castes they have been proposing a theory that English will destroy the 'culture of the soil'.

These arguments again were vulnerable to the assertions that Dalits continued to suffer from a 'colonial hangover' and victims of 'Western hegemony'. It could also be argued that such strategies of emulation are the renewed form that 'Sanskritisation' has taken in modern times.

In contrast, for instance, Nishad Vaibhav from Champaran in Bihar, graduated in Hindi medium and argued that Hindi 'should be allowed', nonchalantly said that 'teachers help to study in English … but I write in Hindi and do not see a problem in this'. One of the modes of assertion of the OBCs, and modes of making their presence felt in public institutions such as the universities, is by demanding that teaching and study material be made available to them in Hindi, as it is officially recognised and is the public responsibility of the authorities. In fact, Mulayam Singh Yadav made a strong pitch for education in mother tongue as against English to give an edge to the lower castes/classes in India. This agenda was at odds with that of the Dalit politics; reflecting on this Chandra Bhan Prasad observed that

> when a couple of years back, we launched English as the Goddess, some prominent OBCs intellectuals were upset with me. I later realized that 'remove English' was the first major political movement the OBCs had launched in the North India. I also understand that, the Dravidian movement accorded excessive importance to Tamil language and saw English with contempt. (Prasad 2008)

The issue of Hindi again overlaps with the conflict between a small—mostly upper-caste—English speaking elites and the vast majority who are well versed in various Indian languages. However, public institutions would now come under a new stress and need to recognise that merely providing reservations to the OBCs is not sufficient but they will also have to make space for other related curricular issues. This could be read as asserting space within the institutions and also questioning the elite bias through which they have been operating so far. In other words, though the Official Language Act provided a provision for the use of all major Indian languages, there were no resources or necessary backup provided to actualise these provisions.[33] It is in this context one needs to realise that the politics of OBCs are posing new set of terms beyond caste, which upturns the stigma of reservations into an open debate on issues that were left unresolved in order to preserve the dominance of a few castes by stealth.

To conclude, it needs to be recognised that 'politics of recognition' that OBCs have set into motion have their own set of terms and dynamics that need to be factored as indispensable to any process of democratisation. These are bound to be in conflict with received forms—read dominant-upper-caste discourse—of articulating issues of democracy, equality and dignity. The politics of OBCs have now brought into the public domain issues that are likely to change the very terms of discourse in which the debate on reservations was pursued for the last three decades. Overcoming stigma of reservations is most likely to impact not merely the OBCs and other beneficiaries of such affirmative policies but is in fact set to influence the very grounds on which public institutions, policy and political processes have so far been perceived and pursued in Indian politics. This, in turn, is bound to have profound impact on the workings on democracy in India, in terms of challenging the hegemony of traditional middle classes and recasting the relations and modes of empowerment for the subaltern classes.

Endnotes

1. This shift towards integrating various dimensions of justice underscores the changes not only in the discourse on development but also the liberal theory through the Rawlsian theory of 'distributive justice' and his 'difference principle', and also the discourse on human rights founded in the international declaration on the 'Right to Development' (refer to Gudavarthy 2008b).
2. This distorted version was coined by the upper-caste students pursuing the MBBS course in one of the medical colleges in Delhi. This college also

witnessed violent attack on students from the scheduled castes, eventually resulting in government intervention and suspension of some those involved in the assault.

3. In fact, it was around this issue of how much and how to combine the material with the cultural or psychological that Ambedkar strongly differed with Gandhi. The Gandhian strategy almost replaced the issue of the material with the moral, while Ambedkar was attempting to combine the two, where instead of negating both these dimensions of justice—recognition and redistribution—mutually reinforced each other (refer to Gudavarthy 2008a).

4. Ambedkar, with this strategy in mind, founded the Republican Party of India (RPI) in order to forge the unity of all deprived castes and take political power. He believed that the modern state and its law-making function were extremely significant in overcoming caste-based practices.

5. The British Prime Minister announced the 'Communal Award' wherein he granted both separate electorates and reserved seats to the depressed classes in 1932.

6. We will revisit this point on the role of elites while discussing the case of the OBCs.

7. One of the critical dimensions of a caste-ridden psyche is to generate self-contempt amongst those suffering under the caste hierarchy. The caste system reproduces itself when the victim himself/herself believes that he or she is not worthy of respect. This is made possible through various rituals, philosophical propositions such as *karma* theory that are converted into common sense, and other related performative dimensions of the caste system.

8. In fact, Thomas Pantham argues that there were two distinct phases. Till about 1934 Ambedkar sought emancipation through reform of Hinduism and welfare measures of the state; however, after 1935 the primary goal was that of gaining social equality outside Hinduism (Pantham 2009: 186).

9. It does not mean that this strategy has been given up by the Dalit movement. As recently as 2006, 20 lakhs people converted to Buddhism, in order to celebrate the 50th year of Ambedkar's *Deeksha* (Verma 2010b: 61).

10. The strange inference drawn, within the dominant public discourse, from this process of demanding reservation for the converted is that the Dalits are now not interested in overcoming their caste identities since they get undue privileges and largesse of state policies.

11. Thirumavalavan is a Dalit activist in Tamil Nadu, and was a Member of Parliament in the 15th Lok Sabha. He is currently the vice president of the political outfit called the Liberation Panthers Party. He is known for his arguments that Dalits need to stop conversion and will find a durable solution in a renewed Tamil Nationalism that questions the Sanskritic traditions, wherein lie the roots of the caste system. He has recently taken up a campaign to change Sanskritic names, as part of which he famously renamed his father! (refer to http://wikipidia.org/wiki/thol_thirumavalavan)

12. The other strategy that caste groups 'invented' in order to infuse mobility into their caste status was what sociologist M.N. Srinivas referred to as the process of 'Sanskritization'. To put it in his words:

   The lower castes always seem to have tried to take over the customs and way of life of the higher castes. The theoretical existence of ban on their adoption of Brahmanical customs and rites was not very effective, and this is clear when we consider the fact that many non-Brahminical castes practice many Brahminical customs and rites. (Srinivas 1992: 44)

   However, even this strategy of emulation had a limited positive impact on de-stigmatising the so-called lower castes, as Srinivas observes, 'But Sanskritization does not always result in higher status for the Sanskritized caste, and this is clearly exemplified by the Untouchables. However thoroughgoing the Sanskritization of an untouchable group maybe, it is unable to cross the barrier of untouchability' (Srinivas 1992: 58). Thus, the impact of this failure is perhaps visible in the shift in contemporary Dalit identity that is being carved out of a middle path between 'assimilation' and 'radical separatism'. Instances such as those of the *Ravidas Deras* in Punjab stand out as a good example for such an alternate path (Ram 2008).

13. The backward class movement in India still has no single icon around which it can be mobilized. Though for the purposes of rhetoric Ram Manohar Lohia is cited as a leading beacon, he has very little following in the south due to the fact that he was a champion of Hindi being the official language, and even in the north, as he has a dominant image of being essentially a socialist. The recent reinvention was attempted by the Aam Aadmi Party (AAP), which invoked the image of Ram Manohar Lohia, alongside Jay Prakash Narayan, for his anti-graft struggles.

14. I am thankful to my colleague Sudha Pai for both discussing various aspects of the OBC politics and sharing some of her published and unpublished works.

15. Even around occupation the MBCs could be differentiated between the specialized service castes such as Lohar and Sonar and the artisanal service castes such as Julaha and Kumbhar.

16. There was an attempt in Uttar Pradesh to subdivide the reservation in accordance with the recommendations of the Hukum Singh Committee, through an amendment to the Uttar Pradesh Public Service Act. However, the Supreme Court in its order dated 14 December 2001 and 21 January 2002 stayed the implementation of the provisions of the Amended Act (Verma 2010a: 12).

17. Fieldwork included intensive interviews with about 50 students and professionals from the OBC communities for a period of one year between January and December 2010. The first round was carried out in Delhi, and the second round was conducted in Hyderabad. The interviews included questions about family background—parents' educational qualifications and income; candidates' educational background, experience regarding movement from his/her village

to the city and urban lifestyle; views on reservations—both for the SC/ST and the OBCs—and on the issue of 'creamy layer' and merit; intra-OBC division; and perceptions about the relation with other dominant castes and the Dalits. Names and case history of those cited are given in this chapter without any change. Prior permission of the candidates has been obtained.

18. Reservations for the poor among the upper castes were suggested by the Mayawati Government in Uttar Pradesh.

19. Since India has an extensive caste system where every group has another group both above and below itself, groups and individuals within them do not have a complete sense of the self. It is only Brahmins who have self-referential identity as delineated by ritual status and as prescribed by the sacred scripts; rest are all condemned and therefore have to get their recognition only in course of face-to-face interaction with other groups. The ladder-like system, I feel, also needs along with the need for recognition to be complimented by confidence to also be (mis)-'recognition resistant'.

20. These internal mechanisms, however, need to be transparent enough not to be either objectified or reified. This is a delicate and therefore a difficult balance to achieve. Dalit movement also made similar claims of exclusive 'lived experience', but it entailed insularity and authenticity that became susceptible to essentialisation (refer to Gudavarthy 2008a).

21. Mulayam Singh Yadav was the former chief minister of Uttar Pradesh and presently heads the Samajwadi Party (SP). He was a wrestler before he came into active politics.

22. Third Five Year Plan in 1961 abandoned the OBC lists prepared by the states to offer post-matric scholarships and instead preferred to go by family income (Galanter 1984).

23. Many scholars have argued that the 50 per cent cap has no sociological basis except the anxiety that efficiency would be compromised and enough opportunities should be left for the upper castes (refer to Balagopal 2009).

24. ₹1 lakh of annual income was decided as the ceiling to decide who fall within the creamy layer criterion. It was later increased to ₹2.5 lakhs in 2004, and currently it is fixed at ₹4.5 lakhs.

25. MRPS is being led by a dynamic and young Krishna Madiga as its leader, who was the first to add 'Madiga' as his surname and proclaimed that they had a long and glorious history; however, it needs to be pointed out here that he was seen to be primarily opposed to the demand of a separate state of Telangana, unlike the OBCs who actively championed the cause. Dalit politics have always remained constrained within a singular focus on caste.

26. This line of argument continued till the recent judgement by the Chief Justice Altamas Kabir on 31 July 2013, arguing that there cannot be reservations in jobs that require super-specialisation, for instance specialising as surgeons within the medical profession or as pilots in the Air Force who require to fly fighter jets, and so on. The assumption being those from reserved categories

cannot be trained to acquire these skills; in the process arguments and assumptions of these kinds reinforce the stigma and prejudice attached to the policy of affirmative action.

27. In fact some of them argued that successfully getting reservations implemented, against the opinion of upper castes, is itself a sign of how effective and meritorious OBCs are.

28. In spite of the critique of economic reforms and globalisation, one of the advantages of a growth rate over 8 per cent has been the increased budget for education, which in turn allowed the government to create extra seats and also make additional appointments of teachers to maintain teacher–student ratio and also resulted in pushing the age of retirement from 62 to 65 in universities under the central government, in order to maintain the services of qualified staff till they find suitable alternatives, especially with regard to professional institutions such as the IITs.

29. This, however, is not the complete story; the same OBCs also increasingly moved towards the far-right Hindutva variant of politics. The pride and aspects of self-respect seem to have also been drawn as the basis for a resurgent Hindutva ideology (Shah 2002). In this context, the recent faceoff between Nitish Kumar and Narendra Modi stands out as a representative example of two contrasting impulses existing side by side. Nitish Kumar insisted on maintaining the social alliance between the OBCs and the Muslims, and therefore opposed Modi's candidature for leading the National Democratic Alliance (NDA).

30. This possibility became even starker with the emergence of Modi as the frontrunner in the forthcoming General Elections in 2014. Modi has carefully crafted his image as a representative of the OBCs and non-Brahmin majority by picking up Vivekanand as the symbol of his campaign for Assembly Elections in Gujarat in 2013, and later in the run up to the General Elections he addressed meetings sharing the platform with Baba Ramdev on 26 April 2013 at a function organised by Baba Ramdev to inaugurate the Acharyakulam school in Haridwar.

31. It would not be perhaps inappropriate to mention here that SC, ST and OBC reservations are not applicable to institutions run by or meant for the minorities. Recently, Jamia Milia Islamia University was declared as a minority institution by the Government of India and the bulk of public debate was that more seats would now be available for Muslims as reservations for SC, ST and OBCs are no longer applicable. It is important to note the general and the specific resentment of the groups that stand to lose out due to such a move. This could create and sustain new and old cleavages across religious communities, and how the debate gets displaced into a conflict *between* backward and economically weak communities. Similarly, the Government of Andhra Pradesh attempted separate reservations (up to 5 per cent) for Muslims in 2007, but was struck down by the High Court as there is no constitutional provision for reservations on exclusive religious grounds.

32. However, the Congress under the leadership of Rahul Gandhi has also been active in foregrounding the issue of regional backwardness of Bundelkhand. It found a special mention in the Union budget in 2010, and was allocated ₹1,200 crores, and a year before that the United Progressive Alliance (UPA) government announced a special package of ₹7266 crores 'to implement its drought mitigation strategy and integrated development schemes' (*The Hindu*, 30 April 2011). I am thankful to Jagpal Singh for suggesting relevant material on Bundelkhand.

33. Mulayam also made statements against use of computers, which he later retracted. This agenda against English also has, ironically, similarity with the agenda of leaders such as Raj Thackeray of the Maharashtra Navnirman Sangathan (MNS). It also therefore offers a new relation between the middle, backward and subaltern classes and the process of globalisation.

4

Subaltern Classes: Governmentality, Resistance and 'Political Society'

What is the impact of the mobilisation of the old urban middle classes and the 'new' and aspiring backward classes on the subaltern that includes the urban poor that figures below the poverty line, working class that is entering the informal sector, rural landless and peasants who are victims of agrarian crisis and forced into distress migration, suspect Muslims in urban ghettoes and peripheries, tribals in central India, Dalits and Dalit women subjected to varied forms of violence, and migrants who are at the receiving end of the 'sons of soil' kind of political machismo, to name a few. Have they also been able to expand their agency alongside the other distinct social and class groups? Or have they vacated the streets for them to be occupied by the emergent urban activism led by the old and new middle classes? Have the subaltern then been pushed into a vortex of de-mobilisation or have they taken to more militant modes of mobilisation, best represented by the Maoist movement in India?

It is in this context of wide-scale difference over how to approach the question of subaltern agency that the postcolonial theorist Partha Chatterjee has offered his rather fresh and novel concept of 'political society'. This arena, according to him, is marked by those practices which the subalterns adopt and are essentially political but look uncivil from the point of view of civil society. It is, therefore, a domain that is not only different but *separated* from civil society that is inhabited by urban middle classes, and, in fact, takes shape in course of struggling to survive while negotiating with the exclusionary practices of both the state and civil society. It is a method of pursuing strategies that rework the modalities of the state and civil society to work in favour of and yield benefits to the bulk of the 'population' groups, which are either left out of or remain mere 'target groups' in the techniques pursued to achieve the large-scale developmental goals of the modern state.

Among the various meanings that the idea of civil society, which is inhabited primarily by the urban middle classes, has assumed for itself over a period of time, Partha Chatterjee finds it useful, in the context of democracy in a postcolonial society, to refer to it, as Marx does, as a 'bourgeois society'. Civil society is delimited by modern associational practices such as autonomy, freedom of entry and exit, deliberative procedures of decision-making, recognised individual rights and duties, among other such liberal practices (Chatterjee 1998a: 60). In complete contrast 'those in political society make their claims on government, and in turn are governed, not within the framework of stable constitutionally defined rights and laws, but rather through temporary, contextual and unstable arrangements arrived at through direct political negotiations' (Chatterjee 2008a: 57). These negotiations could vary from protecting the illegal water and electricity connections and occupying government land to operating the levers of governmental structures and institutions in order to get basic and subsistence provisions. In order to even understand how these negotiations work, we need to step out of the frame of comprehending political processes as confined to the interface between the state and civil society. For instance, these negotiations could occur not through associational activity but with communities—the 'missing-link' in western political theory—as 'some of the active agents of political practice' and therefore democratisation occur in and through the 'much less well-defined, legally ambiguous, contextually and strategically demarcated terrain of political society' (Chatterjee 1998b: 282); Chatterjee here resonates a core concern of the subaltern studies project—'the capacity to hear that which one does not already understand' (Chakrabarty 2002: 36). In effect, Chatterjee wishes to argue that 1990s has not only witnessed the inauguration of a free market economy but also an expansion of welfare policies—which we earlier referred to as neo-welfarism—and thereby the governmentality of the state.[1] There is, according to him, a global mood that is exerting a moral pressure on the state to deliver welfare for the subaltern classes, which are thus negotiating the governmental apparatus of the state to wield benefits, and it is in this 'contextual negotiation' in the domain of 'political society' that we need to see an expansion of new modalities of subaltern agency.

A Brief Biography of Political Society

Political society is a contemporary exposition of the project of subaltern studies that began way back in the 1980s. 'The starting point of Subaltern Studies was that any historiography that concentrates on the control of the masses is by definition elitist' (Amin 2002: 11). Instead, historians engaged in subaltern studies have argued that the relevant question would be: 'how do we make the subalterns genuinely the subjects of their history?' (Chakrabarty 2002: 33). Subaltern studies emerged as a project that rejected the elitism of the colonial version as entrenched in Cambridge historians, who believed that politics was the result of the cultural institutions, such as the universities and the administrative bodies introduced by the colonial rule in India (Amin 2002: 11). In the same breath, it also rejected the nationalist historiography, which believed that the subalterns pursued the politics introduced to them by the Congress and its leaders such as Gandhi and Nehru. As against both these trends, subaltern historians have argued that in order to recover the subaltern history and its agency, we need to understand that politics itself occurred in two domains—one of the elites and the other of the subalterns.

Partha Chatterjee himself developed this logic of two domains of politics, which was initially suggested in the writings of Ranajit Guha (Guha 1983). Chatterjee argued that 'the establishment of a sovereign state authority, based on bourgeois legal and constitutional principles, in the pre-capitalist social formation does not immediately imply the real incorporation of all relations of domination within the political processes instituted by that state' (Chatterjee 1984: xxxviii). Thus, politics is split into two domains: 'one organised by the legal-political principles laid down by the state, the other lying outside it' (Chatterjee 1984: xxxviii). However, while the two domains are structured differently, they interpenetrate each other and can never be completely separated. As Shahid Amin observes,

> The methodological task that Chatterjee set for himself and for others in Subaltern Studies was to study the 'evolving process of interpenetrating of the two domains of politics', a process in which one domain seeks to enter into, breakdown, transform and incorporate the other into its own form of exercise of domination. (Amin 2002: 14–15)

The domains interpenetrate not merely because they operate in an 'integrated material reality', but also or primarily because the colonial categories and institutions that are exclusionary and entail violence also simultaneously and inextricably offer a vision of justice and freedom. The subaltern perspective has 'to seek another relation with European thought; it has to attempt an alternative thinking of equality, democracy, citizenship or human rights. In other words, postcolonial scholarship has to question Enlightenment categories in the very spirit and even name of these categories' (Skaria 2009: 53). In other words, the subaltern perspective does not draw a wedge or dichotomise the two domains of politics but resignifies the so-called universal for the imperatives of the 'specificities' of democracy and radical social transformation in postcolonial societies. Therefore, the postcolonial project is, as Dipesh Chakrabarty in his work *Provincialising Europe* explicitly argues,

> not a project of rejecting or discarding European thought .... European thought is at once *indispensable and inadequate* in helping us to think through the experiences of political modernity in non-western nations, and provincialising Europe becomes the task of exploring how this thought—which is now everybody's heritage and which affects us all—*may be renewed from and by the margins.* (Chakrabarty 2000: 16)

In fact, Chatterjee himself argued in his essay *Our Modernity* that the lessons of reason that modernity has taught us enable us to 'identify the forms of our own particular modernity'. Thus, 'ours is the modernity of the once-colonized. The same historical process that has taught us the value of modernity has also made us the victims of modernity. Our attitude to modernity, therefore, cannot but deeply be ambiguous' (Chatterjee 1997: 20).

Is this ambiguity now being replaced by a strategy that dichotomises politics into neatly self-enclosed domains where modernity stands against democracy? Has this search of how to reorder categories at the point of their interpenetration—'indispensable and inadequate'—given way to the temptation of drawing a series of new binaries such as modernity/democracy and civil society/political society in this new formulation on political society by Chatterjee? Is there then a break from the earlier methodology of the subaltern and postcolonial school in the new approach enunciated by Chatterjee in his recent formulation? The question which is of critical significance is whether or not the idea of political society, following this shift in approach, is thus counterproductive to the goals of democratisation in arresting the agency of the subaltern to a self-contained domain.[2]

Political Society and Resistance as Radical Politics

Political society refers to those aspects of subaltern negotiation that are marked by the growing 'governmentalisation of the state' that transforms or derecognises the 'ethical connotation of participation' associated with citizenship into 'population' groups that are mere 'targets' of administrative policies. Chatterjee argues that the dominant moment in subaltern politics today is to negotiate with the administrative bodies of the state in order to compel them under the 'moral rhetoric of community' to yield benefits to the marginalised social groups. He observes that 'India has never been more governed than it is today', and therefore there is as a result a shift in the modalities of the subaltern politics. He argues that 'there was undoubtedly a strong force against governmentality that motivated peasant resistance in an earlier era, even in the middle of the twentieth century; I see very little of it today' (Gudavarthy 2012a). If vying for governmental subsistence benefits marks the new political reality, what then is its relation with radical protest politics? Have they been displaced by the emergent 'politics of the possible' or 'politics of everyday life'? Is aiming for micro-politics or 'molecular' change the new reality that has emerged in light of the changes that have been initiated by the flexibilisation of both governmental strategies and the economy?

However, can we account for the nature of the subaltern politics bereft of a critique of the new model of development that has been pursued with the current phase of globalisation? Do the new institutional changes introduced as governance reforms that aim for a minimalist yet an interventionist state say something about the need for large-scale 'governmentalisation of the state'? Is this a new mode of 'management' of increasing structural inequalities? Wouldn't such dependence on subsistence governmental benefits either from the administrative bodies or from the market emerge in a particular context of initiating neoliberal economic reforms marked by 'uncivil development' that does not account for the social costs of production? It could well be argued that 'while it is democratic to recognize the strategies for survival, it is struggles that lie beyond survival strategies that are imperative for any meaningful idea of democratization' (Gudavarthy and Vijay 2012). Chatterjee on the other hand believes that the new emergent micro-politics hold the promise of bringing in structural changes over a period of time. Political society would in fact point towards the possibility where 'the actual transactions over the everyday distribution of rights and entitlements lead over time to substantial redefinitions of property and law within the actually existing modern state' (Chatterjee 2004: 75).

Political society is, therefore, a domain limited to pointing towards the growing negotiations for governmental benefits and is 'explicitly not a concept of revolutionary politics'. However, it would, perhaps, not be inappropriate to argue that this domain in terms of 'real-concrete' politics will have something to do with radical protest politics that are also visible within the same spatial and temporal dimension. Political society then can actually be referring to the modalities through which antagonisms are being 'deflected, deferred or nullified in the postcolonial society' (Sarkar 2012). However, Swagato Sarkar cautions that 'yet, we must be careful to not treat political society as a *successful* strategic field, structured to overcome the problematic of "dominance without hegemony", i.e., the development of non-coercive and persuasive political condition for capitalist transformation' (Sarkar 2012). In other words, would it be right to conclude that political society is only offering us a descriptive account of the emerging condition in a postcolonial democracy and not a normative evaluation about transformative politics? Or would it be more appropriate to say that political society in fact valorises the strategy of 'contextual negotiation' as the only mode through which 'popular politics' can be articulated in contemporary postcolonial democracies?

This confusion—normative suspension as valorisation—seems to be at the heart of the very concept of political society. Part of the reason for this seems to be the fact that Chatterjee has not, or at least not yet, reflected on the interface between the strategies of political society and those of radical protest politics that lie outside it, except that at times he vaguely encompasses everything including political parties, social movements and non-party political formations as part of political society, without ever raising the more fundamental question as to whether or not all these strategies can so unproblematically coexist within the same political domain. For instance, can 'contextual negotiations' coexist along with organised political movements? Or do they come in lieu of the former? If so, is there a new context in which mobilisational politics are on a retreat? Is there a generic scepticism with organised party politics and unwillingness on the part of the subaltern to become party to planned strategies by organised political movements? Are we moving beyond, as a range of new writings have suggested, 'politics of events' that have come to signify instrumental reasoning? (refer to Holloway 2002; Laclau 2005).

Political strategies being adopted, as part of exerting pressure on the state to recognise their rightful demands, by the marginalised social groups in India have been varied and too complex and demand a framework that can make sense of currents that run concurrently and at other times, in mutually exclusive ways. Subaltern response has varied from patiently building mass protest movements such as the Narmada Bachao Andolan or the movement for the Right to Information (RTI), to militant armed struggles best represented by the Maoist movement across central India spreading to the south of Vindhyas, raising issues such as implementation of minimum wages to the more basic issue of 'land to the tiller'. Amidst these protest forms, there is also a trend of a generic decline in the mobilisational capacity of political organisations of all hues on the one hand and farmer's suicides on the other. The subaltern classes seem to be caught between *militancy and powerlessness* that are closely related and negatively reinforce each other.[3]

The decline in organised mobilisation could be attributed to both the subtlety of power in the new capitalist forms of production without a clear target to mobilise against and the fact that anthropologists such as Jan Breman have pointed that beyond a level of distress the underprivileged are in no position to sustain and nurture resistance. Could it then be possible to, not merely descriptively but analytically, link the nature of protest politics to the nature of political economy? For instance, in what ways and to what extent does the growing informal sector determine the decline as well as the fragmentary nature of subaltern protest politics? Supriya Roy Choudhary in her study of the urban poor in the city of Bangalore observes that 'the informal sector, vast and diverse, presents formidable problems of conceptualization. However, the nature of informal work and the associated vulnerabilities may hold an important key to understanding the domain of the urban underclass' (Gudavarthy 2012a). This in turn influences the modes of protest they choose or not choose. Again Jan Breman observes that it is 'widely known that organized and sustainable collective action is relatively uncommon in the untransparent and fragmented landscape of the informal sector economy' (Breman 2007: 432).[4] Similarly, human rights activist K. Balagopal observed that neither armed nor non-violent protest politics have been by and large successful in India in forcing the rulers to pull back their policies (Balagopal 2009). On the contrary, in those places where the armed movement has retreated, due to state repression, it is very difficult to build a movement by the marginalised social groups since they see the futility and understand the state–society relation very differently from what Chatterjee has depicted in his account of the political society.[5] In fact, the growing militarisation of political movements, such as the left-wing Maoist led struggles, could itself be a sign of desperation due to the increasing difficulty in organising agitational politics.[6]

What and who fills up the streets that are vacated by the marginalised? As we had observed in the previous two chapters in this section, streets are being taken over by unlikely social groups, such as the newly rising social classes that already wield economic and political power and are now looking for social power, and caste groups such as the Rajputs, Marathas and Jats, who are 'demanding' the status of an OBC and Gujjars that of scheduled tribes. They are also being taken over by either urban middle-class professionals such as doctors, lawyers, teachers and urban youth who are taking to street protest, agitation and confrontational modes to demand better payments, urban postings and refusal to take up postings in 'remote' and rural areas, or upper middle classes simply protesting against crime through candle light marches and against graft as represented and led by the Team Anna campaign. While these protest forms make the dominant social classes more self-righteous, the underprivileged are pushed to take up more militant modes of protest to be heard. There seem to be subtle links in the way spaces open and close for different social groups. Thus, the state becomes 'righteously suppressive' and the uncertainty generated by militant protest forms 'can be the justification for lawless enforcement of law, the more lawless the more righteous the anger it can whip up in society' (Balagopal 2009). These social classes then become the social base for the state's strategies of exceptionalism, as we had argued earlier, to violate the rule of law with impunity and launch state-led organised vigilante groups such as the Salwa Judum in Chhattisgarh. These social classes seem to have travelled some distance from representing the nation to becoming the nation (Deshpande 2003).

The social groups that 'operate' are no longer the educated middle class and professionals, as those that 'agitate' are no longer the lower-class workers. Democracy has turned on its head, where

> those groups with fewer economic resources have weaker, more loosely established associations and have a more difficult time mobilizing members of their occupational group to participate in time-consuming and expensive strikes and demonstrations. Strikes are particularly costly and almost impossibly so for most lower-class workers. Therefore they tend to use less costly, less risky means of making demands upon the state: filing petitions, using the judicial system, making appeals to district- and state-level administrative authorities, voting in elections, and so on. The middle-class occupational groups, on the other hand, have the resources necessary to build up powerful associations, attend organizational activities like meetings, and participate in contentious action. They do use formal, procedural means such as those listed above, and utilize informal channels such as personal connections. However, they quickly lose patience with such time-consuming processes and resort to agitation, as it usually brings a speedier and more satisfactory response. In India, protest is for the privileged. (Wood 2012)

Does Chatterjee's account of political society take into consideration any of these changes that have taken place in the modes of protest? Chatterjee seems to provide very little explanation as to why the poor have moved to 'contextual negotiations' and what this means in a context wherein the privileged have taken to protest politics. As he puts it, his analysis is limited to looking at something 'new' taking place, but does it sufficiently account for the larger context in which this new trend is becoming visible? The ensuing 'politics of silence' that accompanies the concept of political society seems, at times, to give the impression that it valorises the new modalities of subaltern politics that have been resorted to—as an active 'choice' they make to avail of governmental benefits. This is also due to the dichotomised mode in which Chatterjee has presented his concept, where patterns and strategies of democracy necessarily stand outside modernity. Thus, he argues that the subaltern are resorting to modalities that are based on community, which is itself not a given aspect of the social structure but has been created in the course of the political action. According to Chatterjee, this is new and different from the earlier forms of protest, but the reasoning or lack of it, that he offers seems to bring into relief the limitation with an explanation that has modernity as the fault line. In identifying the subaltern exclusively with community-oriented strategies, such as the use of religious symbols—not on the basis of goals for which these forms are employed—does he not end up reinstating the tradition/modernity dichotomy that he in fact wishes to criticise and overcome? Could this then be the implication of postcolonial approach as such that it ends up with a process of 'ethnicisation of the subaltern' that it set out to critique in the first place (Gupta 1985; also refer to Mannathukkaren 2010).

While it is clear that what is missing is an engagement with the complex mosaic of protest politics, and its changing dynamics, Chatterjee has however incisively argued that the idea of the political cannot be restricted to the domain of protest or street politics alone. Instead, he has attempted to expand the scope of the idea to provide a new political subjectivity to the subaltern. He argues that those arguments which foreground certain essentialised ideas about political subject often end up victimising the victim, i.e., they blame the subaltern for the lack of a proper political subjectivity that will bring about a radical change in the state of affairs. He cites the intriguing example of a woman from Malda in West Bengal who succeeded in surviving by 'daily manipulating the local levers of an utterly banal political machine'. However, he finds it 'unconscionable to exclude her from the domain of political subjectivity'. He further adds,

> I will voice my full-throated support for a political order that will bring destitution of this kind to an end or arrange that unfortunate persons like her find guaranteed shelter and care, but I cannot blame her for not having the subjectivity to will such an order into existence, since those who claim to be such subjects have not thus far found a way to bring it about. (Gudavarthy 2012a)

In other words, Chatterjee has fundamental objections to attributing an external normativity to the actions of the subaltern and analyse or rather evaluate their actions against an externally constructed idea of politics or political subjectivity. Such modalities, which are part of both radical politics and theory such as that of the Maoists, have often only burdened the subaltern with a utopia that regulates rather than liberates them. Chatterjee further adds to this order of analysis by arguing that such emphasis on street politics often neglects the 'everyday politics' that lie beyond 'heroic events' that get the attention of critical theory. He asks, 'does the political subject vacate the scene when everyday politics is resumed? Or does she pursue a different mode of political action?' Thus, 'in looking at political society as a condition of un-heroic everyday politics, I am trying to find that which is new in the quotidian' (Gudavarthy 2012a).

Both the issues of imposition of external normativity and the argument about everyday politics seem to have certain analytical linkages and beg the question: How do you then study politics without offering a mere positivist account of what you see? How do we go beyond discursive empowerment of the subaltern? While it is important to dignify the modalities subaltern chooses in deciding the course of their own history, how do we make the point, without being either judgemental or essentialising the cult of subaltern, that often those 'choices' could be the outcomes of how dominant social groups close or structure the access to resources and thereby to political action? Ranabir Samaddar, therefore, reminds us of the 'significance of materiality in studying politics'. According to him,

> in the history of political writings in India we have this divide—the culturalist and the materialist (or the speculative and the journalist, if you like), and Chatterjee occupies a crucial but enigmatic position in this context. He studies politics, but likes to study this through the cultural glass, which makes his writings interesting, full of possibilities, but never able to grasp the roughness of the political world. (Gudavarthy 2012a)

Chatterjee's analysis seems to follow the overall shift that came about with the 'cultural turn' inaugurated by the combination of post-structuralism and the postcolonial theory. State on the one hand is essentialised in terms of the 'technologies of power' such as the techniques of enumeration, obfuscating issues of historical specificity such as the social forces and class alignments—between the feudal, bourgeois and the corporate. However, this essentialisation of the state is combined with an uncritical cult of the popular culture or subaltern participation. The latter, in turn, avoids deeper analysis regarding how social hierarchies that are part of popular culture need to be negotiated, even if they are occasionally acknowledged as possessing a 'dark side', especially with regard to caste and gender. Such critical analysis, as against 'naturalization of culture', is possible with the interpenetration of culture, politics and economy as three different but closely interrelated dimensions of domination and exclusion. Such a 'trivalent approach', as Fraser (1999) has suggested, allows us to study culture, not as a 'metaconcept' that is able to trump all other concepts, but as an irreducible dimension of economy and the political. However, on the contrary, '...culture came to be seen not merely as one exemplification of constructed-meaning, but *the* overdetermining paradigmatic instance of it' (Scott 2003: 107). Any analysis that is only an internal moment of culture fails to raise questions regarding modalities of combining recognition with redistribution, or political economy with cultural analysis (Fraser 1999).

This attempt to recombine culture with economy, in turn, has consequences for framing issues of subaltern agency. It allows us to better understand as to when do demands for 'identification can become not liberating but oppressive' (Appiah 2006: 20); or when foregrounding the 'lived experience' of the oppressed can render '...invisible the historicity of experience and reproduce(s) the very terms and conditions upon which that experience is in fact founded and therefore cannot contribute to transformation' (Scott 1992: 24). This recombining would also allow us to recognise the need to analyse resistance against structures and coercive powers in relation to and in tandem with the more everyday politics, and not as two separate or dichotomised moments of subaltern action.[7] It is perhaps not misplaced to argue that Chatterjee's approach comes forth as a dichotomised one, which attempts to study these two modalities of politics at separate levels, when he argues that 'political change in necessarily molecular, local and perhaps impermanent and even reversible. But partly it is also a provocation to think of democratic politics outside the familiar mode of undivided concentration on resistance to coercive power' (Chatterjee 2008b: 93). While it is a significant attempt to expand the scope of the political, but can this happen as a mere 'provocation' against or 'outside' the focus on 'resistance to coercive power?' We will be able to better frame this question and the issue of agency in the context of Chatterjee's renewed analysis of the role of middle men and the manner in which they are 'operated by' the subaltern.

Politics of *Pyraveekar* and the Question of Subaltern Agency

Chatterjee argues that the molecular change, everyday politics and putting the governmental state and its authorities under moral pressure are made possible by a new context where the marginalised social groups are no longer tied down by the 'old form of patron–client relations between local notables and their protégées' and the 'prevailing hierarchies of class and status'. It does not mean that these relations have disappeared but the marginalised seem to mobilise these structures for their benefits. For instance, caste is no longer just about ritual practices (as we pointed out with relation to the mobility of the OBCs and accompanying modes of stigmatisation in the previous chapter) and 'moral hierarchy', but matters in practical everyday transactions as to who gets what, and the leadership of the caste groups is decided by individual's ability to move the system and get concrete benefits for specific caste groups. Similarly, in the larger social arena what matters is the ability of political parties, political representatives, NGOs, or, as in West Bengal, school teachers to mediate with the system, and the higher echelons, institutions, procedures of the governmental structures to obtain various kinds of concrete benefits for the subalterns. In other words, the subalterns are able to bridge the class-divide with the middle class by negotiating with the state structures through the urban middle classes; they are converting the cultural capital of these classes into resources for their own mobility.

As Chatterjee puts it, 'rapidly expanded governmental activities in the rural India were providing the grid for population groups to be mobilized into the moral form of communities with voice and identity' (Gudavarthy 2012a). Political society 'often *creates* a community where none existed before, or else it *gives new form* to older community structures'. Giving a new form is made possible by using the 'creative fuzziness of the community' where the marginal groups find a 'way in which the imaginative power of a traditional structure of community, including its fuzziness and capacity to invent relations of kinship, has been wedded to the modern emancipatory rhetoric of autonomy and equal rights' (Chatterjee 1998b: 281). This could include the squatters of Kolkata, who 'create' a community to negotiate with governmental agencies 'responsible for administering welfare' since they matter for reasons of 'political efficacy'; or it could be older communities such as religious minorities including the Muslims who can use, for instance, their numerical strength by voting en-mass—by converting or creating a 'vote bank'—to push through their demands; or caste groups that can forge new alliances with other such groups—*Bahujan*—to create a political community that matters for getting electoral gains. To realise these demands, they can work their way through in order to negotiate with institutional—rules, legal principles and norms—framework of the political system, through a range of mediators, acting on their behalf, including political or public representatives, and global or national NGOs, depending on each individual case and the access and proximity they enjoy with such agencies.

The moot question is again: what then is the relation of the new modes of negotiation with the older hierarchies of social structures? As Chatterjee himself puts it,

> this is not to insist, of course, that the older forms were suddenly obliterated. For many people, especially in rural India but also in the cities, the connection to the political world continued to be mediated through powerful patrons such as landlords (or, in the cities, slumlords), or caste leaders, or religious authorities. (Gudavarthy 2012a)

If these relations do continue and matter to the way in which the political system and the economy (for instance, mafia operating in industrial areas) work, what is the interlink with the new emerging mode of negotiation? Does it entail social and political conflicts or is the situation changing, independent and bereft of such conflicts, solely on the basis of the 'social capital'—as in fact Robert Putnam claims—that the poor are able to muster?

Ram Reddy and G. Haragopal, interestingly in a study prior to Chatterjee formulating his concept of political society, argue that there are a number of reasons why the rural hinterlands are dependent on fixers or as they put it *pyraveekars*. This could include the need of skills to deal with 'time-consuming and complicated procedures' including technical aspects associated with legal matters; knowledge of official language, which in many instances is English; the gap between the sociocultural ethos and the 'politico-administrative culture of the system'; the centralised planning involved in the various developmental activities; lack of access to information, such as the funds available with the panchayat;[8] and finally, in the 'absence of organized local units of political parties, *pyraveekars* have come to play the role of party cadres'. These are the conditions that allow for a unique role of the middle men, which is why Reddy and Haragopal argue that

> while the *pyraveekar* with one hand applies pressure, pushes files, lubricates the process, and extracts the benefits from the system, with the other hand he passes on incorrect information, misleads the target groups, and makes a private fortune. It is the negative and exploitative dimension of the institution that speaks against it and calls for its elimination through appropriate measures. (Gudavarthy 2012a)

Although they claim that the

> professional *pyraveekar* can be traced to the feudal system, the negative characteristics of the institution are not restricted to social structures accompanying this system but are also seen to infiltrate the modern governmental structures, not least through leakages of the financial assistance programmes and poverty alleviation schemes meant for the disadvantaged sections of society. (Gudavarthy 2012a)

If expanded governmental activities provide the grid for new forms of community action to emerge, they are also the instruments through which old forms of power and hierarchies are reproduced. Within the state terrain, there are instances or rather a pattern of the regulative rentier class, such as the politicians, bureaucrats and village leaders, monopolising their hold over the administrative system. As we had pointed out in Chapter 2 on the middle classes, in the rent-seeking economy patron–client relations could continue in the selection of a state-sponsored programme, or by extracting a rent for disbursement of public funds. For instance, as regards the People's Plan Campaign in Kerala, the public works were to be supervised and managed by the people themselves through various beneficiary committees. However,

> on the ground these do not work as intended. The engineers and contractors colluded to make things difficult for the beneficiary committees, which suffered from the lack of skills needed to undertake the works. The engineers, for example, refused to give technical advice to the committees, deliberately

prepared wrong estimates, refused to supervise the works, and so on. As a result, in many cases, even though the beneficiary committees were in existence, the actual work was (illegally) done by contractors or the committees were filled with nominees of contractors who were masquerading as beneficiaries. (Mannathukkaren 2010: 305)

Along with the expansion of governmental activities, there has also been a massive expansion of the contractor class—including the civil, liquor and mafia segments—and its hold on the state. The saga of the Reddy brothers in Karnataka is just one case in point. In most states, there has been a shift of political power to this newly emergent contractor class, with a sizeable number of them holding various ministerial positions in the Cabinet. For instance, in a city like Mumbai, most of the city's 36 MLAs are either builders or contractors.[9] It would not be an exaggeration, as we had pointed out earlier, if one were to say that in India the state has moved from being a contractual state to a contractor state. While this depicts, on the one hand, the characteristic features of a crony, casino capitalism, on the other hand, it continues with feudal social relations.[10] However, within Chatterjee's framework, though he does take into consideration the recent rise of the corporate capital and non-corporate capital, he does not study in any depth their control on the state and the changes that have come about at the ground-local level, for instance due to this rise of new non-productive classes, largely, as was pointed, out of the leakages of state funds.

Here again, there is culturalisation of the categories, wherein they are analysed more in terms of their relation to modernity. Ranjit Guha argued that looking at feudal as remnant or survival makes them elitist interpretations because people live in those social relations. Thus, according to him, 'relationships in India that looked feudal when seen through a stagist view of history were contemporaneous with all that looked modern to the same point of view' (Chakrabarty 2002: 14). The issue as to how power and patronage within these social systems can be studied remains underproblematised, and thereby, it seems that the thinning of subaltern agency is difficult to capture in such frameworks. Similarly, it also remains relevant to ask if various versions of 'Indian feudalism' are unacceptable as relevant categories to capture the nature of social relations, and why or how modified versions of modernity as 'Our Modernity' and unmodified versions of corporate capitalism qua corporate capitalism remain useful within the same frameworks. Vivek Chibber has argued in his recent work that

> Chatterjee argues that the turn to modernization came about because of national elites had internalized Western discourse, but I will show this argument to be entirely mistaken. Nationalist elites promoted modernization not because they were victims of indoctrination but because of the pressures of governing in a capitalist world economy. What Chatterjee presents as an effect of discourse was in fact a recognition of real, material pressures from global capitalism. This is an example of how Subalternist theorists simply whisk capitalism out of the picture, even where it played a central role. (Chibber 2013: 25)

In other words, capitalism as a material order is undermined in much of postcolonial theory and projected merely as an ideological and a cultural system that affected the elites but not the subaltern, and it is in this imagined space that they find expanding subaltern agency.

Corbridge et al. on the basis of their ethnographic account of the state agree with Chatterjee that political society does represent a distinct set of cultural norms, actors and institutions that is often constructively engaged in providing links between 'government' and 'the public', and is the site where 'technologies of development are reworked by agents' and 'provide service to local people'. However, they too find the limitations integral to political society in providing mobility to both the communities seeking amelioration and the mediators who 'operate' the system. In their comparative fieldwork in Bihar and West Bengal, they found that political society is susceptible to internal fragmentation, prone to conflict within and between the various social constituents, and mobility is limited and temporary. The poorer and the weaker of the marginalised without even that minimum capacity to forge networks are left out, and sometimes become victims of the practices of political society. For instance, adivasis and tribals are not equipped to mobilise the governmental authorities in fulfilling their demands for various reasons. Some of it is definitely due to their limited capacity to hold 'political efficacy'. Unlike Dalits and Muslims, both geographically and demographically, they are more spread out, and in no single state are they in any kind of majority. In general elections, Dalits can influence the decision in 300 constituencies as against only

50 or 60 constituencies with the tribals (Guha 2007: 3308; see also John and Deshpande 2008).

Even though participatory institutions such as the panchayat have been active in a state such as the West Bengal, the 'mediators' themselves have limited capacity, in terms of acting on grievances of the local communities. Most of them enter public life but fail to move beyond the panchayat. The best they can do is to manage a contact with the block offices or work for the local MLA, and such dependence is hardly helpful in either moving away from the patron–client relations or for achieving effective democratisation. Thus, Corbridge concludes that 'poorer people were provided with sightings of new state officials and new sites of corruption, but not with sightings of the new model state that has been mandated by New Delhi' (Gudavarthy 2012a).

Thus, it could be argued, much against the grain of the subaltern perspective forwarded by Chatterjee, that the dynamics of political society would seem very different when viewed from the point of view of those neglected and dominated. 'Popular culture' and demands of forging networks could actively reproduce the dominant values and interests. In course of their field work with the organisations of widows in Kerala, J. Devika and Rajasree reiterate the point that mediators such as the political parties, that Chatterjee emphasises, do not work in the favour of 'deeply disempowered' both due to strategic reasons and the fear of transgressing the dominant social–moral codes. Such a condition opens up space for global NGOs to mediate on behalf of widows. Such NGOisation, in turn, limits the capacity of these organisations to politically negotiate their issues and form alliances between different organisations working on similar grievances. These limitations, inherent to the way political society as a site is structured, push women activists, in this case the widows themselves, to 'occupy the mediator's position'.

The urge to both mediate for themselves and go beyond the strategies and social–moral frameworks offered by the dominant political parties comes from the aspiration to ask for more than mere subsistence demands. What the widows were looking for was not just everyday benefits, but 'public happiness' and the pride of negotiating with the public officials on equal terms. These organisations of the widows 'do not regard themselves as mere pressure groups for government benefits'. They were, in fact, looking for the possibility of counter-hegemonic politics 'that critique the founding conditions of widowhood itself'. They articulated issues that went beyond being a mere 'governmental category', including issues of loneliness, sexual deprivation and resisting desexualisation; 'these activists were actually arguing moving against the conservative interpretation of widowhood that would have probably have brought greater benefits in terms of public sympathy' (Gudavarthy 2012a).

Strangely enough, in political society, as has been conceptualised by Chatterjee, the subaltern seems incapable of raising issues beyond that of subsistence and of achieving them outside of merely 'operating' the system. The agency of the subaltern, therefore, seems to be in perpetual dependence on mediators, who do not necessarily always belong to the political society. Gayatri Spivak interestingly remarks about Chatterjee's work—*Politics of the Governed*—that 'the book ends on a superb note of productive contradiction—when the author leaves popular politics and speaks in praise of "gathering of self-conscious people" to counter urbanization in the services of neo-liberalisation'. Could this 'contradiction' entail a mode of extending refracted patronage in understanding the role of the subaltern, within the limits of the dominant narrative? Wouldn't it be important to study the moves to go beyond or against governmentalisation even to grasp as to what extent subsistence demands alone can capture the contours of subaltern agency?

Struggling for dignity, it seems, entails moving beyond both a governmental category and a moral category. As Devika and Rajasree argue, like many other contemporary feminist writers,

> any effort to build a 'moral community' around the widows and deserted women may be flawed … because it may draw upon the norm of chaste widowhood, which is not shared by other similar groups. … Such alliances can be built only if the widows are able to forge political alliances that do not rely upon such moral unity, but highlight shared experiences of oppression and deprivation. (Gudavarthy 2012a)

What then could be the interlink between these two dynamics of political society? Could Chatterjee's repeated use of the idea of 'moral passion' and 'moral community' as the basis of the formation of political community then signify that such morality—as against the political—is only available to certain dominant section, as it does—through the language of civility—within the contours of civil society? Would it be right to argue that both morality in political society and civility in civil society seem to empty the social dynamics of conflict, and create communities and associations respectively bereft of internal power dynamics? As civil society, in many of the theorists of that idea, has come to represent a social space without power, is political society also weak in articulating the conflicting dynamics internal to it? Are there then similarities and complex overlaps and continuities between the domain of civil society dominated by urban middle classes and political society that help us articulate better, both modes of domination and forms of resistance, rather than construct a binary in drawing the two domains as completely segregated from one another?

Middle Classes/Civil Society and Subaltern Classes/Political Society

Chatterjee makes a strong argument that political society is a domain that is completely segregated from that of civil society. They are both constituted by different actors, institutions and practices. While civil society is delimited to a very small section of the urban middle classes, political society in contrast denotes the dynamics of the majority of 'population' groups. Civil society refers to the modern elite groups that are 'walled up within enclaves of civic freedom and rational law' (Chatterjee 2004: 4). Political society, in contrast, is defined by 'populations'—such as 'slum dwellers'—which are the 'targets' of state policy and state control, but do not enjoy the modern state's recognition of the 'ethic of participation' that is the basis of citizenship. They predominantly transact outside the modalities of formal—read liberal—institutions and their norms and procedures. This could include transgressing 'strict lines of legality' and at times use of violence, crime and other such acts that are considered uncivil from the standpoint of those inhabiting the 'civil' sphere. In terms of economy, this alternative sphere is dominated by non-corporate capital and includes all those working within the informal sector, such as the 'peasantry, artisans, and petty producers'. Politically, this means that these groups access state resources through political negotiations and not as 'legal rights' and thereby are 'not under the moral-political leadership of the capitalist class' (Chatterjee 2008a: 57). In effect, political society draws its conceptual strength from being a domain that is imbrued with processes that are the obverse of civil society.

Ironically, however, the concept of civil society (in India) is left untheorised. In fact, as Chatterjee himself observes, it has been at the centre of debate in capturing the processes of democracy in India. It is precisely for this reason it should have warranted some exploration from him. He, instead, argues that he would use the concept as Marx did to refer to it as a classical bourgeois society, without surprisingly being sensitive to its variations in the Indian context. Thus, civil society is left to stand 'as an ideal-type' with which political society can be contrasted.

> However, because political society is construed as the sphere of those excluded from civil society, it is impossible to fully understand the significance of the workings of one without comparing this against the workings of the other. Chatterjee's account therefore risks replacing one black box with two black boxes, as the way in which interactions occur through both civil and political society are never fully unpacked. (Harrison 2012)

Does this concept then draw its distinctiveness and thereby its 'political efficacy' in some measure from the interstices of this conceptual silence? What could be the political effects of drawing a binary and in undermining a part of the binary by reducing it to the level of pure abstraction and an ideal type?

It is possible that this approach actually ends up reifying the concept of civil society. One is made to believe that there is a civil society in India that operates around the liberal principles of association with 'positive presence of liberal organizations'. This could include respect for individual rights, rule of law, ethics of participation, free flow of information, intermediary institutions working on neutral norms and procedures, freedom of thought, and above all a liberal and democratic state that has the capacity and will to create such a civil society.

> Civil society is, in other words, a context created by the state. If that context does not exist, then the sorts of organizations that Chatterjee describes are nothing more than liberal clubs in an illiberal world, perpetually vulnerable to the uncivil violence of other citizens and the state. ... Chatterjee's concept of political society thus quite fundamentally describes the state's failure to maintain its role as the neutral, dispassionate enforcer of rules. Because the existence of political society means that the state is not guaranteeing

the space of negative freedoms, the very concept of political society is antithetical to the classical concept of civil society. Civil society and political society cannot exist side by side, as they do in Chatterjee's depiction, and thus his theory is inherently flawed. (Kutty 2012)

This flaw then makes it imperative to raise a range of questions, apart from whether or not in reifying the civil society Chatterjee's theory becomes susceptible to circumventing the state, if not legitimising it; it is significant to also ask: what is the nature of civil society in India?[11] And why while there is a need to move beyond such hegemonic zones as civil society, as Chatterjee points out, it might not be the best of strategies to demarcate domains constitutively 'outside' of it, in the process letting-state-off-the-hook and undermining the possibility and the need to resignify and democratise the scope of the 'technologies' of the state and civil society?

Civil society in India is indeed distinct due to the nature of social history and contemporary politics, and can, therefore, hardly be summarised as a bourgeois society. If modern elites are the dominant classes in the civil society, there are various layers ranging from the neo-rich born out of the processes of liberalisation of the economy to the middle classes that include the highly paid professional and managerial classes. There has been a rapid expansion of the middle classes in the past couple of decades or so with the inflow of what Chatterjee refers to as the corporate capital.[12] However, what is distinct, is that this class, which was the social base for democracy and civil society, a stable and autonomous intermediary institutional base in Europe, has been accompanied by the transient nature of the economy, due to the advent of neoliberal reforms, and the accompanying uncertainty and insecurity in India. Both rapid mobility and uncertainty are inextricably linked, marking the new 'risk society' that accompanies the globalised world and characterises the social nature of the classes that emerge from these processes.

The urban middle and the neo-rich classes while experiencing upward mobility are also witness to massive retrenchment, financial crisis and recession, withdrawal of social security measures such as the pension schemes and their replacement with unique proposals such as 'golden handshake' and VRS, casualisation of white-collar workers, outsourcing, increased techniques of surveillance (such as punch cards), and more accurate weekly assessments of productivity and working hours (Fernandes 2000a, 2000b). The insecurity that affected the industrial workers has now become generic. Jan Breman argued that, in the context of Gujarat, communal riots had occurred as a result of the change in the nature of industrialisation. Since 1980s, textile mills, especially in Ahmedabad, the epicentre of riots in 2001, have been driving the workers into the immiserisation of the informal sector that failed to offer the security of the formal sector. With the collapse of the social infrastructure, and social solidarity built by the trade unions, it adversely impacted the inter-communal networks leading to initial breakdown of trust and later ghettoisation of Muslims. This marked, according to Breman, the shift from 'welfare capitalism to lumpen capitalism based on the ideology of social Darwinism' (Breman 2002: 1487).[13]

These processes, however, have not been limited to the working class and seamlessly seem to have gripped the bulk of urban processes too. Alongside the ghettoes of the poor, the middle classes and modern elites increasingly built 'enclaves' and 'citadels' and operated in urban spaces as 'gated communities' with their own private security, power supply and other infrastructure (see Marcuse 1997).[14] The impact of such 'privatisation of the public sphere' was so pervasive that it reflected in the social processes as the growth of individualism without respect for individual rights; in the economy as the protection of private property without an accompanying civic responsibility towards public property; and in the political process as the base for the emergence of a securitised state—democracy that is dependent on bureaucracy—that violates law with impunity, and the rise of right-wing politics represented by the BJP and Shiv Sena that are strongest in urban metropolitan cities.[15]

Modern elites, if anything, can hardly be characterised by their respect for the rule of law and cannot be neatly juxtaposed against a domain outside the civil society that can be exclusively marked by 'transgressions into illegality'. Instead, the interrelation between the state and the dominant civil society is inextricably marked by the violation of laws and the phenomenon of growing 'illegality of law' that smudges the difference between legal and illegal. In fact, as Rob Jenkins argues, economic reforms through which the modern elite has expanded in India were itself introduced through 'underhand tactics', which he refers to as 'reforms by stealth'. According to him, democratically elected governments use obfuscation and betrayal as routine methods to achieve ends and 'arguably democracy makes such tactics both necessary and possible' (Jenkins 1999: 5). Bourgeois' liberal principles such as the rule of law no longer remain in their pristine form but instead take on the shape and purpose constructed during the period of 'structural adjustments'. As Mattei and Nader observe in their recent work, the rule of law itself becomes an instrument for corporate capital and mode of compelling countries to accept free trade, open markets, corporatisation, informal economy, special economic zones, among other such policy options. In the process, 'the distinction between what is legal and what is illegal blurs in a world in which rule of law is reduced to a dull rhetoric or to Orwellian double-speak' (Mattei and Nader 2008: 5). In such a situation, the illegalities of the political society are fashioned around and gain their rhetorical legitimacy from the illegalities of the civil society. Political society, then, seems to be neither a residual nor an obverse of the practices of civil society but is in fact a structural fall-out of the larger pilferage that seems to be endemic and integral to the growth of the new classes.[16] As we argued in Chapter 2 on middle classes, their role has expanded in the market as against state bureaucracy, and which is what prompts them to launch struggles against graft in public institutions, in many parts of the world, which is not to show that civil society operates on pure norms, while subalterns thrive in violating them. Even if Chatterjee argues that there is no 'moral legitimacy' to the illegality of the civil society, as against that of the subaltern, it does not seem to work in any radical way in favour of those inhabiting the political society.

Nandini Sundar and Aparna Sundar argue that 'if there is a distinction between those whose rights are legally recognized and those whose aren't; this is not a distinction that members of a so-called political society themselves make' (Gudavarthy 2012a), as they do certainly think that while they violate law, it is the nexus between the state and civil society that is glued through practices that violate law.[17] In such a context what is the scope of law in protecting the rights of the marginalised? Sundar and Sundar believe that 'some of the most significant political movements today are precisely over the legal recognition of rights' and 'whose definition of property and whose definition of law will prevail'. In this battle, they see very little of 'moral passion' that Chatterjee thinks the state is pressurised by, and it is precisely because the state is not responsive and certainly not a 'welfare state' that poor cannot stop short of asking anything less than radical changes in the law.[18] This according to them reflects the 'extent to which a liberal political subjectivity is emerging/becoming generalized, even when expressed in the form of a Maoist armed struggle'. This also allows us to foreground the point that as a subaltern theorist, it is ironical that Chatterjee does not lay emphasis on what subalterns themselves think and how they see the discourse of rights, even as it is made available exclusively for those residing in civil society.

The law remains a highly contested terrain that allows us to comprehend the complexity of the emerging subjectivities. While, on the one hand, the rule of law itself is made illegal by the state and the hegemonic social groups, the subaltern is attempting to expand the very scope and content of the available legal provisions. For instance, in Andhra Pradesh, the rule of law was resignified by the human rights groups not to exclude militant protest and armed struggles but to argue that dialogue—a civil society practice—is necessary to contextualise as to why marginalised social groups take up arms. In other words, here it was not rule of law versus violence—as they are bifurcated in a civil society-oriented articulation—but rule of law to contextualise violence, which seems to stand beyond a liberal frame.[19] The debate, therefore, seems no longer constrained between 'liberal subjectivity' and 'transgressions of legality'; instead it moves beyond in terms of appropriating law by resignifying its very content and scope.

Finally, Chatterjee reasons that the category of community has been suppressed in most of the Western political theory, as a result of which the options available within community practices have not been explored. He avers that one of the strategic questions of significance today is to decide to choose

> legal reform through state initiative from the top or mobilization of initiatives within the relatively unmobilized spaces of the communities themselves. To choose the former is to underscore the moral primacy of the modernizing state. To advocate the latter is to accept the risks of walking through a normatively uncertain political terrain. If my critics demand that I state my preference between the two, I would say that while the former strategy has not necessarily exhausted itself, I believe that the real challenge lies in exploring the possibilities of the latter. (Chatterjee 2001: 17)

Chatterjee believes that in the process of resisting the top-down approach of state and imposition of its modernisation project, 'the subaltern classes embark on a path of internal transformation'.

While it is democratic to accept the need for autonomy and to recognise internal processes and transformation that communities are capable of as also their right to be different, one must, however, realise that modern power operates in the very interstices of these discourses—difference as domination. In recognising that social groups are different and have a right to remain different, we need to explore the adverse possibility of naturalising those differences, and making the naturalised differences instruments of socialising segregation. Slavoz Zizek refers to this as a process of 'racism at a distance' where in recognising differences, social prejudices and hierarchies remain unchallenged—externally by segregating some social groups such as Muslims or internally when Muslim community re-imposes patriarchal structures on women of 'its own' community. How then, we might ask, is the postcolonial/communitarian approach going to entail a difference in negotiating internal–external power from that of western–liberal approaches based on 'politics of difference' as enunciated in the modern discourses of multiculturalism? In its current version, the postcolonial/communitarian approach seems to reinforce a certain social location of the dominant castes/culture (for instance, the Bhadralok culture) in claiming a difference vis-à-vis the 'western'/liberal societies that they have—normatively superior—community life while much of the West has undergone a process of individuation, while they also claim vis-à-vis the subaltern—Dalits and women—within the community that they have access to modernity (as in modern education) and the capacity to recombine the two in unique ways. In other words, the interface between community and modernity, the way it occurs in postcolonial/ communitarian frame reinforces, willy-nilly—the social location of the social elites in India.[20]

While the existing liberal language of rights and citizenship is inadequate to address the emerging social complexity, they perhaps undergo a transformation under the pressure from protest politics to become in a renewed sense the terrain for democratisation. This is a story that can be captured only in all its continuities and breaks and not through either a selective reading or strategic silences that might lead us unto not just 'uncertain political terrain'—internal to communities—but sometimes into very known historical forms of strangulating democratic aspirations. Sanjeeb Mukherjee cautions us that

> instead of celebrating the populist democratic assertions of the poor or political society, we need to highlight the thicker meaning of democracy,

to include institution-building and institutional norms, like the rule of law and rights and respect for dissent. In the absence of these norms and values, democracy slides from majoritarianism to authoritarianism, fundamentalism or fascism. (Gudavarthy 2012a)

To conclude, Chatterjee has indeed made a bold attempt to foreground certain new challenges that are emerging due to the recent changes in the reach and nature of governance in India, even when he does not locate these in the complete texture of the political terrain and the various possibilities it offers.[21] What we observe in contrast to many of his formulations is the shrinking space for subaltern agency, with the rise of the kind of exceptionalism of the state and the new moral rhetoric of the middle classes in civil society, which pushes the subaltern either into desperation or into militant modes of struggle—between *militancy and powerlessness*. The kind of 'contextual negotiations' that Chatterjee alludes to best represent the residual space available to them in the workings of contemporary democracy in India, at the altar of new development model and global capital flows, and certainly not an expansion of subaltern agency.

Endnotes

1. Chatterjee however reads this as the policies of a welfare state, which I do not. Instead, I have argued that what is distinct about the current welfare policies is that they are formulated without a welfare state, and therefore there is a need to refer to them as neo-welfarism. Therefore, India has welfarism without a welfare state, because it is the same state that run 'Operation Green Hunt', displaced tribals without rehabilitation, formulated special economic zones (SEZ) that run without basic labour rights, watered down trade unions, among other such measures.

2. It would not, perhaps, be inappropriate to mention here the critique of Althusser by E.P. Thompson, whose writings were recognised as closely related to the subaltern school. Thompson in his classic work titled *Poverty of Theory* had precisely argued that Althusser by understanding structures as regionally separated and self-enclosed domains had disallowed any space for human agency. What then are the consequences of this regional separation by Chatterjee? We will reflect on this issue of agency in the next section of this chapter (refer to Thompson 1978, and also Gudavarthy 1998).

3. We have made this point earlier in the introduction. Refer p. 34.
4. However, scholars such as Rina Agarwala have argued to the contrary that

    changes in the structure of production do not necessarily signify the end of all class struggle (and thereby the utility of class analytics). On the contrary, I argue that the circumstances of informal employment that pushed workers to initiate an alternative form of class politics that articulates their unique class-based interests and attempts to improve their basic security. (Herring and Agarwala 2008: 97)

5. This point was observed by Balagopal in course of personal communication. He also observed that there is, perhaps, some innocence required for those from the marginal backgrounds to believe in and make it possible to take part in organised political protests. We have alluded to this point in Chapter 1 on the Maoist movement.
6. Writer and Novelist Arundhati Roy had once commented that peaceful protest is no longer respected by the state, and this gives legitimacy for movements to take up more militant modes of protest. It is a different matter that militant movements are controlled through massive state repression, while the state is indifferent to peaceful protest politics. The choice really is between indifference and repression.
7. I have offered a more detailed critique of such dichotomised understanding of politics elsewhere (refer to Gudavarthy 2013a).
8. Which is what has been the focus of the recently promulgated act—Right to Information; this was achieved after a long drawn battle organised by social activists such as Aruna Roy in Rajasthan.
9. In instances, where social activists attempted to use the RTI to fight back such a system of patronage, there have been a spate of murders organised by these vested interests.
10. Refer to Sainath 2010. Here, he argues that in the recent Common Wealth Games, 2010, hosted by India, the scale of corruption involved reminded us of the kind of crony capitalism that has seeped into all the activities of the state.
11. Chatterjee's theory does not raise the question of state power. How and what do you do with it? It circumvents it and believes that the proliferation of autonomous non-state processes will in itself restrict the scope and power of the state. It is, therefore, not surprising that the Italian translation of his book *The Politics of Governed* was introduced as a work of an autonomist Marxist from India—personal communication with Chatterjee.
12. It is estimated that the middle class in India stands at 300 million (National Council of Applied Economic Research 1996).
13. Lumpen capitalism is co-existing with welfare policies in the current phase of development in India, which is what I refer to as neo-welfarism.
14. Growth of modern elites in India is accompanied by the expansion of the private sector that violates laws in the name of efficiency, pushes over social costs

to vulnerable groups and encourages lack of transparency through dispersed global presence and faceless interaction locally. It is accompanied by massive expansion of unproductive middle-men classes such as the contractors and urban mafia that indulge with impunity in land grab, violation of property laws including evading tax, double registration, illegal occupation, to mention a few; urban culture that is fraught with, not civility, but aggression, and ego reflected in their intolerance to caste reservations, religious minorities, to the more everyday road rage and corruption.

15. In Gujarat, middle classes actively took part in riots and the state pogrom against Muslims. In fact, the ideological spread was so thick that in pockets even the mobile Dalit and OBC castes were part of the organised riots, leading to various Dalit intellectuals enquiring into the new and emerging interface between Dalits and Hindutva (Teltumbde 2002).

16. Recent instances of violation of norms by the mining lobby led by the Reddy brothers in Karnataka, or environmental norms by the UK based Vedanta Mining Corporation in Odisha, are only the most glaring of examples as to how corporate capital grows only through massive violation of law and becomes the 'exemplars' for the society. On my way to the university, often the auto drivers who are unwilling to go by the metre give the examples of corrupt ministers and government officials to argue that what they are earning is very insignificant and cannot amount to a 'malpractice' or corruption.

17. Sundar and Sundar refer to the struggle by the rickshaw pullers in Delhi. It is law that criminalises them and also makes it necessary to offer bribes to survive. For instance, the civic body rulebook states that the rickshaw puller must be the owner of his rickshaw. Since many of them are migrants and do not own a rickshaw, they cannot survive without offering bribes to the police; criminal mafia owns the bulk of rickshaws and makes it impossible for a poor man to own one, even if one has the resources on a rare occasion. According to an estimate, street vendors of Delhi pay about ₹500 crores and rickshaw owners pay ₹360 crores as bribes ('Voice of the Underdog', *The Hindu*, 17 April 2010). When there is illegality all the way from the state officials down to the poor, is there a distinction one can meaningfully make between a law-abiding civil sphere and the illegality of a political society?

18. It is, however, important as we pointed out earlier that there have been a series of welfare measures starting with the general election in 2009, and return of the Congress to power in the centre. The welfare seems to be an appendage to a state that cannot be characterised as a welfare state, as Chatterjee does. This could well be what is unique about the second phase of liberalisation, beginning 2004, in India. The first phase beginning 1990s was based on an exclusive growth agenda without an accompanying rhetoric or policy framework of welfarism.

19. Similarly, feminists have repeatedly argued the need to move beyond law, since law in terms of its very structure is not capable of articulating the demands of a women's movement (refer to Menon 2004; Kapur 1996).

20. This needs a more elaborate conceptualisation and will be part of my forthcoming work on community.
21. It could also be, perhaps, argued that postcolonial theory itself might need to enter into a new phase to remain relevant in raising pressing political concerns on the ground. Some of the 'dark sides' of communitarian practices, culturalisation and essentialisation of culturalised categories, unhindered celebration of popular culture, to mention but a few areas where postcolonial theory has maintained a rather discomforting silence, need to be put more upfront on the table for further deliberation.

Globalisation

5

Politics of Global Human Rights in India

Human rights have emerged as the new framework for global or transnational justice. The new language and instrumentalities in the era of globalisation have had deep impact on the workings of democracy and those social groups engaged in bottom-up mobilisations. A whole range of issues have come to articulate themselves in the language of rights, as instantiated in various international declarations and conventions, which in turn have found their way into national legislations, and interpretations by the courts. Among many 'new' rights, the most prominent that have been at the centre stage in Indian democracy, in the last couple of decades, after the globalisation of the economy, include the right to information, right to development (RD), right to city, right to memory, right to privacy, rights of internally displaced peoples, rights of the indigenous people, right to habitation, rights against environmental degradation, right to work, right to food, forest rights, apart from debates on Geneva Convention, internal civil war, capital punishment and rule of law, global debt, child labour, health and the HIV/AIDS crisis, humanitarian aid, modern technology, including access to Internet and digital technologies, and many others.[1] The practices of global human rights have then been imparted distinct meaning in different and contrasting localised contexts through the various forms of mobilisations and protests articulated by a variety of social groups. As Samuel Moyn observes,

> If there ever really was a 'global human rights revolution', it has occurred only since the 1980s, when a variety of groups around the world, and all the governments, learned to speak the language. Close to the ground, one of the most hotly debated issues is whether this process of 'vernacularization' of human rights was one in which ordinary people in different places winnowed their demands in the direction of acceptability to Western audiences, or whether they were able to use them from below in creative and transformative ways. (Moyn 2010: 218–219)

The workings of Indian democracy are imbricated in these global discourses, which have become a site for contestation. In tune with the first two sections of this book, we shall focus on the intersection between those global discourses that have worked their way in articulating the specific issues of militant struggles such as those led by the Maoists; the old middle classes and their equation with the global human rights language; the growth of new middle classes among the Dalits and the caste-based political articulations at the global level; and the subaltern classes, and their growing concern with issues of poverty, development and the state.

Indian state's response to the militant protest forms has drawn from the ongoing global discourse of 'war on terror', and the felt need thereof to make changes to the legal regime. After the end of the Cold War and the collapse of Soviet Union, there had been a relative decline in war between sovereign nations, and this was replaced by warfare within sovereign nations, around the new-found threat of global terrorism by the non-state actors, especially post-9/11. The United States directed its foreign policy with the new purpose of fighting the 'Global War on Terrorism'. The 'War on Terror', in turn, laid justifications for 'State terror' and violations of human rights and resignifying the principle of rule of law from its interface with substantive justice to maintenance of 'law and order'. In India, this took the form of the emergence of the public discourse on 'Suspect Muslim' that was part of the Global War against Terrorism, represented by groups such as the Al Qaeda. At another level, this led to a framing of various militant movements and the political violence they used, through the discourse on terrorism, so that there was a steady conflation between Maoism and terrorism as 'Red Terror', turning democracy against Maoism.[2]

There was wider justification built to deal with political violence through the prism of 'law and order' rather than as a socio-economic problem. This shift was in consonance with the shift in the global discourse on terrorism. As Richard Falk notes, 'this disturbing encroachment on constitutional democracy in the name of counter-terrorism became the essence of homeland security in the United States' (Falk 2012: 247). He further argues,

> whatever the eventual historical unraveling of 11 September, the response certainly demonstrates that the vulnerability of a democratic society may be greater from its own manipulative forces than it is from those who are feared as 'evil' and as 'enemies'. These anti-democratic domestic forces are often concealed in the deep recesses of governmental bureaucracy, and are ready

to make common cause with their right-wing allies when opportunities exist, especially at times of national crisis. (Falk 2012: 248)[3]

It is these anti-democratic impulses, connected to the global discourse on 'war on terror', that are implicit, as we shall argue, in legal–institutional changes brought about to circumvent and subvert 'fundamental'—civil–political—rights.

Globalisation at one level has eroded the state's sovereignty in terms of de-territorialised economic processes and at another level in terms of framing justice through a transnational discourse. As Nancy Fraser argues,

for many, it has ceased to be axiomatic that the modern territorial state is the appropriate unit for thinking about issues of justice, and the citizens of such states are the pertinent subjects of reference. The effect is to destabilize the previous structure of claims-making—and therefore to change the way we argue about social justice. (Fraser 2008: 275)

In India, this process of de-stabilisation has taken place alongside or in conjuncture with the rise of middle classes among the backward classes and the Dalit groups. The 'new' middle classes among these groups have reframed the ways of accessing social justice beyond the Westphalian structure of claims-making. Dalit groups, in particular, have reframed the injustice of caste around the global discourse of race. As we shall argue in this chapter, 'politics of recognition'—'caste is race'—became the new mode of negotiating claims to sovereignty, including the ability of the state to bestow citizenship rights and arrest human rights violations that compromise basic dignity and recognition to the marginalised social groups. In other words, mere territorial control, monopoly over coercive authority and military control do not sufficiently signify/reinforce claims to sovereignty by the modern state.[4]

Finally, with regard to the subaltern classes such as the rural-lower caste women, beyond the margins of middle classes and urban metropolitan cities, the global discourse on human rights impacted both the state-policy regime and the novel protest forms in foregrounding issues of global poverty, debt and 'development'. The interface between globalisation, human rights and mobilisations by the subaltern classes is explored in this chapter through the ongoing debate on the RD that has laid a renewed emphasis on the *indivisibility* of rights. The global human rights discourse itself has undergone a significant change after the invocation of the declaration on the RD and

> it was precisely in the 1970s that the high tide of anti-colonialism found expression in the attempt to craft a subaltern politics of development, international agencies as well as state and private actors in the decades since have devised schemes of development in which honoring human rights is conceived as both the means and the end. (Moyn 2010: 224)[5]

It is this emphasis on the indivisibility of rights that finds a resonance in the subaltern groups such as the rural women, in their struggle for the prohibition of liquor and redefining 'development' through the imperatives of quality education, food, shelter, leisure, health and their interconnections with the formation of rent-seeking classes in the rural hinterlands of India.

India and International Human Rights Law

At the heart of thinking, practicing and implementing human rights is the dilemma between making them sufficiently general, abstract and universal so as to entitle individuals and collectives across gender, race/ caste, colour, class, language, age, sexual preferences, and religious distinctions, and the imperative of making them context specific, concrete and particular so as to effectively implement them to protect specific individuals and groups experiencing particular modes of marginalisation and denial of socio-economic mobility. Human rights, therefore, essentially refer to those rights that are accrued to us for just being human, and thus 'the subject[s] of human rights are not members of this or that society, but of the community of humankind' (Vincent 1986: 9).[6] It is this vision that is enshrined in the Universal Declaration of Human Rights (UDHR) as a 'common standard of achievement for all people's and all nations'.[7] Various conventions, declarations and other documents further developed rights based on this vision, the most prominent among them being the International Covenant on Civil and Political Rights (ICCPR) and the International Covenant on Economic, Social and Cultural Rights (ICESCR) that were adopted by the United Nations (UN) in 1966 and came into force after being ratified by the UN member states in 1976.

There were conventions that focused on the rights violations of specific social groups such as the various misrecognised racial, ethnic and indigenous groups, women and those that were relegated to a minority status, such as the immigrants. For instance, International Convention on the Elimination of All Forms of Racial Discrimination (ICERD) was adopted by the UN in 1965, and the Convention on the Elimination of All Forms of Discrimination against Women (CEDAW) was adopted in 1979.[8] The international discourse on human rights underwent a transformation with the addition of the 'third generation rights' that yet again focused attention on the common concerns of the humanity by foregrounding issues of interdependence. This was reflected in the various declarations and protocols on environmental issues, along with the declaration on the RD that was adopted in 1986 by the UN.

Much of the international human rights law has close connection, both conceptual and in terms of its actual implementation, 'with the principles of domestic constitutional law embodied in the fundamental laws of various countries'. Domestic laws have been both the source and effects of international human rights laws. It is significant to note, with reference to India, that the Indian Constitution was framed at a time (1947–1949) when the General Assembly of the UN had given its approval to the UDHR. However, the Constitution making process was also preceded by a struggle for civil liberties as an integral part of the anti-colonial struggle. The first probable organised initiative was taken by Jawaharlal Nehru to form a civil liberties organisation on 7 November 1936 by founding the Indian Civil Liberties Union (ICLU) with Rabindranath Tagore as its president. Rights were articulated not only as guarantees against arbitrary state action that was so much part of the British colonial rule, but also as necessary means to achieve a more just and egalitarian socio-economic order. It was this two-pronged strategy that was the basis of the anti-colonial struggle and the various instruments it set up, including the Motilal Nehru Committee of 1928 and the Karachi session of the Congress in 1931, which adopted the resolution on fundamental rights (Gudavarthy 2013a). The strategy was a derivative of the conceptual distinction between the natural rights and the positivist tradition of articulating rights. In the natural rights tradition, rights are envisaged as inalienable, having their own origins in nature, while in the positivist tradition 'rights not only originate in the action of the state, but are also entirely dependent on it for their existence' (Singh 2005: 32).

It is this conceptual distinction that the Constitution of India has enshrined in the various principles and provisions of human rights in Part III (Fundamental Rights) and Part IV (Directive Principles of State Policy). Fundamental rights protect broadly six types or categories of rights that include right to equality, right to personal liberty, right against exploitation, right to freedom of conscience and expression, rights dealing with cultural and educational rights (with special reference to minorities), and finally right to judicial or constitutional remedies. Based on the constitutional vision, the Supreme Court in India, besides the review of legislative and administrative measures, gave the writ jurisdiction a creative shape, entailing judicial activism for protection and expansion of human rights, through the innovation of public interest litigation (PIL) or social interest litigation (SIL) since 1980. In the cases of *Gupta v. Union of India* (1982) and *Nakara v. Union of India* (1983), the Supreme Court did away with the 'orthodox bar of *locus standi*', and it extended the possibility of approaching the Court even by a letter (named by Upendra Baxi as epistolary jurisdiction), which can be 'treated by the Court as a writ petition' (Singh 1999: 75). The courts also expanded the scope of enumerated rights by reading in new rights into the fundamental rights. Among others, they included the right to literacy and primary and secondary education; right to health; right to food, drinking water and integrity of environment; right to minimum wages; right to compensate for torture, cruel treatment; right to speedy trial (including the right to free legal aid) (Singh 1999: 79).

These efforts to both protect and expand the content of rights by the courts were possible, apart from the pressure from the civil rights and other political groups and movements such as that of women and Dalits, due to the fact that India is a signatory to the major international human rights instruments including the UDHR, ICCPR, ICESCR, ICERD and CEDAW, to name a few. The Supreme Court has invoked the Articles of International Conventions to pronounce judgements. For instance, relying on Article 24 of the ICCPR, the Supreme Court expanded the ambit of Article 21 that refers to the 'right to life and personal liberty'. In *Sheela Barse v. Secretary, Children Aid Society*, the Court made stringent provisions for protecting the rights of children detained in observation homes. Similarly, in *Jolly George Verghese v. Bank of Cochin*, the Supreme Court relied on Article 11 of the ICCPR, which provides that no one shall be imprisoned merely for inability to fulfil contractual obligation, in interpreting section 51 of the Civil Procedure Code of India (Joshi 1999: 97).

However, notwithstanding these invocations, what these rights actually refer to depend on the more specific historical, social and cultural context, both across and within particular societies. The interface between global and domestic human rights, while enabling the implementation of human rights, continues to raise politically and philosophically significant questions (for the jurisprudence of rights) regarding the Eurocentric character of the global human rights. For instance, Immanuel Kant argues that 'freedom (independence from being constrained by another's choice), insofar as it can coexist with the freedom of every other in accordance with a universal law, is the only original right belonging to every man by virtue of his humanity' (Kant 1995: 238). Such a foregrounding of the idea of freedom could be problematic, in the sense of being Western and Eurocentric, from the point of view of those societies that wish to protect their communities and pose certain limits on free speech, or for certain sections within a society, such as women who might argue that a notion of freedom without obligations presupposes atomistic individuals hyper-separated from the complex network of social relations.[9] Thus, the question that begs attention is how do we retain the emancipatory, rather than the hegemonic, potential of the universal nature of human rights, and transmute them into particular, rather than localised, mechanisms accessible to different social groups in varied political contexts.

Civil–Political Rights, the 'War on Terror' and Maoism in India

Cranston in his celebrated essay 'Are There Any Human Rights' argued that human rights need to have a restricted reference to only the 'first generation rights', such as freedom of speech, that are based on the principle of non-interference and therefore are cogent and encompass the 'feasibility of guaranteeing complete and comprehensive fulfilment', which in turn makes it possible to legislate and make these rights justiciable. Without legality being the defining feature of human rights they end up, as Bentham once put it as 'bawling upon paper'. Human rights become effective only as legal rights emanating either from national legislation or international conventions and declarations 'rather than on the basic humanity (or humanness) of the persons involved' (Sen 2006: 2). According to Cranston, 'The traditional political and civil rights are not difficult to *institutionalize* for the most part, they require governments, and other people generally to leave a man alone. ... The problem posed by claims to economic and social rights, however, are of another order altogether' (Cranston 1983: 13). This centrality of legality seems to be linked to a certain understanding of not just human rights but of law itself. The idea that law by its very nature 'holds for everyone' and it is a 'sort of thing that demands equality in its application' (Bilgrami 2007: 318). Furthermore, it is abstract enough to inform us or enable us to make sense of uncertain situations and institutionalise certain standardised practices, even under conditions of emergency or social crisis of various kinds. It is with this understanding that the ICCPR in Article 6 explicitly states that 'every human being has the inherent right to life. This right shall be protected by law. No one shall be arbitrarily deprived of his life'.[10] Similarly, it states in Article 9 that 'no one shall be subject to arbitrary arrest or detention. No one shall be deprived of his liberty except on such grounds and in accordance with such procedure established by law'.

In contemporary liberal democracies, it is the principle of rule of law that assures the individuals the 'governments respect for the sovereign authority of the people' and therefore the guarantee against the violation of 'basic' civil and political rights. It is this promise in the rule of law that Marxist historian E.P. Thompson attempted to foreground and extrapolate, contrary to either reducing it to a mere 'juridical illusion' or ideological hypocrisy of liberal democracies. Thompson therefore argued that the rule of law meant 'the imposing of effective inhibitions upon power and the defence of the citizen from power's all-intrusive claims' (Thompson 1975: 266). However, with the growing global 'war on terror',[11] analysing the rule of law, in order to comprehend the efficacy of human rights (civil–political rights) as legal rights, would perhaps point towards two dominant forms that it has taken in contemporary times, quite in contrast to its promise of 'inhibiting' the 'all-intrusive powers'. First, the rule of law is 'receiving so much attention now because of its centrality to both democracy and the market economy in the era marked by a wave of transitions to both' (Carothers 1998: 97). Strengthening the rule of law refers to institutionalisation of the 'basic elements of a modern market economy such as property rights and contracts' (Carothers 1998: 97), making it possible therefore to 'export' the rule of law (and democracy), and confirming its inextricable link with market that Hayek had proposed in his campaign for the libertarian right. Second (in many complex ways linked to the first) is the very erosion of law as norms outside of exception and instead becoming a mark of 'normalization of the exception'. As Agamben has pointed out, the 'state of exception' 'is not a special kind of law' meant to deal with conditions like war, but normalised to the extent of becoming 'a paradigm of government', and 'constituting the very basis of modern state power' (Agamben 2005).

The plight of human rights—as civil political rights—in India is marked expressly by this shift to the 'normalization of exception'. The growing 'war on terror' has translated into a public discourse and state policy where on issues of 'national security' and 'public order' there can be no constraints that law (and democracy) can impose. In fact, in its renewed avatar the raison d'etre of law has to be to protect security and order, marking the rise of a new securitised state. Various acts have been promulgated to put this new role of law into action. Among them, the Terrorist and Disruptive Activities (Prevention) (TADA) Act, the Prevention of Terrorist Activities (POTA) Act and Armed Forces (Special Powers) (AFSPA) Act have gained prominence in terms of their role in the violation of the civil and political rights of citizens of India, as well as the activists struggling on behalf of the citizens as part of a vibrant human rights movement in India (Gudavarthy 2008b). These violations are not aberrations but implicit in the way these legislations have been both envisaged and put to use. For instance, under AFSPA, Section 4(a) states that any commissioned officer

> if he is of opinion that it is necessary so to do for the maintenance of public order, after giving such due warning as he may consider necessary fire upon or otherwise use force, even to causing death, against any person who is acting in contravention of any law or order for the time being in force in the disturbed area prohibiting the assembly of five or more persons or the carrying of weapons or of things capable of being used as weapons or of firearms, ammunition or explosive substances.

This can be contrasted with, as Noorani has argued, the provisions of the Code of Criminal Procedure (CrPC), wherein Section 130(3) explicitly states that the officer of the armed forces should use 'as little force and do as little injury to person and property' (Noorani 2009: 9). In spite of the contrast with the CrPC and the outrageous powers to kill, the Supreme Court has upheld the constitutional validity of AFSPA in the *Naga People's Movement of Human Rights vs. Union of India* (1998) (2 SCC 109).[12]

The process of 'normalization of exception' is being further entrenched in not only upholding 'special powers' but in fact making them part of the CrPC itself through the recently constituted *(Malimath) Committee on Reforms of Criminal Justice System*, which has proposed extensive changes to the criminal procedure code carrying in many of the 'special powers' into regular criminal justice system. It suggests for some very fundamental changes in its proposals:

(a) To dilute the provision of 'guilty beyond reasonable doubt' and replace the Evidence Act with the provision that it is sufficient that 'the court is convinced that it is true' (Para 5.13).

(b) Withdrawal of the right to silence to the accused by 'amending the code to provide for appropriate inferences from the silence of the accused' (Para 3.40).

(c) Removal of the distinction between 'cognisable' offences and 'non-cognisable' offences.

(d) 'The confession before a Superintendent of Police or a higher ranking official should be admissible in evidence subject to the condition that the accused is informed of his right to consult a legal practitioner' (Para 7.35.2).

(e) Review of the sunset (time-bound expiration) provision in acts such as the POTA.

We have observed in some detail in Chapter 1 on Maoism the shift of the Indian state to new modes of governance through a paradigm of exceptionalism. However, the changes in the legal regime pointed to in this chapter are in consonance with the change in the global discourse on terror led by the United States. This discourse has actualised itself through the way liberal democracy in India was wedded to global corporate economy, rise of urban/professional middle classes in clout (as we pointed out in Chapter 2 on middle classes) and the new meanings attached to principles such as the rule of law, and the manner in which the language of human rights has itself been framed by Western powers to impose conditionalities on the developing countries through international financial agencies, such as the World Bank, and to strike regime changes, mostly in African, Middle East (coup in Haiti stands out as a glaring example in the past, and in Middle East, including Libya and Syria more recently) and Latin American countries. These changes seem to be closely related and find resonance in the way it has been made global over the last two decades. The resonance between practices of preventive strikes and 'shock and awe' pursued by the United States in Iraq, recent modes of 'total war' in Sri Lanka and the 'Operation Green Hunt' in India has striking resemblance both in terms of methods and ideological justifications they have sought.

The interdependence in the times of globalisation and thereby mutually linked vulnerability have generated a global discourse of 'war on terror'. We, perhaps, cannot make sense of these changes without looking at this convergence and necessarily global terms in which this perceived battle is being fought, conflating all forms of violence by non-state actors into a single epithet called 'terrorism'.[13] Richard Falk, with regard to this convergence and its consequences in a democracy, rightly notes:

> Returning to the post-September 11 framing of terrorism and state terror, it is worth observing that President Bush often accused the terrorists of waging a war against civilization, and as thereby being the embodiment of evil. But what is it that is being labeled as 'civilization' except a governmental actor that has a shameful record of engaging in state terrorism on a scale that dwarfs any understanding by 'the terrorists', that is, the political violence of non-state actors. (Falk 2012: 252–253)

Civilisation as the fault line attempts to bring together various forms of state excesses on the one hand and collapse various forms of political violence on the other. This then offers a global discourse for various states to draw justifications and legitimacy from; in India, this was drawn to justify unprecedented surveillance of Muslim communities and legitimise unprecedented state violence against the Maoists.

Global Cultural Relativism, Dalit–Middle Classes and the 'Caste Is Race' Debate

Human rights are also unique as they allow for imagining them to be universal as much as being culturally relativistic to each individual society with its different social traditions. It is therefore possible to argue that the notion of human rights to be found in the UDHR or the UN can be traced to the historical experience of Western civilisation. When the UDHR was adopted most 'third world' countries were still under the yoke of colonial rule. However, does this historical fact make human rights essentially Western, in the sense that they originate exclusively from Western culture or tradition and therefore there is nothing universal about human rights? By that logic would human rights then be inadequate in allowing nation states to arrive at a common language in the era of globalisation and delivering transnational justice for the subaltern groups?

Jack Donnelly, in one of the early interventions to the debate on 'cultural relativism versus universal human rights', argued that there are broadly four ways to approach the interface between them. Through 'radical cultural relativism', culture becomes the sole source of human rights,[14] while a 'radical universalist' approach argues that culture is irrelevant and there are values and rights that are eternal and relevant across space and time. Contrary to the above approaches are two other approaches, namely 'strong cultural relativism' and 'weak cultural relativism'. While the former argues that rights are culturally determined but universality of rights serves as a check on 'potential excesses of relativism', the latter foregrounds culture as an important source but allows 'relatively rare and strictly limited local variations and exceptions' (Donnelly 1984). According to Donnelly, the weak cultural relativism is possibly the best way to reconcile relativism and universalism. Such an approach, while emphasising the need for universalist categories, allows for variations in 'form'. For instance, right to work needs to be recognised as a universal right in all societies, encompassing issues such as right to seek employment, right to be compensated for unemployment, among others. However, further specification regarding the length and amount of unemployment benefits could vary (Donnelly 1984).[15]

In the more contemporary of debates, scholars have attempted to foreground principles around which a universal framework of human rights can be sustained. Nussbaum has argued, based on her Aristotelian approach of 'general characteristics of human beings', that it is possible to identify characteristics that are fundamentally human and 'not as a member of a particular group or local community' (Gould 2004: 55). She says,

> my proposal is fairly universal and 'essentialist'. That is, it asks us to focus on what is common to all, rather than on differences (although, as we shall see, it does not neglect these), and too see capabilities and functions as were central, more at the core of human life than others. (Nussbaum 1995: 63)

She believes that needs such as food, drink, shelter, sex, mobility, related-ness, humour, among others are common across societies. Amartya Sen has further argued, in basic agreement with Nussbaum's approach, that there is an impending need to develop common standards in accessing development, such as nutrition and education, as they form the 'capabilities' to function in various ways and are essential to the universal 'freedom to achieve'. Cultural relativism, therefore, cannot be meaningful in con-texts where it undermines the 'capabilities' necessary to function. Thus, for instance, Okin argues that the 'respect for cultural practices must be subordinate to the requirements of women's equality' (Okin 1999: 12).

Universality in such a framework emerges 'as a potential framework or horizon for interaction', which grows with inter-societal conversations. In contrast to abstract universality, we could, following Gould, refer to it as 'concrete universality' that is 'constructed by individuals in concrete and differentiated social relations ... in networks of relationships and networks of engagement, themselves interconnecting' (Gould 2004: 62). It could be possibly developed around the universal values of care, sympathy and solidarity, and was referred to as 'non-Eurocentric universality' by Bhikhu Parekh, premised on a unique dialectic between the particular and the universal where 'particularity or difference is valued but not particular-ism, which absolutises it. The universal is valued but not universalism, at least not of the kind that sets itself in opposition to and despises the particular' (Parekh 2008: 3).

This discussion is of particular significance in understanding the politics and discourse of human rights in India. As the state increasingly becomes non-responsive and governs through a paradigm of 'state of exception', marginalised social groups access rights moving beyond the nation and talking of a language that is post-Westphalian in nature, playing out the unique dialectic between the universal and the particular. At the World Conference against Racism, Racial Discrimination, Xenophobia and Related Intolerance (WCAR), held at Durban in August 2001, Dalit organisations led by the National Campaign on Dalit Human Rights (NCDHR) spearheaded a campaign to include caste discrimination as part of racial discrimination and discussed the modes of eliminating it by putting international pressure on the Government of India, as its obligation for having ratified the ICERD in 1969. The UN (universal) framework to understand discrimination based on birth was exclusively West centric in its recognition of only race and colour, and in ignoring experiences that were specific to Asia and Africa. Article 2 of the Convention proclaims that 'no state, institution, group or individual shall make any discrimination whatsoever in matters of human rights and fundamental freedoms in the treatment of persons, on the ground of race, colour or ethnic origin'. Though racial discrimination was defined in terms of exclusion based on descent, the Convention did not mention or include 'discrimination arising from non race-colour-ethnic identities' (Thorat 2004: xvi). It was only in 1996 that the ICERD made an explicit reference to caste-based discrimination and the practice of untouchability: 'The committee states that the term "descent" mentioned in Article 1 of the Convention does not solely refer to race. The Committee affirms that the situation of the Scheduled Castes and Scheduled Tribes falls within the scope of the Convention'. The Dalit groups in India taking a clue from this demanded a more elaborate discussion on caste-based practices under Paragraph 109 of the agenda of the Durban conference, which referred to 'discrimination on the basis of work and descent'.

However, the Government of India objected to this demand of the Dalit groups. Caste was described as strictly an 'internal' matter, not to be debated in international fora. The official position of the government clearly stated that

> communities which fall under the definition of Scheduled Castes and Scheduled Tribes are unique to Indian society and to its historical process and do not come under the purview of Article 1 of the Convention. Caste-based discrimination should not, therefore, have been brought within the discussion in this committee, which is charged solely with the responsibility of looking into racial discrimination. (Thorat 2004: xxiii)

In claiming caste as 'unique to Indian society', Government of India was making a 'cultural relativist' argument that cannot easily be made sense of by the international organisations, which function with a universalist discourse on human rights. Intriguingly, while the Dalit groups themselves had to puncture the Western centric bias to get caste included within the scope of the ICERD, the Government of India also critiqued the universalist nature but precisely not to debate caste within the purview of the ICERD. The debate took interesting twists in India; many of the scholars sensitive to protecting the 'self-determination' of India argued that taking caste to international fora also meant that 'we are looking for foreign help to fight everything, including the caste system' (Gupta 2004a: 53).

Similarly, those alert to the 'imperialism of categories' objected to the forceful reading of caste as race, while the weakening of the caste system is possible only 'if caste is presented as a caste and not forcibly fitted into the category of race, and at the same time, an attempt is made to pro-mulgate an international charter against caste discrimination' (Seth 2004: 96). This alone would actually realise the initial attempts of the Dalit groups to recognise the specificity of caste-based discrimination, rather than conflate caste with race. Furthermore, this kind of conflation may even lead to a change in the way caste is understood and provide an opportunity for the state to withdraw some of its social welfare policies, such as affirmative action.

Dalit groups and activists working on their behalf were attempting to foreground a 'concrete universality' that is sensitive to the specificities of caste-based discrimination but comprehend universalisation as increasing interconnections and looking for commonalities in discrimination prac-ticed in various social contexts. They therefore argued that 'whether it is Australian attacks on Indians or atrocities committed on dalits by Indians or discrimination and oppression of the people of the north-east [which is racial in nature], they are basically issues that concern humanity and cannot be prevented from being internationalized' (Teltumbde 2009: 18). While there is commonality as discrimination against humanity, which is important to recover, there is distinction in the way they are privileged or neglected in concrete social and historical contexts. Therefore, while caste-based discrimination is neglected, racial discrimination of Indians living elsewhere gets focused since they belong to specific (privileged) caste backgrounds. In essence, what Dalit groups were attempting was a double-edged approach of distinguishing caste from race, yet using race, which is globally a more recognised form of discrimination, by reading caste unto race to make use of the political spaces opened by the latter. As a result of concerted efforts by the organisations such as the International Dalit Solidarity Network, United Kingdom outlawed caste-based discrimination. As part of Equality Act, 2010, the Parliament brought an amendment accepting caste as an 'aspect of race'. 'The House of Lords had voted twice in support of the amendment, but the House of Commons had reservations against it. MPs overturned their earlier decision and decided that caste would in future be treated as "an aspect of race"' (*The Times of India*, 26 April 2013). This was recognised as a major legal protection for the four lakh Dalits residing in the United Kingdom.[16]

The 'Caste is Race' represents the unique dynamics between democracy and globalisation. While democracy allowed for, through its policy of affirmative action, formation of new middle classes within the Dalits, globalisation and the accompanying discourse of human rights gave the framework to articulate anti-caste demands through a post-Westphalian frame. The new middle classes, within the Dalit groups, resignified the claims to sovereignty by the state, beyond mere physical control of the territory, into providing basic dignity and recognition, drawing a new equivalence between *Reservations, Recognition and the Republic*. They not only offered new meanings to caste as a sociological category but also, in the process, made it possible to forge new alliances between the various marginalised social groups, across the globe and beyond national territories—forging a new 'fourth world'.

> Human Rights will be vigorously defended by the Fourth world and the multiple social justice movements mobilizing across the globe. ... By a felicitous convergence of meanings and histories, the term 'Fourth World' brings together actors and ideas that share marginalization along with the will to end it by globalizing human rights. ... [T]his term (also) refers to peoples who live in extreme poverty and to the indigenous peoples who make up a third of the world's population—the 5000 to 6000 nations within states that did not consent to having their land and sovereignty appropriated by the modern state. (Fischlin 2007: 211)

Globalisation, in tune with democracy, provides for this unique dynamic for contemporary Indian politics.

Third-generation Rights, RD and the Subaltern Classes

Third-generation rights were not merely new, or merely rights that were not covered under the first two generations of civil–political and social–economic and cultural rights but signified radically new principles beyond the scope of the language of rights in the first two generations. Apart from the end of the Cold War, there were various social and political developments that led to a new language of rights among which prominent was the rise of movements for environmental justice, for peace and for nuclear disarmament. Environmental struggles brought into relief the principle of 'intergenerational equity' further problematising the idea of equality. The World Commission on Environment and Development stated that 'needs of future generations will not be compromised while present generation's needs are met' (Brundtlard Commission Report 1987: 170). Movements for peace articulated new ideas about 'collective interests' that have to be fought by humanity as such and there are no natural (social) constituencies that would struggle for peace. Such issues could be fought not solely around interests but common concern about the well-being and the very future survival of humanity. It is the spirit and the vision of some of these novel principles that were encapsulated in third-generation rights, such as the RD.

The RD, adopted in 1986 by the UN General Assembly and reaffirmed in the Vienna Declaration of 1993 World Conference on Human Rights, marked a new beginning. It envisaged a new model of development around principles of fair and equitable distribution, political participation, social well-being, cultural recognition and dignity beyond the parameters of development as expansion of gross national product (GNP), industrialisation, export growth and capital flows, and marking a break from the top-down process of 'developmentalism'.[17] It is indispensable to recognise the strong interdependence of various kinds of civil–political and socio-economic rights and the futility in attempting to either achieve one against the other or selectively privilege a set of rights.[18]

In order to effectively convert this vision of indivisibility into tangible policies, the declaration on the RD made, among others, four fundamental formulations. First, the RD reiterated the principle of indivisibility of rights.[19] Article 6(2) states that the prime object of the declaration is to 'eliminate obstacles to development resulting from failure to observe civil and political rights as well as economic, social and cultural rights'. In other words, the RD works as a hinge connecting various rights into a 'vector' that 'measures' human well-being. 'The value of the vector improves if at least one right improves and no right deteriorates. If any right is violated, then the vector deteriorates and the Right to Development is violated' (Sengupta 2006: viii).

Second, the emphasis on the right to participate replaced human being as an object of development and made him/her an active subject. Article 1 states that 'Right to Development is an inalienable right by virtue of which every human person and all peoples are entitled to participate in, and enjoy economic, social, cultural, and political development, in which all human rights and fundamental freedoms can be fully realized'. Without the right to participate, human societies are reduced to 'target groups' to be administered state-initiated policies and bureaucratic intervention. For instance, peasants are reduced to 'pure' economic categories such as 'small farmers', undermining as Escobar argues a 'whole way of life' (Escobar 1997).[20] The societies are made 'manageable' and the imperatives of 'governmentality' undermine the agency of social groups reducing them to the status of mere 'populations' (Scott 1998).

Third, the RD recasts development as neither a means nor an end; instead, it lays premium on development as a process. In other words, 'the outcomes of the process are human rights, but the process itself would also be claimed as a human right' (Sengupta 2006: 12). As we understand democracy not only as an end but also as a means to an end, development is also 'not a finite event but a process over time' (Sengupta 2006: 17). This mode of approaching development makes it open to 'social ethics and public reasoning', as well as makes it a collective right to be available to specific social groups as much as individuals within those groups (Sen 2006: 2).

Finally, the RD lays emphasis on its realisation on the mutual interdependence within the 'international community of states'. The RD argues for the primary responsibility on the individual national states and cooperation from the international community. It expects 'policies at the national level with equitable economic relations and a favourable environment at the international level' (Sengupta 2006: 18).

The responsibility of international community is articulated as an 'imperfect obligation', addressed to all those states which are in a position to help. An instance of such a role by the international community could be found in the recently forged alternative regional organisations such as MERCOSUR and ALBA in Latin America. With the initiative under these regional organisations, there has been, for instance, extensive medical services made available by Cuba to Venezuela, keeping in mind not merely profit but also social benefits to the people of both the countries (which shall be the focus of the next chapter).

Increasingly, there has been the realisation that any effective and meaningful implementation of human rights has to integrate various aspects including the civil–political rights for political participation with social and economic rights for fair distribution, means with ends as an ongoing process and domestic policies with international cooperation. This move towards integrating various rights is visible in some of the prominent judgements by the Supreme Court in the recent past. For instance, in the *Francis Coralis Mullin vs. Union Territory of Delhi*, the Supreme Court argued that

> the right to live is not restricted to mere animal existence ... but it also includes the right to live with human dignity, and all that goes along with it, namely the bare necessities of life such as adequate nutrition, clothing and shelter and facilities for reading, writing and expressing ourselves.... (SCC. 608, 1981 1)

Right to education was read into the fundamental rights through right to life. Article 21A was inserted that recognised the right to education as a fundamental right and imposed a duty on the state to provide free and compulsory to all children from the age of 6 to 14 years. It is these judgements that led to the 86th Amendment to the Constitution in 2002 granting legislative recognition to right to education, finally fructifying in the Right to Education Act, 2010. While state institutions such as the judiciary have to some extent demonstrated an integrationist framework, political movements of various hues, forged by the subaltern classes, have worked for long within such a framework.

Women's struggles at the grassroots, for instance, have been for long indicating that domination and systematic marginalisation of women has been possible due to complex interaction between the political, economic, social and cultural dimensions. Therefore, in dealing with specific forms of violations of rights, such as dowry-related deaths, domestic violence, sexual harassment among others, their manifold interactions have to be taken into account in developing strategies that can effectively undermine the entrenched modes of domination. It was such an integrationist strategy that was being proposed in a struggle that drew incisive links between a political economy driven by the collection of revenues from the sale of liquor and the masculine culture of controlling the 'private' sphere through physical violence against women. The anti-arrack movement, as it was referred to, began in August 1992 in a remote village of Dubagunta of Nellore district in Andhra Pradesh. Women of the village stopped vending of arrack in their village after three men lost their way and drowned in a tank. Women stopped arrack carts and jeeps from entering the village, and demanded complete prohibition of the sale of liquor in the state. The movement went beyond the traditional and conventional divisions between the public and private in order to comprehend the hidden linkages between family, domestic violence, the state and the liquor lobby. They understood that behind their abusive husbands was the whole support structure led by the arrack contractors, police, 'goondas', legislators, ministers, officials and bureaucrats (Reddy and Patnaik 1993: 1064). Women consistently articulated the language of including various social (domestic stress, dignity, mental anguish, education and health), economic (constant debt, hunger, falling standard and quality of living) and political (unholy nexus between the politicians/representatives, police, and the liquor lobby contractors) issues in the developmental agenda. They further argued that without necessary economic empowerment, social change, political participation and struggle against cultural practices, mere legal (rights) intervention can be formal and counter-productive. Thus, when the Government of Andhra Pradesh refused to prohibit liquor and restricted women's right to forge political movements, and instead suggested availing legal options by making use of the Domestic Violence Act (2005), women's groups argued that it has the effect of making law insular to the needs of women.

Firstly, the victims become more 'vulnerable' by the compulsion of opening up before an unsympathetic judiciary and police stations. Secondly, the provisions of the law are incapable of addressing the larger issues of women.

A close look at the appeals that women have made in relation to the domestic violence law 498A in the last two decades shows that they are seeking relief which extend beyond those that can be offered by courts and police stations. Women are seeking responsible husbands, a role in decision-making, self-respect and a dignified family life, which in itself often contributes to the violence they experience. (Suneetha 2005: 4102)

Finally, such legal interventions add to the logic of the technocratic state in pulling social problems outside the domain of politics and projecting solutions in fine technical interventions. 'Such an "enclosure" in the legal realm individualises the woman into a case and leads to a depoliticisation of the discussion of women's battles in the family. Is it this closure, which is producing the silence that we are noticing?' (Suneetha 2005: 4103).[21]

Thus, women's movements at the local level are reiterating the points made at the international level in the declaration on the RD that development needs to be posited around principles of indivisibility, right to political participation by the agents, and perceive it as an ongoing process forging complex links rather than a single event. In this case, political movements, more than the state, have adopted the frame of indivisibility of rights. While globalisation has made the global discourse on human rights a new modality to negotiate justice, paradoxically it has also heightened inequalities between the nations and between classes within the nations. The aggrieved subaltern classes have been looking for possible ways of reconciling these two dimensions of globalisation.

Endnotes

1. To cite an instance, Amnesty International in its latest report titled 'Death sentences and executions, 2012' observed the rise in death penalties in India after 2004. Suhas Chakma, Director of Asian Centre for Human Rights, observed that 'during 2001–2011, lower courts granted death sentence to at least 5,776 convicts ... of these death sentences 4,321 were commuted into life sentence' (*The Hindu*, 15 April 2013). This growth corresponds with the growing sentiment, especially among the urban middle classes to award larger number of death sentences for various types of crime.
2. It was in fact believed that for the NDA regime prior to 2004, 'Suspect Muslim' or Islamic terrorism was at the centre stage of framing politics, while for the

UPA, after 2004, Maoisim was the bogey to undermine even non-violent protest politics.

3. Echoing the sentiment expressed by Richard Falk, Barack Obama promised to be proactive in closing down prison at Guantanamo Bay that had become a symbol of excesses committed by the Bush regime; on his second day in office in January 2009, he ordered the prison to be closed within a year. Its existence since 2002, he said had, 'likely created more terrorists around the world than it ever detained' (*The Hindu*, 7 May 2013). It is a different matter though that Obama did not actually close down the prison; 'meanwhile the Guantanamo authorities are seeking an extra $200m for refurbishments...' (*The Hindu*, 7 May 2013).

4. It is interesting to observe that this erosion of sovereignty across the axis of physical control might in itself lead to a heightened use of coercive mechanisms, as the Indian state does with regard to the challenges it faces from the Maoist movement. The anxiety of sovereignty's de-recognition through the global discourse on recognition and basic human rights coupled with real challenges through militant-armed mobilisations, in fact, paradoxically reinforces the wanton use of coercive powers and imposition of 'exceptionalism' by the modern state.

5. The phrase 'Right to Development' was coined by the Senegalese jurist Keba M'Baye in 1972; after that it was formally incorporated into the African Charter on Human Rights in 1981. The UN General Assembly passed its declaration on the Right to Development in 1986.

6. The idea of what constitutes human can be approached in very many different ways. While it could refer to a basic difference from animals, in terms of our capacity to possess reason and self-reflection, it could also refer to the ability to recognise, and 'feel' pain and therefore foreground ability to empathise with the suffering of others, including that of the animals.

7. This was adopted by the General Assembly of the United Nations on 10 December 1948.

8. During the same period, the European Convention on Human Rights, and the Organization of American States proclaimed the American Declaration of the Rights of Duties of Man.

9. For communitarian perspective refer to Parekh (1993, 1997), and for a feminist critique of the liberal idea of freedom refer to an interesting debate between Nancy Hirschmann and Carole Pateman (Hirschmann 1989; Pateman 1992). In the context of India, Gandhi has been a champion of the idea of obligation, which could, notwithstanding its critique of individual-centric rights or freedom discourse, entail politically problematic consequences. I have attempted to explore this elsewhere (Gudavarthy 2008a).

10. ICCPR was adopted and opened for signature, ratification and accession by General Assembly resolution 2200 A (XXI) of 16 December 1966.

11. Marxists such as Perry Anderson have argued that 'bourgeoisie-democratic power is simultaneously and indivisibly dominated by culture and determined by coercion' (Anderson 1976: 42).

12. Noorani notes that in its judgement the Supreme Court does not even refer to Article 21 of the Constitution which recognises the right to life of every person, citizen or foreigner. Refer to Noorani 2009.

13. This kind of conflation and popular sentiment against terrorists found its way into legal pronouncement by the Supreme Court of India. In *Devender Pal Singh Bhullar v. State of NCT of Delhi*, the 'Supreme Court sees as paradox in "terrorists" seeking mercy under the Constitution when they showed no mercy themselves' (Surendranath 2013). Furthermore, Justice Singhvi and Mukhopadhaya in Paragraph 40 of their judgement state that 'the bandwagon to espouse the cause of terrorists involved in gruesome killing and mass murder of innocent civilians and raise the bogey of human rights' (Surendranath 2013).

14. Such an approach can both invoke 'mythical cultural past', like the dictators in Africa, and right-wing cultural organisations such as the RSS in India, which either no longer exists or is a distortion of history; it can also disregard (as most often it does) those rights, as Donnelly points out, that have no cultural basis such as arbitrary arrests, detention, etc.

15. For instance, while the United Kingdom has social security benefits and monthly allowances for all those unemployed, India has its own version in the recently promulgated NREGA, which allows for 100 days of employment and is geared towards protecting the interests of the rural poor.

16. Meanwhile, groups such as Hindu Alliance in the United Kingdom gave a call to boycott the amendment. This amendment directly undercut Indian Government's 'claim that caste prejudice was indigenous to Indian society and it could not be a subject of policy at international fora like the UN' (*The Times of India* 30 April 2013). Furthermore, 'experts said it would trigger lobbying for similar legal protection in the US, Canada, South Africa and Australia—countries that have a strong presence of Indian Diaspora, but have little awareness of caste' (*The Times of India*, 30 April 2013). It would provide for international scrutiny of India's record on caste-related discrimination, as it was done previously with issues related to gender and child labour.

17. The United States opposed and will continue to oppose the Right to Development; it argued that 'development accrues thanks to economic liberties and private enterprise rather than a claimed Right to Development' (Baxi 2007: 129).

18. As we pointed out earlier, this shift towards integrating rights in redefining justice underscores the changes not only in the discourse on development but also the liberal theory through the Rawlsian theory of 'distributive justice' and his 'difference principle', and the discourse on human rights was itself founded on this principle of indivisibility in the international declaration on the RD.

19. Indivisibility in fact was first emphasised in the UDHR in 1948, but was consistently undermined during the days of the cold war. It took more than

four decades thanks to the new political movements that provided the political and discursive context, as elaborated at the beginning of this section, for indivisibility to be brought back into the human rights discourse.

20. In fact, Escobar suggests the use of the term post-development, which, according to him, refers to 'a discursive anti-colonialist insurrection'.

21. I have borrowed arguments in this section from my previous book (Gudavarthy 2013a).

6

Globalisation and Regionalisation: Mapping the New Continental Drift

Liberalisation, privatisation and globalisation are conjoined processes that mark what is distinct about the current phase of globalisation. It is this distinctness and its consequences for the global economy, and for the various classes in democracies across the world that needs to be evaluated, rather than an abstract idea of globalisation per se. Jan Nederveen Pieterse argues,

> contemporary globalization can be described as a package deal that includes informatization (applications of information technology), flexibilization (de-standardization in the organization of production and labor), and various changes such as regionalization and reconfiguration of states. Since the 1980s, the growing impact of neoliberal policies adds to the globalization package, deregulation (Liberalization, Privatization), marketization (unleashing market forces), financialization and securitization (conversion of assets into tradable financial instruments, and the ideology of lean government. (Pieterse 2010: 84)

The globalisation of these processes was initiated through 1980s as 'structural adjustment programmes' initiated by the International Financial Institutions—World Bank and the IMF—which eventually fructified into a new 'Washington Consensus', after the dismantling of the Bretton Woods System (1944–1976). 'The main tenets of the Washington Consensus are monetarism, reduction of government spending, and regulation, privatization, liberalization of trade and financial markets, and the promotion of export lead growth' (Pieterse 2010: 92).

The central tenet of this philosophical (as well as an economic model) shift was the new-found belief that democracies can be vibrant only when practised alongside 'free market economy'. State regulation leads to retarded markets and the overreach of bureaucratic state apparatus. 'Less State' then unleashes the 'animal spirits' and entrepreneurship in the economy and transparency and accountability in the functioning of democratic regimes. This new global order had promised higher growth rates, new opportunities for the Global South and a guarantee of sorts against economic crisis, with the belief that markets have inbuilt modes of 'managing the crisis'.[1] However, the global financial crisis of 2007 revealed a different story about the current version of globalisation based on economic deregulation and liberalisation.

> So far, the first global economic recession since the Great Depression of the 1930s has already destroyed at least 50 million jobs around the world, at least half of them in supposedly advanced economies and pushed another 90 million people in the global South into 'extreme poverty', defined by the World Bank as living on less than $1.25 a day. (Birch and Mykhnenko 2010: 256)[2]

The economic crisis also broke open the social alliance between various classes that the state had laboriously attempted to build in favour of liberalised economies across the globe. The new economic model represented the interests of a new emergent 'transnational capitalist class' carefully crafted by what B.S. Chimni refers to as the evolving 'global imperial state' (Chimni 2004).

> In most cases, these emerging neoliberal social alliances also incorporated parts of the middle classes, and they could often count upon the temporary support from marginalized population segments. Thus, neoliberalism came to constitute the major force driving the dismantling of the predominance of Keynesian and developmental state strategies in the Capitalist core states and the periphery, respectively. (Schmalz and Ebenau 2012: 488)

However, 'the raid action by the major governments worldwide in a bid to save giant transnational corporations from the financial meltdown has ultimately shattered the ideological disguise carefully constructed by the twentieth-century neoliberal doctrines' (Birch and Mykhnenko 2010: 256–257). It 'burst asunder' the illusion regarding the non-interventionist role of the state, as well as the myth that this kind of globalisation was in the 'best interest of society at large', around which the states attempted to build a consensus on. Instead, the 'new' role of the state in managing the financial crisis made it clear that the interests of 'giant transnational corporations' and 'transnational capitalist class' undermined the autonomy of the state, unravelling its class character.

Flexibilisation of the economy also included massive shift from the organised to the unorganised sector, steadily pushing the social costs of production to the labouring poor, end of the post-war welfare state and de-unionisation, among other such processes.

> Ruthless exploitation of labour has become the source of increased corporate profit as well as international price competitiveness in a globalised world. Between mid-1960s and mid-1990s, the poorest 20 per cent of world's people's share of global income has declined from 2.3 per cent to 1.4 per cent, while the share of the richest 20 per cent has risen from 70 per cent to 85 per cent. (Banerjee–Guha 2010: 9)

David Harvey refers to this process as 'accumulation by dispossession', involving large-scale displacement of the poor and creation of immigrants, land acquisition from the farmers for the industries with low and inadequate compensation, creation of special economic zones, longer working hours at less wages, accompanied by 'widespread erosion of public sympathy for the citizenship rights of the dispossessed'.

In between the interests of the 'transnational capitalist class' and the immiserisation of poor owing to the process of 'accumulation by dispossession' lay the place of the middle classes. The middle class itself is 'heterogeneous and polymorphous', constituted by the dominant, middle and lower-middle sections. As we have pointed out earlier in Chapter 2 on middle classes, their role has expanded with the coming of market economy and the expansion of the knowledge base of contemporary societies—knowledge society. 'At the global level, information technologists, software experts, engineers, and the managerial classes have been making advances' (Misra 2010: 157). These classes, to a certain degree, have become globally integrated and adopted global cultural tastes, lifestyles and consumption patterns. This dominant fraction of the middle class, which is part of the liberalised economy, has gained in finding new employment in multinational companies and has benefitted from the current processes of globalisation in terms of both expansion and mobility that it witnessed. However, the lower end of this class, which found jobs through outsourced activities, such as the BPOs, have had lower pay packages, bleaker life chances, longer working hours and poor work conditions. 'This segment is also characterised by feminisation of work', where women are employed in less skilled jobs for lower levels of payment. Further, even the dominant sections of the middle class have had the experience of retrenchment, loss of employment and social security during the current phase of financial crisis.[3] 'Then again, what has become clearer is the real and actual beginning of "austerity" for the majority of taxpayers on middle and modest incomes' (Birch and Mykhnenko 2010: 262). While this has opened new cracks in the social alliance for the current phase of globalisation, these sections have remained steadfast supporters and played the role of generating ideological legitimacy for globalisation (Fernandes and Heller 2008).

Alongside these changes in contemporary globalisation, it has also been witness to the 'rise' of the Global South. With many of the countries in the Global South identified as 'engines of growth', and the impact of financial crisis on the countries of the Global North, in terms of slowing down growth rates, and constant flow of capital flows into new spaces, in search of cheaper labour and raw materials, the international order has witnessed the rise of new modes of regionalism between these nations.

> As the current crisis has unfolded, the USA and its western allies have found themselves confronted with an emergent multi-polar world. The once almighty Group of Seven (G7) major capitalist economies (Canada, France, Germany, Italy, Japan, the UK and the USA) has become another victim of the global financial crisis to clear the way for a Group of Twenty (G20)—a new top gathering which includes, besides the old 'advanced industrialized nations' of the now defunct G7, the EU and the emerging market economies of Argentina, Australia, Brazil, China, India, Indonesia, Mexico, Russia, Saudi Arabia, South Africa, South Korea, and Turkey. (Birch and Mykhnenko 2010: 258).[4]

This has led to a visible shift in the momentum, from North–South relations to South–South relations. Initially, the new regional organisations were floated within each—Asia, Africa and Latin America—of the southern continents. They included organisations such as the AU and NEPAD in Africa, ASEAN and SAARC in Asia, and MERCOSUR and ALBA in Latin America. The new and alternative regionalism has further undergone a change with a new momentum towards inter-continental organisations between the countries of the Global South, which includes new forums such as IBSA and the BRICS.

What then has been the historical role of this shift from North–South to South–South regionalisation? Have the new South–South organisations been able to chart out a new form of 'alternative globalisation'? Are there new possibilities available in the 'alternative regionalism' of the intercontinental regional organisations in the Global South? Further, do they present new opportunities for a more equitable growth between various social classes within each of these nations? For instance, the regional bloc referred to as IBSA has articulated, at its conference held in Rio de Janeiro in 2005, the slogan of 'economic growth and social equity'. Similarly, BRICS nations have recognised that economic growth has not eliminated large-scale poverty in their own nations, thereby emphasising the need for a new international community that can confront this issue. Can they map a new historical role for global middle classes and change the equation of the subaltern classes with democracies across the Global South? Can they abate the growth of militant modes of protest and 'political violence' through more equitable forms of economic organisation? In other words, does 'alternative regionalism' offer space for articulating 'alternative globalisation'?

Problematising Alternative Globalisation

Problematising alternative globalisation is an arduous task not only in mapping the alternative political, cultural and economic principles that are agreeable without excluding or being disadvantageous to any of the developing countries but also in making them practical enough in terms of their immediate implications and implementational mechanisms. We shall attempt to elaborate the core economic, political and cultural principles and also the possible conflict between them. These shall serve us as the guiding principles in making an assessment of the historical role of the phenomenon of regional organisations.

Economic Guidelines: From Maximisation to Redistribution

The thrust of economic organisation has to move beyond the singular focus on economic growth and trade, to arrive at human-centric 'sustainable', 'humanist' or 'whole' development. This involves moving beyond the 'profits system' for the corporates as the prime aim of the economy and concomitantly the failed logic

> that the huge global problem of poverty, both absolute and relative, can be solved by seeking to maximize overall economic growth, on the questionable assumption that this will push up living standards across the board. In these circumstances it will have to be recognized that the only alternative way of solving the problem is through redistribution of income and wealth, both within and between the nations. (Shutt 2001: 109)

There is, perhaps, an immediate need to re-establish the point that there is no alternative to reasonable and just redistribution of wealth and means of production. This shift from 'maximisation to redistribution' helps us to make a crucial distinction between market economy and market society, i.e., the market needs to have a delimited role and cannot be the lone driving force for the development model to be pursued by the countries of the South. Increasingly, the Northern countries have ended up as market societies with hedonistic consumerism as the most significant motivational factor, allowing the consumer logic to dictate the social life-world, which is what Habermas referred to as a process of 'colonisation of the life-world'. It needs to be recognised that since the World War II the global growth rates cannot for long significantly exceed their historic average of 2–2.5 per cent over the long term (Shutt 2001: 108). Thus, the alternative development model, as against the neoliberal model of economy, needs to postulate alternative priorities such as follows:

1. Sustainable environment that is being disrupted by overconsumption of scarce non-renewable resources. Focusing on the ecological issues invariably has global dimensions and cannot be restricted to the local or the national. However, the issue of distribution of responsibilities between the North and the South needs to be elaborately discussed not to adversely impact the basic growth required for any meaningful development.
2. Draw a causal link between population growth and poverty that works both ways. Thus, to break the vicious circle between the two, eradication of poverty and upgrading of social conditions are the first priority.
3. Universalising the effective appropriation of all human rights— civil, political, social, economic and cultural, where both forms of

rights are indispensable to any meaningful idea of development. As Amartya Sen has observed, for 'Development as Freedom' both civil–political and socio-economic rights are both means and ends simultaneously. Thus, development is considered as a combination of economic issues such as income and jobs as 'social bases of self respect', and any account of justice and development needs to conjoin the equal distribution of basic capabilities (Sen 1998).[5] In this context, the objective of full employment appears as central to the implementation of economic and social rights. 'The more so that unemployment and severe underemployment affect 30 per cent of the world work force and the realistic projections do not warrant any optimism unless employment-oriented development strategies replace the growth-oriented ones' (Royal Danish Ministry of Foreign Affairs 1996: 205).

4. Labour of the primary producers is valued at a level compatible with basic human dignity, rather than the starvation wages which currently condemn so much of the Third World's rural population to subsistence living. This reinvigoration of labour into the development model should subsume two important factors: (i) proper economic value to the role of 'carers' (including those engaged in child rearing or tending disabled relatives); (ii) policies on labour should move beyond mere 'reactive social policies' that bring relief to the victimised populations dealing with unemployed, underemployed and excluded, rather than with unemployment and exclusion (Royal Danish Ministry of Foreign Affairs 1996: 205).

Political Guidelines: From Democracy to Democratisation

In the political arena, the crucial issue is that of initiating the process of democratisation as differentiated from democracy. The crucial issue seems to be that of conceptualising the role of the state, in the third world, which is undergoing contradictory pulls. On the one hand, the rise of the new empire and a growing 'imperial global state' constituting the new financial and international institutions, such as the World Bank, IMF, NATO, G7, Inter-American Development Bank and global corporations, warrants a strong state in the southern countries to retain autonomy to pursue independent policies (Chimni 2007). In other words, there is a strong need to preserve the sovereignty of the nation state. On the other hand, within the nation, the process of democratisation implies and entails a state that is within the control of the local, and is porous enough to account for the public opinion. As we have argued earlier, subaltern classes, be it the basic classes led by the Maoists or the Dalits led by new international organisations in their quest for justice, have undermined the claims to sovereignty by the state. Are these—preservation and democratisation of sovereignty—reconcilable objectives? Three broad views emerge on this:

1. One set of scholars argue that 'to resurrect the nation state to protect against the global capital' is a misguided nostalgia and must be rejected. Antonio Negri argues that

   > we claim that Empire is better in the same way that Marx insists that capitalism is better than the forms of society and modes of production that came before it. In the same way today we can say that Empire does away with the cruel regimes of modern power and also increases the potential for liberation. (Negri and Hardt 2000: 43–44)

   'Global Cosmopolitanism' demands that the state be pushed into a process of 'withering away'. Even scholars from the South have begun to accept 'some erosion of national autonomy in the short term to improve economic performance in the medium term on the premise that, ultimately, it is economic strength which provides nation states with political clout in the international community' (Nayyar 1996).

2. Manuel Castellas argues that 'a new form of state is emerging, and supranational institutions, national states, regional and local governments, and even NGOs are linked together in a network of interaction and shared decision making that becomes the prevalent political form of the information age: the network state' (Castellas 1996: 27). In such a formulation, domestic concerns have become intertwined with 'external' factors as to make the distinction between national and global merely semantic. We need to therefore acknowledge that globalisation has encouraged the formation of multiple modes of organisation and alliance at a transnational level, which is also advantageous to protest movements across continents.

3. Finally, James Petras and Samir Amin would argue that contemporary globalisation predominantly is a form of imperialism. According to Petras, the expansion of capital should be seen as an imperialist conquest, exemplified by the concentration of world economic power in a few <u>US based</u> multinational companies. We are witnessing transnationalisation of global elites in nexus with the domestic elites of the third world countries with an increasing disintegration of national societies and local communities. The current process is therefore best conceptualised as 'mercantilist capitalism', according to Petras, where 'the imperial state (the United States) combines protectionism at home, monopolies abroad, and free trade within the empire' (Petras 2000). Similarly, Samir Amin believes that protecting against the imperialist onslaught first requires a kind of de-linking before we re-globalise in order to pursue certain 'protectionism' internally and development without expansionism (Amin 1997: 123). The marginalised therefore need the nation state 'as a buffer from the world economy'. According to Kapstein, 'the fate of the global economy ultimately rests on domestic policies in its constituent states' (Kapstein 1996).

The process of contextualising the role of the state in augmenting democratisation and empowerment of the marginalised is a complex issue; however, alternative globalisation has to continuously push the state to move beyond the demands of mere representative democracy and provide for substantive opportunities to the vulnerable to take part in the policy making. This is possible if democratisation refers not just to procedural neutrality and representation but also to effective 'local control' of resources and decision making, including autonomy for the indigenous peoples coupled with new modes of planning, 'by redirecting existing resources and organizing education and production in terms of locally determined goals and available resources and revenue generators' (Bray 2002: 120). On the other hand, the state needs to be compelled to curb the power of the corporates; apart from the popular pressure at the institutional level, there need to be restrictions on the funding of political parties by the corporates, and control of the ownership of the mass media should be regulated so that minority opinions are heard and openly debated in the 'public sphere' and not monopolised either by the 'transnational capitalist class' or the urban middle classes. Finally, popular control cannot not be restricted just to an organised and institutionalised 'civil society' but should also take into account the various radical and militant protest politics across the globe, including movements such as the Zapatista in the Latin America and the Maoist struggles in South Asia. In other words, merely taking on board the NGOs is not a sufficient account of the process of democratisation.

Cultural Guidelines: From Recognition to Solidarity

Finally, cultural parameters are as important a source of conflict and discrimination in the contemporary world as the problems of economic inequality and redistribution. A broad alternative culture as part of the alternative globalisation has to have its roots not in market and competitiveness but in the processes of generating substantive solidarity. Solidarity connotes the human capacity to cooperate and trust to generate a sense of security and development and preserve spontaneous exchanges between individuals and social groups. This includes both the process of avoiding commercialisation and marketisation of society and relations, and the continuous need to legislate on—legalise—most relationships. Solidarity has many dimensions. It could include solidarity between nations, often reflected in the new phenomenon of regional integration; solidarity with future generations includes taking the responsibility for the climatic changes and damages thereof due to excessive industrialisation, and solidarity among social groups and classes can be expressed in the payment of taxes. Recently some of the countries have officially introduced 'solidarity taxes', which are directed at alleviating unemployment or poverty in general. It thus needs to be recognised that alternative globalisation has to preserve solidarity as a founding, rather than as an instrumental, value. In other words, individuals, groups and nations have to realise the intrinsic value of the 'act of giving'.[6] This in course of time should make it possible for the nations to recognise a global order based not on uniformity and standardisation but 'graded obligations'. The more developed will have more obligations towards the developing countries. Entrenching such an inverse relation will alone ensure lasting global peace.

Similarly, closely related to this is the need to realise the claims to recognition. These include respect for the immense global diversity and avoiding the 'civilising missions'. It is equally pertinent to realise the claims for recognition in their own right rather than as a dependent or a derivative variable of economy. In other words, claims for redistribution and recognition are two dimensions of justice, where both are 'co-original' and 'co-primary'. As Nancy Fraser argues:

> Bivalently oppressed groups … suffer both maldistribution and misrecognition in forms where neither of these injustices is an indirect effect of the other, but where both are primary and co-original. In their case, neither the politics of redistribution alone nor the politics of recognition alone will suffice. Bivalently oppressed groups need both. (Fraser 1999)

In other words, the move from recognition to solidarity is possible only in duly recognising and realising the claims to recognition, and also in looking for possible ways of combining them with redistributive mechanisms.

Alternative globalisation has to be thus based on these three broad principles of moving beyond economic growth and trade-driven development in the economic field: shifting the focus from maximisation to redistribution, differentiating between democracy and democratisation in the political arena and augmenting substantive solidarity by combining the claims for recognition in the cultural domain with those of redistribution in the political and economic realms. These principles provide us the possibilities of the emergence of a new tri-continental perspective between Africa, Asia and Latin America. However, in order to move closer to this new 'world view', there is a need to 'de-link' in order to re-globalise the alternative vision. What has been the historical role of regional organisations in the Global South?

Pan-African Regionalism—AU/NEPAD: Market-driven Economic Model

African unity was based on the ideal of 'Pan-Africanism', which constituted both 'global' and the 'continental' perspectives. While the global Pan-Africanism envisaged a unity of 'all those people with African origin' and joined a worldwide movement for solidarity, the 'continental' perspective emerged in an attempt to unite the postcolonial states. It was in 1958 when the first Pan-African movement was finally launched with the Conference of Independent African States (CIAS). After that in 1960, the phase of political independence for very many African nations, young African leaders took the initiative for African Unity and formed the Organisation of African Unity (OAU) in 1963. Their primary aims were liberating the other remaining African countries and fighting against discrimination, racism and hierarchies of all hues, along with the right to self-determination in running the internal affairs of the independent nations, OAU brought out the Lagos Plan of Action (LPA) in 1980 (Biswas 2003: 21). It was anchored on two principles—collective self-reliance and self-sustaining development. However, for various historical reasons, such as lack of infrastructure and continued dependence on the metropolitan powers among others, the initiative for African unity around these principles was derailed.

Yet again, on 9 July 2002, leaders of 43 African countries met in Durban, to replace the 39-year-old OAU, with the new African Union (AU, perhaps named taking inspiration from the European Union). The major shift was the 'civic foundations' of the AU.

> The OAU did not even pretend to include civil society in any of its activities. Not until the emergence of the AU did the norms and principles of democracy, civil society ... come to be recognized as essential to accelerate the African integration project. This recognition is a big step from the OAU days and the state-centered ... approaches of the past. (Habib 2006: 16)

Civil society is to participate in the AU through the Economic, Social and Cultural Council (ECOSOC). ECOSOC should be composed of 150 civil society organisations, including groups such as the NGOs and community-based organisations, organisations of workers and employers, traditional leaders, and religious and cultural associations. There will be 24 transnational sectoral civil society organisations selected at regional and continental levels (Habib 2006: 16). The economic programme for the realisation of the African integration envisaged by the AU was formulated through the NEPAD.

The African leaders adopted NEPAD at the Lusaka Summit of the AU on 21 July 2001. The operationalisation of the AU was interconnected to the implementation of NEPAD. NEPAD was envisaged as an alternative regional level programme to reverse the dire socio-economic conditions in Africa.[7]

> Amongst 340 million, half the population lives on less than US$1 per day. The mortality rate of children under five years of age is 140 per 1000, and life expectancy continues to be low at 54 years. Only 58 per cent of population has access to safe drinking water. The rate of illiteracy for people over 15 is 41 per cent. To reverse this situation the proposals in NEPAD are expected to help Africa achieve a growth rate of over 7 per cent per annum. (Biswas 2003)

To achieve this, NEPAD has certain core principles around which it proposed to work:

1. *Good governance*: It primarily referred to building institutions for the markets. It included among other things the idea of 'corporate governance', which refers to 'the mechanism through which the corporations—whether private, publicly traded, or state-owned—and their managers are governed' (Hope 2002: 391).[8] Similarly, it also emphasised that governments can no longer 'monopolise' programme delivery and instead need active participation of the private sector and NGOs.

2. *Economic policy making and execution*: Under this, NEPAD believes that economic liberalisation needs to be deepened to encourage greater private sector activity. It stressed the need for the government to withdraw from 'interfering' in all the sectors of the economy. There was an urgent need to give priority to revitalising regional cooperation and integration frameworks. The primacy seems to be given to emulating the models of the European Union and North American Free Trade Agreement (NAFTA).

3. *Productive partnerships*: The focus as per forging new partnerships was the need to recognise that the NEPAD secretariat work closely with the World Bank, IMF and the African Development Bank. In fact, the Poverty Reduction Strategy Papers were finalised under the guidance and approval of the World Bank and the IMF. NEPAD was seeking active partnership with the industrialised countries to attract Foreign Direct Investments (FDIs) and the international donor community. To realise this, NEPAD was interested in

establishing a market-oriented economy based on open trade and investment policies; the protection of property rights; supportive taxes and expenditure policies; appropriate monetary, financial and exchange-rate policies; the control of corruption; explicit promotion of the private sector activity, including the privatisation of the state-owned enterprises (Hope 2002: 395).

4. *Enhancement of democracy, peace and security*: Democracy here refers to increasing political pluralism, allowing for the existence of various political parties, and periodic organisation of open elections. To achieve security, the focus again has to be on peacekeeping, peace enforcement and post-conflict reconciliation and rehabilitation.

Given these broad policy formulations of NEPAD, it is perhaps justified to conclude that its notion of regional integration was primarily driven by a market-dominated economic model. Throughout the document and the programmes taken up there was only emphasis on global integration but no sustained criticism of the global corporations and their prioritisation of profit-making mechanisms. Instead, the global corporate capital was repeatedly looked upon as the sole alternative, giving up the previous emphasis on protectionisms and building indigenous industries. 'Imperialism' was not the ideological language used by NEPAD. Similarly, there was no mention of redistribution of any kind in removing poverty; instead, the emphasis was on the protection of property rights and the logic seems to be to reinforce the neoliberal belief in 'maximisation leading to upliftment of living conditions'. Even democracy is conceptualised more in procedural terms rather than around substantive principles. Governance reforms are sought to be implemented in consonance with civil society organisations, especially local and global NGOs. Most of the regional organisations working along with or as part of NEPAD had a limited notion of participation. For instance, 'SADC encourages non-state actors and stakeholders to form associations with which it will sign memorandum of Understanding' (Landsberg 2006). The 'stakeholder' language shifts the focus where people are expected to act more as 'consumers' rather than as rights bearing citizens protecting political rather than just commercial interests.

Even the institutions designed to implement the programme of integration, such as the African Peer Review Mechanism, were technically functioning and largely depoliticised. Problems were identified as functions to be solved by putting together 'experts'. Complex socio-economic processes were reduced to technical problems. There was no effective provision for 'local control' or to accommodate the demands of radical protest movements; instead they relied on civil society that essentially represented the NGOs. While the AU was critiqued as state-centric integration, NEPAD becomes 'people centric' by virtue of withdrawal of the state, and replacement with the market and the NGOs. Virtually, civil society and the market become synonymous to each other. However, selective state intervention was demanded, as in any other neoliberal model, when the state had to serve the interests of the market. Therefore, it is believed that 'integration (around the imperatives of the market) will not be succeeded if sufficient political muscle is not applied to make it succeed' (Mistry 2000: 560).

Thus, regional integration as a mode of global integration needs to factor in the historical fact that Africa is not being 'integrated' for the first time with the global capital. Mere emphasis on market, growth and FDIs gives an impression that Africa is underdeveloped because it was marginalised in terms of its global integration. These myths according to Samir Amin are strengthened because the exports of Africa represent only a minute proportion of the world's trade. Amin argues,

> In fact it matters little that Africa's exports have represented only a minute part of world trade yesterday and today. Capitalism is not a system which sets out to maximize production and productivity, but one which chooses the volumes and conditions of production which maximize the profit rate of the capital. The so called marginalized countries are, in fact, the super exploited in brutal manner and therefore, impoverished countries, are not countries located 'at the margin' of the system. (Amin: unpublished)[9]

The peripheries are integrated into the global system in a 'passive way', i.e., they adjust without playing a significant role in shaping it. All regions are equally integrated; the point is in which way they are integrated. The AU and NEPAD seem to proceed on the assumption that they are the harbingers of a new global integration, and in the process are strengthening the global market and thereby the already existing marginalisation of the African people. To reverse this, we need a certain kind of 'delinking' from the global market before we can reglobalise, and build a self-sufficient economy for which it is imperative to go 'far beyond what is generally suggested under the labels of "good governance" and "political multiparty democracy"' (Amin: unpublished). Political pluralism does not necessarily represent wider socio-economic groups; they can very well represent the nexus between the domestic and the global elites.

Finally, NEPAD's regional integration does not take into account the problem of regional "hegemones" such as the case of South Africa. In Africa, South Africa enjoys a favourable trade surplus—the overall trade balance recently stands at 5:1 in South Africa's favour. Will the South African MNCs reinforce the South African government's foreign policy favouring the development of the entire region or use plans such as NEPAD to gain market access? The foreign policy of the post-Apartheid South Africa aims to create congruence between 'human rights, solidarity politics and its own development needs'. However, South Africa has contradictory policies in relation to Zimbabwe, Lesotho, the Democratic Republic of Congo (DRC), and Burundi. The presence of business is seen as exploitative, profiteering or leading to displacement. NEPAD has not sufficiently focused on any of these issues. It needs to realise that countries like South Africa cannot remain as relative islands of prosperity in a 'sea of poverty and insecurity'. But for this we need to move beyond the considerations of trade as formulated under neoliberal ideological proclivity, which is what seems to be missing in NEPAD.

The recent Revised AU/NEPAD African Action Plan 2010–2015 lays the same emphasis that we identified here. It continues to stress on an export-oriented growth (with special emphasis on the export of energy resources, such as oil), combined with good governance and corporate governance through the language of stakeholders.[10] The only new issues it seems to have identified include climate change and gender development. However, these concerns within the corporate paradigm of NEPAD would continue to suffer due to integration into the corporate economy without any emphasis on human development and issues of protection of ownership of resources for the local people, among many other such similar concerns.

Asian Unity—SAARC/ASEAN—Cultural Entrapments

The most significant initiative, for not just Asian regionalism but that of all the southern countries, was taken by the newly independent Asian and African countries, as part of the Non-alignment Movement (NAM).

An important forerunner of NAM (which was formally inaugurated in 1961 at Belgrade) was the 1955 Bandung conference in Indonesia. The most important aspect was the 'third bloc' solidarity that emerged between the Asian and African countries. China played a prominent role in the formulation of the famous Five Principles (Panchshila) at Bandung. The most significant aspect of Panchshila was its anti-colonial spirit and belief in the autonomy of the nations and practice of non-violence (Vanaik 1995: 26). Finally, it stressed on cultural and racial equality, bringing an important cultural dimension into the idea of solidarity. Further, the economic programme was formulated as part of the Group of 77 (the entire Third World), which expressed this new broad Southern Alliance. The struggle for the New International Economic Order (NIEO) initiated in 1975 envisaged the following:

1. Independent pursuit to develop productive forces.
2. Carry economic affairs primarily at the national level by following the policy of self-reliance and protection to the nascent industries.
3. Though it was effectively a state-initiated programme, it has the popular support of the people of the South.

However, in spite of the spirit, the NAM was a non-starter and so was the initiative to forge regional alliance between the Asian countries. The literal collapse of the political project to economically align the nations in Asia was primarily due to what can be described as cultural reasons. NAM and the struggle for NIEO failed due to various cultural conflicts between the countries of Asia. Historically, in South Asia, it can be traced to China's humiliating defeat of the Indian armed forces in the 1962 border war. With this, the nations began to think in terms of their realist 'national interests' and military prowess. India began to 'position itself so as to benefit from both the US policy of seeking to contain China and from the deepening Sino-Soviet rift' (Vanaik 1995: 29). Next was the 1965 Indo-Pakistan war around the issue of Kashmir. Yet again, it had strong cultural overtones as Pakistan argued that Kashmir belonged to its territory owing to the majority Muslim population in Kashmir. 'Though the war did not trigger a rebellion in Kashmir, it had a major impact on the nature of realignment of forces. First, Pakistan began to cultivate closer ties with the Islamic West Asia, making the religious angle more prominent in the geo-politics of Asia' (Vanaik 1995: 29). The 1971 war finally led to the formation of Bangladesh. The Simla Accord of 1972 put a temporary lid on the brewing conflict, but not without realignment, where the new alliance between Pakistan–China and the United States stood in contrast to the Indian decision to move closer to the Soviet Union. In Sri Lanka, as the repression of the Jaffna Tamils grew and ethnic strife escalated around the question of self-determination and an independent 'homeland' or Eelam for the Tamilians, India began to involve itself, yet again around an ethno-cultural issue. 'On July 29, 1987 the two countries signed the Indo-Sri Lanka Accord wherein the Indian army was for the first time made the guarantor of civic peace in a neighbouring and fully sovereign country with which it was not at war' (Vanaik 1995: 35). There are similar tensions between China and India that continue even today. There is a border issue where part of Arunachal Pradesh is claimed by China as its own territory and there is the sore point of India providing political asylum to Dalai Lama and being politically active in supporting the cause of Tibet. More recently, tensions brew with the Chinese incursion into Ladakh in April 2013. It was alleged that Chinese soldiers had set up a temporary camp 19 km inside the Line of Actual Control (LAC). This also led to the changing geo-strategic relations within South Asia, with both Nepal and Sri Lanka developing closer ties with China. As stated before, these tensions had deep historical and cultural roots, detrimental to the interests of the South Asian region in forging closer ties for common developmental goals.[11]

Amidst such entrenched cultural entrapments, the signing of the Treaty of Rome in 1957 made the first attempt of regionalism. Institutionalised regional cooperation began as late as in 1985 when the SAARC was established. SAARC shunned cooperation in hardcore economic issues and formed the South Asian Free Trade Agreement (SAFTA) at the end of the Islamabad SAARC summit in January 2004 (Dubey 2007: 1238). However,

> there is no specific provision in the Agreement for the adoption of measures of deeper integration. ... And worst of all Pakistan has refused to apply the SAFTA provisions to its trade with India. An FTA in South Asia has very little meaning if it does not cover potentially the largest segment of trade in the region i.e. between Pakistan and India. (Dubey 2007: 1238)

During the 14th SAARC Summit in New Delhi in 2007, the issue of SAFTA remained inconclusive. What comes through is the 'obsession with state security to prevail over human security'. Thus, there are very little provisions to bring in non-state actors that express the popular sentiments in the region. The state is weakened after the process of liberalisation with very little independent policy space left to it to exercise its policy options and for making macro-economic policy decisions. Nation state in this context is in a peculiar position of remaining only as a cultural entity and playing very insignificant role either in generating common political ideologies or in forging new economic alliances. Thus, 'the intra-SAARC trade remains around 4 per cent of the regions total as against 78 per cent of EU, 53 per cent of ASEAN and 50 per cent of NAFTA. Even the late entrant MERCOSUR have substantially enlarged their intra-regional trade' (Srivastava 2004: 148). The recent SAARC Summit held in Maldives in 2011 issued the 'Addu Declaration', yet again emphasising the same old agenda of 'building bridges', recognising the ongoing cultural differences, translating into policy incongruity and inability to forge regional integration.[12]

The ASEAN with 10-member countries has made some attempts to expand and stabilise with its attempts to include China, Japan and South Korea. This was made evident at the Summit held in Bali on 8 October 2003. ASEAN was set up in 1967 as a coalition of anti-Communist countries (Philippines, Malaysia, Singapore and Indonesia) to primarily stop the spread of communism. Ironically, it is this very organisation now seeking integration with China. However, firstly, the APT's (ASEAN Plus Three) emergence raises questions about the relations between it and other regional groupings such as the Asia-Pacific Economic Cooperation (APEC) forum and ASEAN itself, as well as about the overall prospects for its future development. Second, given the history of the region, the cultural, linguistic and political divisions that run through East Asia, it is again difficult not only to incorporate new members but also to stabilise the relations between the old members of the ASEAN (Stubbs 2002: 440).

> The region's democratization means that the rise of popular nationalism will have an impact on decision making at the highest levels. ... In countries such as Indonesia, Malaysia, Thailand, South Korea and even Japan

there are signs that nationalism has intensified in the wake of the crisis. ... The differences in approach to economic policy within the region that have emerged in the wake of the Asian economic crisis and underscore the cultural and institutional diversity of the East Asian region could also limit regional economic cooperation under the APT framework. (Stubbs 2002: 451)

Further, what is making the new regionalism between ASEAN and the new regional powers such as China difficult is the ostensible nexus between Chinese ethnicity and the Chinese capital as a vehicle for regional integration. The increasing economic value of 'Chineseness' catalyses the ethinicisation of economic growth in the region. As some of the scholars have pointed out, 'We introduce the concept of "ethno-class" to encapsulate the diversity of historical, social, and economic factors that have led to the cultural and economic powers held by certain ethnically defined non-state actors' (Wee 2006: 326). Such ethno-class formations then become crucial in determining the political and economic relations between the countries.

> From this perspective, the Malaysian state responded to the historical existence of ethnic Chinese entrepreneurs as an ethno-class by deliberately setting out to create a bumiputra (native) ethno-class of entrepreneurs. The distinctiveness of such ethno-classes then comes to be marked by ethnically based exclusion and inclusion, advantages and disadvantages, opportunities and constraints. (Yuk Wah 2006: 337)

With *bumiputra*, the citizens being granted with rights are not shared with non-indigenous citizens. However, the culture-based interactions can work both ways; for instance, in other contexts, Malaysia has been aggressive in utilising the 'cultural resources' of its Muslim, Chinese and Indian populations to tap into Arabic, Chinese and Indian capital markets, respectively. A logical contradiction has thus emerged between Malaysian Chinese being viewed as national assets on the one hand and as non-*bumiputra*, and hence second-class citizens, on the other hand. Thus, to conclude, the changing relations between China and Southeast Asia are not just international relations between different nation states; they are also inter-ethnic relations internal to each Southeast Asian nation state.[13] The latest, 21st ASEAN Summit held in Cambodia in 2012 was organised under the theme 'One Community, One Destiny', yet again signalling the need to overcome tensions and conflicts of interests involving issues of cultural identities in the age of migration.

Finally, China is attempting new mode of regional cooperation to counter the culture-constrained former experiments with its new currently active Shanghai Cooperation Organisation (SCO), with China, Russia, Kazakhstan, Kyrgyzstan, Uzbekistan and a proposal to include India, Pakistan and Iran. SCO aims to realise free flow of commodities, technologies and services in the Asian region. They have already agreed on 125 joint proposals relating to trade and investment. Between China and Russia alone, bilateral trade has reached $30 billion, which amounts to an increase by 37 per cent from 2004. In order to boost other Asian economies, China has already announced $900 million loans for the other SCO countries. Further, it needs to be noted that

> politically, Russia is a rather weak actor outside the Commonwealth of Independent States. Consequently, it has been seeking external allies that could enhance its international position. Since the mid-1990s, its most important long-term strategic ally has been China. The Shanghai Cooperation Organisation is the instrument intended to defuse the two countries rivalry over Central Asia. (Tudoroiu 2012: 33)

There is also along with SCO the Conference on Interaction and Confidence Building Measures in Asia (CICA) with all the major countries in the Asian region including China, Russia, India and Central Asian countries, Afghanistan, Pakistan, Turkey, Thailand and South Korea. It would be a platform to act on matters of social development in the region addressing concerns such as underdevelopment, poverty, literacy, etc.

Asian experiments in regionalism are marred by strong cultural entrapments. They need to rework around how to infuse their experiments with substantive solidarity where the mutual obligations go beyond mere *quid pro quo* kind and the nations are able to dialectically balance between the claims for recognition on the one hand and realising substantive solidarity on the other. Currently, they seem to be countering each other and thereby retarding the regional experiments. Going beyond culture, without negotiating with in as in the new experiment with SCO, might yield positive results in the short term but might prove to be counterproductive in the long run.

Latin American Solidarity—MERCOSUR/ALBA: 'Open Regionalism'

On 26 March 1991, Argentina, Brazil, Uruguay and Paraguay met to form the Common Market of the South. Mercosur has 50 per cent of the population, 58 per cent the GDP and 40 per cent of the total foreign direct trade of the Latin American Integration Association (LAIA). Mercosur is the third largest trading bloc in the world. The rationale for Mercosur was the notion of 'open regionalism', unlike the protectionism, inward-oriented model of regional integration of the 1960s and 1970s. However, Mercosur did not embrace a complete neoliberal approach. Instead, it was conscious of the political dimensions of regionalisation and was conscious that 'the debate has been monopolized by economists, with an excessive focus on the trade creation–trade diversion issue, thus neglecting the political dimensions of the new regionalism' (Carranza 2003: 70).[14] In this sense, Mercosur was basically aimed at strengthening the bargaining power of Argentina and Brazil in regard to NAFTA, and therefore, Mercosur was essentially 'a political initiative of the governments of Brazil and Argentina'. It does not believe in the free operations of the market to achieve 'inter-regional equilibrium' on the basis of common industrial and agricultural policies.

However, the August 1994 Buenos Aires Prudential Summit indefinitely postponed the formation of common market with a common industrial policy and productive complimentarity of national economies. Argentina abandoned all state-sponsored industrial initiatives and left its national industry completely unprotected. Brazil wanted free access to the Argentina market, while Argentina wanted to preserve its automobile industry, which was hit hard by the Brazilian devaluation. Argentina's 400 auto parts companies feared being wiped out by Brazilian competition. In July 1999, the Brazilian government announced that all negotiations with Argentina have been suspended and even threatened to dissolve Mercosur. The lessons learnt from this crisis were the measured need of state intervention with a 'political perspective' on the need for regionalisation beyond merely trade-driven 'liberalised' integration. Regionalism needs to harmonise the macroeconomic policies around a common vision of development. In turn, this requires a stronger link with the domestic politics and its demands thereof, as against such an assumption in the 'there is no alternative' model. Mercosur needs to develop into something more than free trade.[15]

It is at this crucial juncture in the history of the alternative regionalism in Latin America that Hugo Chavez came up with the programme of ALBA (Bolivarian Alternative for the Americas). It is a proposed alternative to US sponsored Free Trade Area of Americas (FTAA). The core principles of ALBA include a socially oriented trade bloc rather than one strictly based on the logic of deregulated profit maximisation. ALBA appeals to the egalitarian principles of justice and equality; it proposes 'Compensatory Fund for Structural Convergence' which would give financial aid to the most economically vulnerable countries to build economic infrastructure for 'endogenous development'. Agriculture would prioritise food self-sufficiency rather than being a mere export-oriented activity. It is opposed to the intellectual property rights regimes, particularly concerned with the case of medicines—life saving drugs being the focus. Finally, it is for the use of public policy instruments such as the provision of subsidies to regulate domestic prices to guarantee essential public services for the overwhelming majority of the population who cannot afford market-priced services (Anderson 2006).

With this ideological and political perspective, ALBA is emerging as an agreement between Venezuela, Cuba, Brazil, Argentina, Bolivia and Uruguay. The Cuba–Venezuela agreements formalised on 14 December 2004 include among other things the transfer of Cuban health professionals to build a primary health care system in remote areas of Venezuela in exchange for Venezuelan oil. Cuba provides support for the Venezuelan educational missions Robinson, *Ribas, Sucre and Vuelvan Caras.* The nine integration and cooperation agreements signed between Venezuela and Argentina include Petrosur and Petrocaribe. There is also the proposal for *Telesur* to build the Latin American Television Network. ALBA would also build regional alliances not by emphasising on standardisation but on principles of special and differential treatment determined by variables such as population, surface, global production, and endowment of resources, compositions of exports and external vulnerability, level of industrial development, and per capita income (Anderson 2006). Further, under the 'Gran Gasoducto del Sur', a region-wide pipeline is being planned to transport natural gas from Venezuela and Bolivia to the rest of South America. A pipeline between Argentina and Venezuela (worth $20 billion) has already been formalised; there is a proposal for a South American development bank to channelise South American international reserves from the banks in the North and Venezuela has already committed $2.4 billion to Argentina in order to assist it to pay off debts to the multilateral agencies; to improve communication, there is a proposal to build a 'bio-oceanic corridor' connecting the Atlantic with the Pacific side of the continent through Bolivia and Amazonia. It is envisaged that in near future there would be joint projects to enhance technology, infrastructure, security through defence arrangements and energy concerns with special focus on nuclear energy and hydro-electricity.

ALBA is not merely an economic integration but needs to gradually evolve into an Initiative of South American Region (IIRSA) marking the 'physical integration of the region' to emerge as a 'free zone' that is free of illiteracy, street kids and poverty. ALBA also intends to fuse with the radical political movements. These movements go beyond even lessening poverty and redistributing income, and include transforming the nature and application of power. They strive to redefine power between people, place, state, class and social groups. This kind of participatory democracy is sought to be maintained along with developing a 'social state' that works towards maintaining its sovereignty against external intrusions. There are attempts to build creative forms of national and transnational organisations that aid democratic participation. For instance, community participation in health and education are ensured through the newly formed neighbourhood associations, health and school committees and activating local government. Pre-packaged programmes are replaced with active citizen participation under missions such as *Barrio Adentro*. Similarly,

> the idea of 'integral' education is a key component of the Bolivarian Revolution, meaning that education is not seen as separate from other spheres of life; it is seen to be a critical element in efforts to create direct, participatory democracy. Over two million people are active in 'Bolivarian Circles' that organize within local communities to discuss, and implement a variety of community projects in areas such as education, health and sports.

Further, 'direct democracy is evident in land councils, giving ownership and control of poor areas to local residents'. Further,

> by 2010, the unity of the hemisphere culminated in the creation of the Community of Latin American and Caribbean States (CELAC), which

unlike the Organization of American States (1948), no longer had the US as a member. ALBA and CELAC underlined the end of US primacy in the region, a consequence of Chavez's Bolivarian agenda. (Prashad 2013a: 30)

These processes still raise questions as to whether a centralised state as against the global powers can be democratic and representative in its everyday working. Though the Venezuelan experiment does not exhaustively answer this question, it nevertheless reflects the fact that 'more qualitative forms of democracy and redistribution depend on a certain degree of national sovereignty in economic matters' (Gibbs 2006: 277). ALBA comes very close to the agenda of alternative globalisation that we drew at the beginning of his chapter. Notwithstanding the fact that there are very many crucial issues that can only be commented upon in times to come, including the issue of how centralised that state might get given the politics of fighting the global forces and focusing a lot on the discourse of nationalism, nation state and its sovereignty. Part of these apprehensions get reinforced by some of changes that Chavez had initiated with regard to the term of the president and merging many of the political parties. However, there seem to be effective counter-checks in the way power is also being decentralised and radical movements are being taken into count in the agenda setting process, both at national and regional levels. Similarly, in terms of the economy, Venezuela continues to be heavily dependent on the export of oil, which accounts for roughly 95 per cent of its export revenues and 45 per cent of the country's budget, and there has been slow growth in terms of infrastructure and industrial capital. These questions are open to historical scrutiny, more so after the death of Chavez, whose successor Nicolas Maduro took over the reins in April 2013.[16]

From Intra- to Inter-continental Regionalism

Adding a new dimension to this intra-continental regionalism has been the emergent phenomenon of inter-continental regionalism between Asia, Africa and Latin America. The India–Brazil–South Africa forum (IBSA) was launched in June 2003 in Brasilia. 'All three countries share multiethnic and multicultural population dynamics. These dynamics have encouraged policies of social inclusion in each of the countries and prioritized such issues on the broader IBSA agenda' (White: 1). Thus, with the shift to inter-continental regionalism between emerging powers of the Global South also came the focus of inclusion, poverty, growth with social equity, solidarity based on common histories of suffering colonialism and ideas about sustainable development. Further, 'this was the first coalition of developing countries to directly confront the developed world in such a robust and direct manner, and is widely seen to represent a victory for the developing south' (White: 11). Also for the first time IBSA created a development fund for small and medium-sized development projects in the most impoverished countries in the developing world, which initiated a possibility of recognising the need for alternative modes of industrialisation. IBSA is also a forum that has identified the most important issues that are of common concern to all three of them, but also to most of the developing world, among which they identified the issues of agreements on subsidies in agriculture, intellectual property rights and public health and availability of life saving drugs. This alliance emerged as the 'Axis of the South', as it is referred to; however, 'the notion of autonomous development has been replaced by market-orientation among the leading countries of the South, although a facet of that agenda in the form of South–South cooperation persists' (Alden and Vieira 2005: 1091).

The other important initiative at a larger level than IBSA has been the more recent regional formation of BRICS (Brazil–Russia–India–China–South Africa).[17] The first Summit of BRICS was held in 2009.[18] With the formation of such 'alternative regional' organisations, the influence of countries like India in G20 or World Trade Organization has been 'unprecedented', and 'they have an explicit or implicit interest in pushing towards a multipolar international system that would enhance their role in world affairs' (Tudoroiu 2012: 34). During the financial crisis, 'the Joint Statement asked for "greater voice and representation in international financial institutions" for "the emerging and developing economies"' (Tudoroiu 2012: 35). In the Sanya Declaration that was formulated at the third Summit at Sanya, Hainan, China, in April 2011, they made their view clear against the use of force to resolve the emerging crisis in the Middle East, Iran and Libya, and instead argued mainly for multilateral diplomacy, in order to create a 'a more democratic and just multipolar world order' (Tudoroiu 2012: 38). The Sanya Declaration also laid emphasis on the importance of agriculture in developing countries, and the need to fight poverty. 'Analysts claimed that the BRICS collective might within the G-20 is already forcing concession on trade, agriculture and subsidies from the US and EU' (Tudoroiu 2012: 40).[19] However, many of these promising changes introduced to the international order does not mean that BRICS has built a shared vision against neoliberalisation and a more far-reaching welfare regime in their respective countries. What can be argued though is that in the days to come, these regional organisations, in tune with the pulls of representative democracy in these countries, will be sites of contestation, and could be appropriated for an agenda of development, and a far more inclusive social policy. The interaction between regional organisations such as IBSA, BRICS and ALBA, which is limited as of date, can grow in intensity and can mutually strengthen the process of abating the influence of the 'transnational capitalist class' on the global order. This, however, has to happen through local and domestic pressure and in alignment with the counter-mobilisation by the subaltern and 'basic classes' in these countries. For instance, it could be observed in Brazil, where 'a new semi-peripheral social-democratic' class alliance has formed; processes of neoliberalisation have begun to be reversed in most areas; thus, the '"strategic selectivities" of state apparatus have shifted somewhat in favour of marginalized parts of the population' (Schmaltz and Ebenau 2012: 498). Such changes, through popular mobilisation influencing the legal–institutional structure, are possible in countries such as India as well.

Endnotes

1. This understanding was almost like the environmentalist's argument that crisis is man-made; ecology on the other hand has a natural way of adjusting the natural contradictions—a hidden and an invisible hand.
2. Twenty-seven per cent or 6.2 million of the country's 39 million people are unemployed in Spain. Youth unemployment reached 57 per cent of Spain's unemployed people. In France, unemployment was a staggering 3.2 million, its highest since 1977. Major employers such as the carmakers continue to slash jobs in France. 'PSA Peugeot Citreon is scrapping more than 10,000 domestic jobs and rival Renault aims to cut 7500 posts in France by 2016' (*The Hindu*, 28 April 2013).
3. We have made this point in more detail in Chapter 4 on subaltern classes.

4. As the momentum is shifting towards regional organisations, the role and relevance of G20 has also come under the scanner. It has been observed that while G20 played a significant role during the time of the financial crisis and emerged as a premier global economic forum, post-financial crisis there has been perceptible divergence in economic policy around the world. No 'consensus' is visible in such global organisations; instead, the multilateral initiatives have shifted to the new regional organisations. After the recent meet of the G20 in Washington in 2013, it was observed that 'the inability or unwillingness of the G20 to come up with some co-ordinated action points to deal with global level problems, according to perceptive observers, underscores its decline. Nothing useful was expected from the recent Washington meet and nothing came' (Narasimhan 2013). Global initiatives now look more feasible through regional initiatives.

5. It must be stated that Sen is not for redistribution but only for entitlements. He is also for growth and expansion of private capital but with the recognition that market cannot deliver social justice on its own, and therefore the state needs to intervene to ensure entitlements, but not redistribute wealth or change property laws.

6. Right to Development that we discussed in the previous chapter also emphasises the need for 'international cooperation' between nation states.

7. After the structural adjustment programme (SAP) in Africa, there had been a retrenchment of 170,000 public servants by the end of 2002 in Uganda. After the Government of Uganda passed the Uganda Investment Code announcing tax relief, the FDIs increased from $54.6 million in 1993 to $274.8 million in 2000, while the number of jobs created by foreign investment in the entire third world during 1990–1993 is not even equal to the number of people entering the job market in India alone in a single year. In Nigeria, after pursuing the programme of privatisation of water, currently only 60 per cent of the households have access to improved drinking water, and the Sub-Saharan Africa continues to have the largest population without access to water. Between 1980 and 1995, the external debt of Sub-Saharan Africa rose from $84 billion to $223 billion, accounting for an increase by 165.5 per cent, and countries such as Tanzania had to year mark 60 per cent of its exports to pay its debt (while Germany after the Second World War for reparation did not allot more than 7 per cent of its exports). More aid to Africa has been accompanied by decline in the standard of living as GDP per capita has declined over the years.

8. Also refer to Ravi Kanbur, 'NEPAD: An Initial Commentary', www.people.cornell.edu/pages (accessed 15 May, 2013).

9. I am thankful to Samir Amin for sharing this unpublished paper with me when I had the opportunity to meet and discuss with him in Senegal in 2004.

10. Refer to http://www.nepad.org/system/files/AAP%20final%20web%20201301111.pdf (accessed 27 April 2013).

11. 'Chinese Camps 19 km inside LAC', *Indian Express*, 27 April 2013.

12. There was a strong possibility of cancellation of the next SAARC Summit, as many of the countries were in crisis, including Nepal that was suffering from prolonged political instability, Sri Lanka facing 'internal civil war' conditions, Maldives suffering a sudden regime change and escalating tensions between India and China.

13. The latest among such emerging conflict was the one between China and Thailand over South China Sea. China claims almost the entire of South China Sea. 'Efforts by ASEAN to craft a code of conduct to manage South China Sea tensions all but collapsed last year at a summit chaired by Cambodia' (*The Hindu*, 26 April 2013).

14. Also refer to Seligson 1999.

15. After receiving funds from the IMF for well over three decades, Bolivia's per capita GDP remains what it was in 1975. More than 70 per cent of Bolivia's $6.7 billion debt is externally mobilised from the multilateral lending agencies. Since 1994, with the beginning of NAFTA, Mexico has signed additional 11 trade agreements with different economies accounting for a huge rise in its international trade; however, it continues to register low levels of growth, and high levels of poverty and unequal income distribution. Developing countries through trade agreements are increasingly losing policy options to promote industrialisation.

16. 'Mr. Maduro, handpicked by Mr. Chavez as his successor, took 7.505 million votes, or 50.6%, while opposition candidate Henrique Capriles received 7.27 million ballots' (refer to http://online.wsj.com/article/SB1000142412788732 4345804578422352792472978.html, accessed 27 April 2013).

17. BRIC was the initial acronym coined by Goldman Sachs in 2001.

18. South Africa joined the group in December 2010 and became a full member only in February 2011. Thus, the initial acronym BRIC later became BRICS.

19. As part of this success story, Roberto Azevedo was elected as the head of the World Trade Organization (WTO) on 7 May 2013. At WTO, 'he earned a reputation as being a defender of the Global South against the North's very focused attempt to use the WTO as an instrument of its interests' (Prashad 2013b).

Epilogue: India's Violent Democracy: Past and Future

India began with a developmental state that had a social–democratic set-up, and as primarily an agrarian economy. It was a successful democracy, in the sense of holding free and fair elections, with a welfare state and a Constitution that had radical provisions in Part IV under Directive Principles, which had an inclusive perspective of providing resources to all its citizens. However, since its economy grew at, what is popularly referred to as the Hindu rate of growth, about 3 per cent annually, it continued with weak industrial capital, and infrastructure, that eventually landed in the balance of payment crisis by the 1980s. It was at this juncture that the state policy underwent a dramatic shift in 1990s, and the economy was opened up to integrate with the global economy, ushering in free market, and privatisation, keeping in tune with the global shift in the political discourse. It is estimated that between 1979 and the end of 1999, 'more than 130 countries divested or turned over to private management/owner-ship of thousands of state-owned enterprises' (Subramanium 2013; also refer to Ruitters 2013). The claim was to achieve higher growth rates and provide better employment opportunities. From the state it moved to the centrality of market in managing the economy, and from an emphasis on democracy it moved to a policy frame that was based on global governance. In this sense, globalisation was a top-down phenomenon circumventing the imperatives of democratic participation and inclusive growth. From a weak and underdeveloped economy with a social-democratic set-up, India moved to a model of high growth but corporate-market-oriented policy frame. In effect, globalisation was juxtaposed against democracy, as growth stood to counter development, and market supplanted the state, transforming the role of all 'basic' (referred to as 'basic structure' of the constitution) political and economic structures. India is witnessing a strange paradox of a choice between a non-performing economy versus a non-inclusive economy. While the former was theorised as a 'moribund state', 'soft state', 'weak state' and 'retarded capitalism', the latter is being referred to as 'crony capitalism', 'developmental terrorism' and 'preda-tory growth' (Bhaduri 2009) or even 'lumpen capitalism' (Breman 2002).

It is in this context important to realise that militant protest politics, unevenness of democracy and the processes of globalisation have been pulling India in different directions. Maoists have raised very significant structural issues regarding the model of development and limits of Indian democracy, yet remain disengaged and disconnected from available democratic processes. Democracy has shifted the political discourse from mere growth-centrism to neo-welfarism, affirmative action and mobility for certain marginalised social groups, and providing an electoral process for the subaltern to register their influence, yet it has remained formal and been increasingly hijacked by the urban middle classes, and marked by growing exceptionalism of the state. The processes of globalisation has given new status to India globally, more opportunity to influence global processes through alternative regionalism and the language of human rights, and more economic opportunities for a section of the society, yet it has remained insulated from democracy, created a new language of 'global war on terror' and remained well entrenched within the neoliberal discourse. These processes have cumulatively contributed to the rise of India that remains disconnected and a political process that can be best typified as a violent democracy.

Violent Democracy and Paradoxical Convergence

The workings of India's violent democracy has articulated itself through myriad political processes that include the following.

First, governance through emergent forms of righteous lawlessness that includes a combination of spate of extraordinary laws; violation of legal protections for various marginalised social groups and classes, including violation of basic civil and political rights, extrajudicial killings, and custodial deaths; and attempts to change the criminal justice system itself, in the process collapsing the distinction between ordinary and extraordinary laws, and the difference between what is legal and illegal.[1] These processes are in turn aided by the consent offered by the urban/professional middle classes that acts as the conduit or a hinge—social base—between lawlessness and democracy. This leads to associated processes where instead of the rule of law guiding democracy, it is the imperatives of popular/representative democracy that dictate the workings of law, which is marked by a shift from centrality of evidence to pre-eminence to intention, from investigation to creating demonstrative effects in the name of 'collective conscience' and maintenance of 'law and order'. Further, the extraordinary methods have moved beyond restricted 'disturbed areas' to many other parts of India, and from 'security operations' against the Maoists and terrorists to many other kinds of conflicts, including non-violent and peaceful protest politics. These processes in turn lead to augmenting 'frames of war' among militant political mobilisation of the Maoists leading up to a paradoxical convergence, with both Maoists and Anna Hazare led campaign attempting to overthrow the state; rise of the role of intention in the workings of law and in Maoist politics; moralisation of violence by state/urban middle classes through the discourse of nationalism and patriotism and Maoists through the discourse of sacrifice and suffering.

Second, spurt in intra-subaltern conflicts that grow alongside, and at times replacing the conflict with the elites. This is visible in India with the rise of sub-caste conflicts among the Dalits, where elite discourses of merit and efficiency have been reproduced; conflicts between urban women and upwardly mobile OBCs, witnessed during the debate on 33 per cent reservations for women in the parliament; conflicts between OBCs and the Dalits, witnessed in the innumerable violent clashes, some of which we alluded to in earlier chapters; conflicts between Muslims and Dalits, which include evidence of Dalits directly and indirectly participating in riots against the Muslims in Gujarat in 2002; and conflicts between Dalits and tribals, as represented by clashes between Pannnos and Kandhas in Odisha that brought to light practice of untouchability by the tribals against Dalits. This process of growing intra-subaltern conflict has been accompanied by new political discourses and paradoxical convergence of the old and new middle classes represented by the urban India's shift towards right-wing mobilisation, allowing for anti-Muslim rhetoric to frame explanations for or lack of mobility, and new articulations of 'Dalit capitalism', justifying certain forms of exploitation as necessary for mobility. These conflicts and new political discourses in turn make it difficult for Maoist and Dalit politics in particular, and other democratic struggles in general, to enter into any meaningful dialogue.

Third, middle classisation of politics that is reflected in the growing influence of India's global middle classes, alongside the emergent transnational capitalist class. Urban middle classes have occupied streets and attempted to influence state policy through their cultural capital. This phenomenon has occurred alongside neoliberalisation of politics and mediatisation of politics, reflecting a symbiotic relation between the three processes. This phenomenon of middle classisation is however not limited to old urban/ upper caste middle classes; alongside have grown what we referred to as the 'new' middle classes among the Dalits and OBCs. This has led to various political implications, including an overwhelming discourse around urbanisation and 'right to city'[2], which has added to the neglect of rural populations, issues related to agrarian crisis and land reforms; anti-caste being predominantly articulated through the discourse of reservations and a share in the resources of the state as against claims to ritual hierarchy; and as pointed earlier, newer articulation of aspirations by the 'new' middle class to move upwards to occupy and become part of the transnational capitalist class, through creating 'Dalit capitalists/capitalism'. It has also resulted in new political discourses such as the 'caste is race' debate, making caste-based discrimination a global issue in the process undermining issues related to state sovereignty. This again has a paradoxical convergence between anti-caste movement's aspirations to go global with the emergence of a 'new' middle class within and the Maoist movement's mobilisation of tribals and the landless against the very neoliberal model of globalisation and development; while new middle classes undermine state power in reaching out to international organisations, the sovereignty of the state is undermined by the Maoists in using violence and declaring 'liberated zones' out of the reach of the Indian state's sovereign rule. This paradoxical convergence is happening just when the Maoist movement, unlike many other movements, is going in the opposite direction of recruiting not from middle classes but the tribals, and the landless themselves taking over leadership of the movement and emerging as the new 'organic intellectuals'. Middle classisation of politics has in turn adversely impacted the agency of the subaltern, which has moved out of the streets and its traditional forms of popular mobilisation, such as peasant rebellions, trade union movement, among others. 'National-popular' has been replaced by national–urban imagination, reflected amply in the recent refusal of junior doctors to be posted to rural areas or the then Home Minister Mr Chidambaram's announcement that by 2050 nearly 80 per cent of India will be living in the cities. Thus, farmers, landless labourers, urban poor, migrants, among others have either become powerless and remain de-mobilised, such as migrants from Bihar in Maharashtra, or the shift from demanding land reforms to struggling to protect the existing land being grabbed through incursions of land acquisition, or have moved to militant political mobilisation represented by the Maoists. Thus, retreat of the subaltern has to be understood in this context of increasing middle classiation and its accompanying capture of democracy in alliance with the transnational capitalist classes and cannot be understood by the mere study of everyday 'contextual negotiations' of the subaltern or in arguing for their increasing and willing conversion into governmental subjects, or in seeing in all of this an expansion of subaltern agency, as the idea of 'political society' has articulated.

Transference, Neo-welfarism and Transnational Forms of Justice

Are there any real-time possibilities of productively re-connecting this disparate phenomenon of Maoism, democracy and globalisation, and abate the rise and entrenchment of a violent democracy? To a large extent this depends on how we understand the structural limits of each of these processes and resignify and re-mould the practices internal to each of these three political processes. The divide is way too large and the conflict has already assumed a bloody and violent form, but that could well be the context that allows for the logic to become apparent and the need to look for alternatives more pressing. In that sense, it depends on connecting the three processes by realising their contribution as much as their limitations. As for the Maoist movement, we pointed to the various limitations it is facing due to its reduced understanding of political processes, and therefore its spread has remained sporadic and selective. It would be imperative for them to reflect on ways of engaging with available democratic forms and institutional functioning, and also positively conceptualise the nature of mobility that democracy has made it possible for various sections of the subaltern classes, as much as in seeing the kind of structural limits that have been imposed on them. For instance, the mobility made possible through affirmative action policies for the Dalits and the backward classes has led to formation of new classes within these sections; whether that can be viewed through pure structural analysis and critiqued for the formation of new 'hegemonic' classes, or as a long drawn historical process and therefore as a positive change in terms of 'class formation' among the subaltern is the moot question. It therefore needs to be asked in what productive forms this change as a historical process can be aligned to the kind of structural transformation that Maoists envisage. Similarly, can the available modes of institutions and participatory avenues such as electoral politics be simply subjected to the radical critique of formalism or would it also be useful to explore the possibilities for the subaltern and basic classes to register their influence? In that sense, the recent decisions of the Maoists to take part in elections to the local bodies in Odisha, and approach courts, and take part in 'peace talks' with the government have remained important signposts that this kind of churning maybe going on within the rank and file of the Maoist party.

Alongside this, Maoists would have to realise the possibility of what we could refer to as 'political transference' that can occur in popular/ representative democracies, where conflicts and interests can be articulated in manifold forms.[3] For instance, the demand for a smaller state such as Telangana could be another way of articulating agrarian crisis, landlessness, farmers' suicides, among others. This process though could occur the other way round too, where for instance urban middle classes could frame their anxiety to re-occupy urban spaces through protests against sexual violence and crime. In other words, protests against sexual violence are a mode of transference of class demands. The strategies of subaltern could reflect a shift from radical mobilisation and radical political demands to a new kind of political language of reversals. For instance, excluded castes are articulating policies of protective discrimination as de-reserving the privileges of the Caste Hindus. A demand for smaller states is not a fresh demand as much as it is a demand to de-merge; at a global level it is more about de-linking from global corporate economy. At another level, the transference could occur in the seamless shift from left to right. In other words, interests could be articulated through democratic demands, but they could be signified through other exclusionary modes of mobilisation as well. This shift does not adhere to the neat distinctions between left and right, or between democratic and authoritarian. For instance, Telangana was considered by many as a centre for left-wing politics since

Maoists held a stronghold for a very long time; however, with the rise of the demand for a separate state and the Bharatiya Janata Party supporting the demand, there is always the possibility of communal polarisation over shadowing democratic politics. This fluidity in politics, especially representative democracies, is not an aberration but a condition of popular mobilisation, where demands are open to be signified through different and even conflicting frames. This fluidity[4]—transference—in a sense is in excess of the structural analysis that Maoists mostly adhere to. To understand these complexities, Maoists might have to look at alternative experiments by the Zapatistas in Latin America, as much as learn from the failures of the Maoists in Nepal, as not merely for taking part in the bourgeois electoral process but inherent complexities that remain to be addressed through policy frame in a post-revolutionary context. This complexity has to be acknowledged as part of the revolutionary process itself rather than being left for a post-revolutionary situation. As we pointed out in Chapter 1 on the Maoists that many of the challenges they would face in a post-revolutionary situation would be very similar to the ones a (liberal) democratic state is facing, against which they are waging a class struggle. This kind of engagement would not be possible with their practice of combining absolutist critique of the system with a blanket prohibition of any public criticism of their own politics. Alongside their critique of the current phase of globalisation, they would have to seriously raise the following questions: What could be the contours of an alternative model of development? Would they or would they not mine minerals in central India? Do they support large-scale or a localised model of industrialisation? How would they accommodate the conflicting interests of various classes as much as cultural diversity through a single-party rule? What forms of organisational and representative processes they would set in motion? In raising these questions they might have to align with existing forms of democracy in India, radically differently from what they have been doing so far.[5]

An alternative model of development, as we argued in tracing the contours of alternative globalisation, has to be participatory, with an emphasis on absorbing and providing full employment to the skilled and semi-skilled labour force, agriculture should be given priority in policy frame and industry should avoid consuming cultivable and fertile land. Further, 'alternative industrialisation would be characterized by labour-intensive technology, small-scale production by the masses, and maximum direct linkage between consumer and producer' (Bhaduri 2009: 185). Amit Bhaduri argues that alternative industrialisation

> would produce a large range of goods and services for the local market, created through purchasing power generated locally in the hands of the poor. This is the route through which the poor, rejected by today's industrialization, would enter the larger economy with dignity as both producers and consumers. ... [T]he domestic rather than external market must occupy the centre of economic policy, with purchasing power rising at a faster pace at the bottom than at the top of income distribution, and the market used by the poor for local exchanges to suit their needs and priorities. (Bhaduri 2009: 185–188)

The role of democracy in bringing out this shift would be very significant. Already, there is a shift in the discourse of the political parties from the general elections in 1999 that was fought on an assumed consensus on economic reforms and higher growth rates, to 2004, where major advocates of reforms, such as Chandrababu Naidu in Andhra Pradesh, were summarily rejected.[6] This, in turn, has led to a change from mere emphasis on growth to growth with a new kind of neo-welfarism, leading up to a string of welfare policies such as the NREGA, Food Security Bill, Right to Education through Sarva Siksha Abhiyaan, Street Vendors (Protection of Livelihood and Regulation of Street Vending) Bill and reversal of FDI in retail, reversal of land acquired for industry in Singur in West Bengal, halting of transnational operations by POSCO in Odisha, Vedanta in Odisha and Chhattisgarh, and the nuclear energy plant in Kudankulam, to name a few. It is also important to observe the link between neo-welfarism and the steady voter turnout in state and general elections, and the change from the impact of anti-incumbency in elections to a pattern of pro-incumbency for the political party/government in power, which is evident in states such as Andhra Pradesh, Delhi, Chhattisgarh, Madhya Pradesh and Bihar. This shift is in tune with the imperatives of the development process—electorates seem to understand the gestation required for policies to fructify into effective results—and expansion of neo-welfarism.[7] Further, where the parliament failed to strengthen such a process, the Supreme Court intervened, in instances such as holding Palli Sabhas in Odisha to ascertain the tribal viewpoint on opening the Vedanta Aluminium Limited in Niamgiri hills and to know if this in any way violated the religious and cultural life style of the tribal inhabiting these areas. As a result, 12 Palli (Gram) Sabhas summarily rejected the idea of mining the hills for bauxite. Thereafter, 'the Environment Ministry has decided that the claim of even one village council for cultural or religious rights over the hills provides the legal mandate to the Central government to reject the proposal under the Supreme Court orders' (*The Hindu*, 16 August 2013).

India's violent democracy allows for mobility as much as it has increasingly grown into a 'state of exception'. This shift has come not merely in dealing with the Maoists but various other popular forms of protest politics. These strategies of exception of the state have found a social base in the mobilisational politics of the middle classes that have developed a deep sense of discomfort with popular representational politics, even as these classes have taken to street protest politics. Democracy has become increasingly expensive and burdensome for the subaltern classes who have either turned to militant modes or to a sense of withdrawal visible in the spate of suicides, and growing urban crime, even as they continue to register their influence by taking part in the electoral process. Democratic processes in India have to find a way of moving beyond their structural dependence on coercive apparatus, and re-contextualise the debate on 'political violence' beyond the discourse of 'global war on terror'. It needs to be recognised that

> far from representing a hegemonic project, the ruling bloc is faced with growing social discontent and resistance, even giving way to limited state disintegration in parts of India's East controlled by the Maoist guerilla organizations. Despite this, the neoliberal ideology has remained dominant among the elites and the politically vocal middle classes, not least due to the extraordinary economic growth. (Schmalz and Ebenau 2012: 493)

It needs to contextualise instead of moralising political violence, disallowing the moral to supplant the political. The alternative ways of capturing the dynamics of political violence is visible in framing it as a response to 'structural violence', 'routine violence', 'systemic violence', necessitating 'counter-violence'. The structural questions brought to the fore by the Maoists are part of the constitutional vision, and in that sense makes the Maoist movement a 'constitutional struggle', even if there needs to be more public debate on the possibilities of growing militarisation—'frames of war'—of such militant struggles.

Further, democracy has also remained slighted by a process of globalisation that has remained insulated from the imperatives of democratic and participatory processes, through the top-down imposition of global governance models. It has also been marked by the rise of new speculative capital, middle-men type of contractor class, and mafia that engages in illegal mining, speculative land dealings and pilferages of various kinds. There needs to be a fresh consensus on moving from 'reforms by stealth' to 'reforms by participation'. This could be made effective through various legal-institutional mechanisms. For instance,

> the Indian parliament should bring in a law that mandates that 'crucial' international economic and trade treaties are not signed and ratified without its consent, or at least put in place mechanisms to actively oversee their negotiation and conclusion. Such a law can be brought vide Entry 14 of the Union list. (Chimni 2010: 181)

This is imperative since it has already taken shape in terms of the difference of articulation of national versus regional parties, in the recent opposition against FDI in the retail sector. *Federalisation* of democratic processes interrupts top-down economic reforms.

Further, the conflict with globalisation is seen in its worst form over the issue of mining and displacement of the tribals in much of the central India. This clearly articulates as a direct conflict between the imperatives of globalisation and politics of the Maoist movement, with democracy being at best ineffective and at worst turning into exceptionalism. Growth rates in India were incumbent to a great extent on export of raw materials such as the iron ore and bauxite, which is available mostly in the tribal belts of central India, who in turn are being mobilised by the Maoists, becoming a direct site of conflict between globalisation/growth and tribals/Maoists. By August 2013, the growth rates declined from above 9 per cent to below 6 per cent, and much of the reason was sought in the refusal to permit Vedanta and POSCO in Odisha and Chhattisgarh to mine iron ore and bauxite. In 2009–2010, India exported 117.37 million tonnes of iron ore, in 2012 it was down to 87 per cent and by 2013 India was importing five million tonnes of iron ore. Similarly, India has the third largest bauxite reserves in the world; by 2013 it was likely to become an importer of bauxite.[8] Much of this change was due to the unrelenting mobilisation of the tribal by the Maoists, in spite of repressive governance 'Operation Green Hunt', leading to a direct conflict between globalisation and representative democracy at one end and Maoists at the other end.

However, globalisation has also brought to the fore the possibility of global integration through the language of human rights and through alternative regionalism. The question remains whether alternative regionalism can be converted into alternative globalisation. There are expressive possibilities of this demonstrated through the experiments such as the ALBA in Latin America. As we had argued in Chapter 6 on alternative regionalism that the momentum has shifted to the South–South alliances that share a common historical past of suffering from abject poverty and colonial subjugation, this provides for an opportunity to reverse the influence of 'transnational capitalist classes' on the new regional formations. The language of human rights and rule of law could also be imperative checks on the growing exceptionalism of the Indian state. Democracies and popular mobilisations such as the women's movement for prohibition of liquor that find resonance in the international human rights declarations such as the right to development present new avenues to link the global to the local, and realise transnational forms of justice. Post-Westphalian and transnational forms of justice might then provide new avenues and create new pressures to rearticulate the equation between Maoism, democracy and globalisation.

Endnotes

1. For a more detailed analysis on this, refer to Gudavarthy 2013d.
2. The then Home Minister P. Chidambaram had announced that by 2050, 80 per cent of the population will begin to live in the cities.
3. I am borrowing the term from Sigmund Freud, where 'Transference is a phenomenon characterised by unconscious redirection of feelings from one person to another'. I am extending it to a social and political phenomenon (refer to http://en.wikipedia.org/wiki/Transference).
4. I distinctly remember a conversation I had more than a decade back in one of my train journeys from Hyderabad to Calcutta. I had a Bengali couple as my co-passengers and in course of our conversation asked what their next alternative to CPM is, and to my utter disbelieve, they said BJP. I realised how categories such as left and right, or democratic and authoritarian do not seem work in the mobilisations of popular democracy. The same symbols, such as

the Durga Pooja and Rabindra Sangeet, could easily be resignified as right-wing religious symbols.

5. When the Maoist party came for talks with the government of Andhra Pradesh in 2004, the party leadership faced many of these questions from the academics, social activists and journalists. Though they did not have concrete answers, they did acknowledge the importance of these questions.

6. Turning his earlier World Bank driven agenda against subsidies and other welfare policies, for the forthcoming Assembly elections in 2014, Chandrababu Naidu announced a new bounty that included nine-hour power supply to farmers and total waiver of farm loans; free 25 kg rice to BPL families; free medical insurance; ₹1,000 a month unemployment dole; free KG to PG education for poor; free reimbursement to students, laptops for all students and cycles for girl students under the Mahalakshmi scheme, in which ₹25,000 is to be deposited for every girl child; safe drinking water to all villages; and 10 domestic cylinders a year on subsidy (*Outlook*, May 2013: 13).

7. In the run-up to the Assembly elections in Chhattisgarh in 2014, the Chief Minister Raman Singh stressed upon a string of welfare policies his government diligently implemented. This included offering rice at ₹1 per kg to neutralise inflation; food security supplemented by nutrition security to 42 lakh families; health security to 56 lakh families; distribution of sewing machines, cycles, a kit, among many other such schemes for specific target groups (refer to *The Hindu*, 24 August 2013).

8. For more details, refer to Gupta 2013.

References

Agamben, Giorgio, *State of Exception*, University of Chicago Press, Chicago, 2005.

Alam, Javed, 'Emerging Class Formation Among the Oppressed Castes and Its Political Implications', *Social Scientist*, 36(11–12): 5–19, 2008.

Alden, Chris, and Vieira, Marco Antonio, 'The New Diplomacy of the South: South Africa, Brazil, India and Trilateralism', *Third World Quarterly*, 26(7): 1077–1095, 2005.

Amin, Samir, 'Placing Globalisation', *Theory, Culture and Society*, 14(2): 123–137, 1997.

―――, 'The Political Economy of Africa in the Global System' (unpublished).

Amin, Shahid, *Alternative Histories: A View from India*, SEPHIS-CSSC, Calcutta, 2002.

Anderson, Tim, 'Breaking Imperial Ties: Venezuela and ALBA', *Green Left Weekly*, 27 May 2006.

Anderson, Perry, 'Antinomies of Antonio Gramsci', *New Left Review*, 1(100): 5–78, 1976.

Appiah, Anthony, 'The Politics of Identity', *Daedalus*, Fall 2006.

Azad, *Maoists in India*, Friends of Azad, Hyderabad, 2010.

Badiou, Alain, *Metapolitics*, Verso, London, 2005.

Balagopal, K., 'The Maoist Movement in Andhra Pradesh', *Economic and Political Weekly*, 41(29): 3183–3187, July 2006.

―――, 'Beyond Violence and Non-Violence', www.kafila.org, 23 January 2009.

Banerjee, Sumanta, 'Anna Hazare, Civil Society and the State', *Economic and Political Weekly*, 46(36): 12–14, 3 September 2011.

Banerjee-Guha, Swapna (Ed.), *Accumulation by Dispossession: Transformative Cities in the New Global Order*, SAGE Publications, New Delhi, 2010.

Bardhan, Pranab, *The Political Economy of Development in India*, Basil Blackwell and subsequently, Oxford University Press, 1984.

―――, 'Our Self-Righteous Civil Society', *Economic and Political Weekly*, 46(29): 16–18, 16 July 2011.

Baxi, Upendra, *Human Rights in a Post-human World*, Oxford University Press, Oxford, 2007.

Bhaduri, Amit, *The Face You Were Afraid to see: Essays on the Indian Political Economy*, Penguin Books, Delhi, 2009.

―――, 'Corruption and Representative Democracy', *Economic and Political Weekly*, 46(36): 15–17, 3 September 2011.

Bilgrami, Akeel, 'Secularism and the Very Concept of Law', in Rajeshwari Sundarrajan (Ed.), *Secularism*, Permanent Black, Delhi, 2007.

Birch, Kean, and Mykhnenko, Vlad (Eds), *The Rise and Fall of Neoliberalism*, Zed Books, London, 2010.

Biswas, Aparajita, 'Africa's Quest for Recovery in the 21st Century: African Union (AU) and the New Partnership for Africa's Development (NEPAD)', *Africa Quarterly*, 43(2): 17–33, 2003.

Bonime-Blanc, Andrea, 'The Fight Against Corruption Goes Global', *Foreign Affairs*, October 12, 2012. http://www.foreignaffairs.com/articles/137219/andrea-bonime-blanc/the-fight-against-corruption-goes-global (accessed 15 April 2013).

Brass, Paul, *The Politics of India Since Independence*, Cambridge University Press, Cambridge, 1990.

Bray, Donald W., 'Beyond Neoliberal Globalisation', *Latin American Perspectives*, 29, November 2002.

Breman, Jan, 'Communal Upheaval as Resurgence of Social Darwinism', *Economic and Political Weekly*, 37(16): 1485–1488, 20 April 2002.

———, *The Poverty Regime in Village India*, Oxford University Press, Oxford, 2007.

Brown Wendy, 'We Are All Democrats Now', in Georgio Agamben et. al (Eds), *Democracy in What State*, Columbia University Press, Columbia, pp. 44–57, 2012.

Brundtland Commission Report, *Our Common Future*, Oxford University Press, Oxford, 1987.

Butler, Judith, 'Contingent Foundations', in Seyla Benhabib et. al (Eds), *Feminist Contentions: A Philosophical Exchange*, Routledge, New York, pp. 35–58, 1994.

———, *Frames of War*, Verso, London, 2009.

Carlos, Nino, *The Constitution of Deliberative Democracy*, Yale University Press, New Haven, 1996.

Carothers, Thomas, 'The Rule of Law Revival', *Foreign Affairs*, 77(2): 95–106, March/April 1998.

Carranza, Mario E., 'Can Mercosur Survive?', *Latin American Politics and Society*, 45(2): 67–103, Summer 2003.

Castellas, Manuel, *The Rise of the Network Society*, Blackwell, Oxford, 1996.

CAVOW (Committee against Violence on Women), *Salwa Judum and Violence on Women in Dantewara, Chhattisgarh*, CAVOW, Nagpur, 2006.

Chakrabarty, Dipesh, *Provincialising Europe*, Permanent Black, Ranikhet, 2000.

———, *Habitations of Modernity*, University of Chicago Press, Chicago, 2002.

Chandhoke, Neera, 'The Seeds of Authoritarianism', *Indian Express*, 12 April 2011.

Chatterjee, Partha, *Bengal, 1920–1947: The Land Question*, K.P. Bagchi & Co., Calcutta, 1984.

———, *Our Modernity*, SEPHIS-CSSC, Calcutta, 1997.

———, 'Beyond the Nation? Or Within', *Social Text*, 16: 57–69, Fall 1998a.

———, 'Community in the East', *Economic and Political Weekly*, 33(6): 277–282, 7 February 1998b.

———, 'Democracy and the Violence of the State: A Political Negotiation of Death', *Inter-Asia Cultural Studies*, 2(1): 7–21, 2001.

———, *The Politics of Governed: Reflections on Popular Politics in Most of the World*, Columbia University Press, New York, 2004.

Chatterjee, Partha, 'Democracy and Economic Transformation in India', *Economic and Political Weekly*, 43(16): 53–62, 19 April 2008a.

———, 'Classes, Capital and Indian Democracy', *Economic and Political Weekly*, 43(46): 89–93, 18 November 2008b.

———, 'After Subaltern Studies', *Economic and Political Weekly*, 47(35): 44–49, 1 September 2012.

Chenoy, Anuradha, and MitraChenoy, Kamal, *Maoist and Other Armed Conflicts*, Penguin, Delhi, 2010.

Chibber, Vivek. *Postcolonial Theory and the Specter of Capital*, Navayana, Madras, 2013.

Chimni, B.S., 'International Institutions Today: An Imperial Global State in the Making', *European Journal of International Law*, 15(1): 1–37, 2004.

———, 'A Just World Under Law: A View from the South', *American University International Law Review*, 22(2): 199–220, 2007.

———, 'Mapping Indian Foreign Economic Policy', *International Studies*, 47(2–4): 163–185, 2010.

Committee for the Repeal of the Armed Forces Special Powers Act, 'Why the AFSPA Must Go', A Fact-finding Report, Delhi, February, 2005.

Committee of Concerned Citizens, *Negotiating Peace*, CCC, Hyderabad, 2006.

Constituent Assembly Debates (CAD), Proceedings Vol. IX (30th July to 18th September 1949), http://164.100.47.132/LssNew/constituent/debates.html (accessed 5 May 2014).

Cranston, Maurice, 'Are There Any Human Rights? ', *Daedalus*, Fall 1983.

Datta, Nonica, 'Backward Caste Movement Gains Ground', *Economic and Political Weekly*, 34(39): 2630–2631, 11–17 September 1999.

Delhi Solidarity Group on Behalf of Independent Citizens' Fact-finding Mission, Democracy Encountered: Rights' Violations in Manipur Independent Citizens' Fact-finding Report to the Nation, November 2009.

Deshpande, Satish, *Contemporary India*, Penguin, Delhi, 2003.

———, 'Changing Social Composition', *Seminar*, 587, July, 2008.

Dirks, Nicholas, *Castes of Mind*, Princeton University Press, Princeton, 2001.

Donnelly, Jack, 'Cultural Relativism versus Universal Human Rights', *Human Rights Quarterly*, 6(4): 400–419, 1984.

Dubey, Muchkund, 'SAARC and South Asian Economic Integration', *Economic and Political Weekly*, 42(14): 1238–1240, 7 April 2007.

Economic and Political Weekly, Editorial, 'The Anti-corruption Crusade', 46(34), 20 August 2011a.

———, 'Indian Media's Anna Moment', 46(36), 3 September 2011b.

———, Editorial, 'Democracy over Privilege', 46(38): 9, 17 September 2011c.

———, Editorial, 'Mining Violations', 47(40), 6 October 2012.

Escobar, Arturo, 'Planning', in W. Sachs (Ed.), *Development: Dictionary*, Orient Longman, Hyderabad, 1997.

Falk, Richard, *Towards Humane Global Governance*, Orient BlackSwan, Hyderabad, 2012.

Fan, Joseph, P.H., Rui, Oliver Meng, and Zhao, Mengxin, 'Rent Seeking and Corporate Finance: Evidence from Corruption Cases', *Journal of Comparative Economics*, 36(3): 343–364, 2008.

Feldman, C. Leonard, 'Redistribution, Recognition, and the State: The Irreducibility of the Political Dimension of Injustice', *Political Theory*, 30(3): 410–440, June 2002.

Fernandes, Leela, 'Restructuring the New Middle Class in Liberalizing India', *Comparative Studies of South Asia, Africa and Middle East*, 20(182): 88–104, 2000a.

———, 'Nationalizing "the Global": Media Images, Cultural Politics and the Middle Class in India', *Media, Culture and Society*, 22: 611–628, 2000b.

Fernandes, Leela, and Heller, Patrick, 'Hegemonic Aspirations: New Middle Class Politics and India's Democracy in Comparative Perspective', in Ronald J. Herring and Rina Agarwala (Ed.), *Whatever Happened to Class: Reflections from South Asia*, Daanish Books, Delhi, pp.146–165, 2008.

Fischlin, Daniel, and Nandorfy, Martha, *The Concise Guide to Global Human Rights*, Oxford University Press, Delhi, 2007.

Fraser, Nancy, 'Social Justice in the Age of Identity Politics: Redistribution, Recognition and Participation', in Andrew Sayers and Larry Ray (Eds), *Culture and Economy after the Cultural Turn*, SAGE Publications, London, 1999.

———, 'Rethinking Recognition', *New Left Review*, 3: 107–120, May–June 2000.

———, 'From Redistribution to Recognition? Dilemmas of Justice in a "Post-socialist" Age', in Kevin Olson (Ed.), *Adding Insult to Injury*, Verso, London, pp. 9–42, 2008.

Galanter, Mark, *Competing Equalities: Law and Backward Classes*, Oxford University Press, Oxford, 1984.

Gandhy, Kobad, 'Book Review', *Economic and Political Weekly*, 46(26–27), 25 June 2011.

Gibbs, Terry, 'Business as Unusual: What the Chavez Era Tells Us About Democracy Under Globalisation', *Third World Quarterly*, 27(2): 265–279, 2006.

Ghildiyal, Subodh, 'Government Plans to Sell Surplus Land to Ease Fiscal Crunch', *The Times of India*, 3 October 2012.

Gorringe, Hugo, 'When Development Triggers Caste Violence', *The Hindu*, 8 May 2013.

Gould, Carol, *Globalisation, Democracy and Human Rights*, Cambridge University Press, Cambridge, 2004.

Gudavarthy, Ajay, 'Reconstructing Marxism: The Thompsonian Framework', *Social Scientist*, 27(7–8): 64–69, July 1998.

———, 'Gandhi, Dalits and Feminists: Recovering the Convergence', *Economic and Political Weekly*, 43(22): 83–90, 31 May 2008a.

———, 'Human Rights Movements in India: State, Civil Society, and Beyond', *Contributions to Indian Sociology*, 42(1): 29–57, April 2008b.

———, 'The Trap at the Centre', *Indian Express*, 17 April 2008c.

Gudavarthy, Ajay, 'Tangles of Telangana', *Indian Express*, 11 July 2011.

———— (Ed.), *Reframing Democracy and Agency in India: Interrogating Political Society*, Anthem Press, London, 2012a.

————, 'In Defence of the Politician', *The Hindu*, 15 October 2012b.

————, *Politics of Post-Civil Society: Contemporary History of Political Movements in India*, SAGE Publications, New Delhi, 2013a.

————, 'Telangana: Nation, State, and the City', *Economic and Political Weekly*, 48(5), 2 February 2013b.

————, 'The Workings of Modi-fied India', *Deccan Herald*, 21 April 2013c.

————, 'Why Fake Encounters', *Deccan Herald*, 30 July 2013d.

Gudavarthy, Ajay, and Vijay, G., 'Antinomies of Political Society: Implications of Uncivil Development', in Gudavarthy, Ajay (Ed.), *Reframing Democracy and Agency in India: Interrogating Political Society*, Anthem Press, London, pp. 49–72, 2012.

Guha, Ramachandra, 'Adivasis, Naxalites and Indian Democracy', *Economic and Political Weekly*, 42: 3305–3312, August 2007.

Guha Ranajit, *Elementary Aspects of Peasant Insurgency in Colonial India*, Oxford University Press, Delhi, 1983.

Gupta, Dipankar, 'On Altering the Ego in Peasant Histories: Paradoxes of the Ethnic Option', *Peasant Studies*, 13(1): 5–24, 1985.

————, 'Caste Is Not Race: But, Let's Go to the UN Forum Anyway', in Sukhdeo Thorat and Umakant (Eds), *Caste, Race and Discrimination*, Rawat Publishers, Delhi, 2004a.

————, 'Civil Society or the State—What Happened to Citizenship?' in C.M. Ellliot (Ed.), *Civil Society and Democracy*, Oxford University Press, New Delhi, 2004b.

————, quoted in the *Outlook Magazine*, 29 August 2011.

Gupta, Shekhar, 'Current Accountability Deficit', *Indian Express*, 24 August 2013.

Guru, Gopal (ed), *Humiliation: Claims and Context*, Oxford University Press, Delhi, 2009.

Habib, Adam, 'African Integration and Civil Society', *Transformation*, 61, 2006.

Harrison Tom, 'Clubbing Together: Village Clubs, Local NGOs, and the Mediations of Political Society', in *Reframing Democracy and Agency in India: Interrogating Political Society*, Anthem Press, London, pp. 235–252, 2012.

Held, David, and McGrew, Anthony (Eds), *Governing Globalization—Power, Authority and Global Governance,* Polity Press, Cambridge, 2002.

Herring, Ronald J., and Agarwala Rina (Eds), *Whatever Happened to Class: Reflections from South Asia*, Daanish Books, Delhi, 2008.

Hirschmann, Nancy, 'Freedom, Recognition and Obligation: A Feminist Approach to Political Theory', *American Political Science Review*, 83(4): 1227–1244, 1989.

Hindustan Times, 'Being Dalit Not a Boon for Buddhists', 7 January 2010.

HolgerSieg, 'Rent Seeking and Corruption', 3 October 2012, http://www.sas.upenn.edu/~holgers/urban/corruption.pdf (accessed 7 April 2013).

Holloway, John, *Change the World Without Taking Power*, Pluto Press, London, 2002.

Honneth, Axel, 'Recognition or Redistribution? Changing Perspectives on the Moral Order of Society', *Theory, Culture and Society*, 18(2–3): 43–55, 2001.

Hope, Ronald, 'From Crisis to Renewal: Towards a Successful Implementation of the New Partnership for Africa's Development', *African Affairs*, 101: 387–402, 2002.

Illiah, Kancha, 'Dalits and English', *Deccan Herald*, 2 May 2011.

Independent Citizen's Initiative (ICI), *War in the Heart of India*, Delhi, 2006.

Jayal, Niraja Gopal, and Mehta, Pratap Bhanu (Eds), *Oxford Companion to Politics in India*, Oxford University Press, Delhi, 2011.

Jenkins, Rob, *Democratic Politics and Economic Reforms in India*, Cambridge University Press, Cambridge, 1999.

John, Mary E., and Deshpande, Satish, 'Theorising the Present: Problems and Possibilities', *Economic and Political Weekly*, 43(46): 83–86, 15 November 2008.

Joshi, Sanjay, 'The Right to Equality, Life and Liberty Under the Constitution of India', in Abdulrahim et al. (Eds), *Perspectives on Human Rights*, Manak, Delhi, 1999.

Joshi, Sandeep, 'Ministry Fast-tracks Fortification of Police Station in Maoist-affected States', *The Hindu*, 24 September 2012.

Kannabiran, Kalpana, et al., 'On the Telangana Trail', *Economic and Political Weekly*, 45(13): 69–83, 27 March–2 April 2010.

Kant, Immanuel, *The Metaphysics of Morals*, Cambridge University Press, Cambridge, 1995.

Kapstein, Ethan B., 'Workers and World Economy', *Foreign Affairs*, May/June 1996.

Kapur, Ratna, *Feminist Terrains in Legal Domains: Interdisciplinary Essays on Women and Law in India*, Kali for Women, Delhi, 1996.

Karatani, Kojin, 'Critique Is Impossible Without Moves: An Interview of Kojin Karatani by Joel Wainwright', *Dialogues in Human Geography*, 2(1): 30–52, 2012.

Kaviraj, Sudipta, 'A Critique of Passive Revolution', *Economic and Political Weekly*, 23–27(41): 2429–2444, 1988.

———, 'On the Construction of Colonial Power: Structure, Discourse, Hegemony', in Kaviraj (Ed.), *Politics in India*, Oxford University Press, New Delhi, 1999.

Kothari, Rajni, 'Caste and Politics: The Great Secular Upsurge', *The Times of India*, 28 September 1990.

Krishna, Sankaran, 'The Great Number Fetish', *The Hindu*, 26 January 2013.

Kumar, Dharma, 'The Affirmative Action Debate in India', *Asian Survey*, 32(3): 290–302, March 1992.

Kutty, Omar, 'Civic Anxieties and Dalit Democratic Culture', in Ajay Gudavarthy (Ed.), *Re-Framing Democracy and Agency: Interrogating Political Society*, Anthem, London, 2012.

Laclau, Ernesto, *On Populist Reason*, Verso, London, 2005.

Lahiri, Tripti, 'A Dalit Temple to "Goddess English"', *The Wall Street Journal*, 30 April 2010.

Landsberg, Chris, 'People to People Solidarity: Civil Society and Deep Integration in Southern Africa', *Transformation: Critical Perspectives on Southern Africa*, issue 61, pp. 40–62, 2006.

Maddox, Charles, et al., 'Influence of South African Legislation on India's Mines and Minerals Bill', *Economic and Political Weekly*, 47(40): 74–81, 6 October 2012.

Mallikarjun, Prabhu, 'Attacks on RTI Activists in India Raise Questions over Safety Measures', *Indian Express*, 17 January 2013.

Mannathukkaren, Nissim, 'The "Poverty" of Political Society: Partha Chatterjee and the People's Plan Campaign in Kerala, India', *Third World Quarterly*, 31(2): 295–314, 2010.

Marcuse, Peter, 'The Enclave, The Citadel and the Ghettos: What Has Changed in the Post-Fordist US City?', *Urban Affairs Review*, 33(2):228–264, 1997.

Marcuse, Herbert, *The One-Dimensional Man*, Routledge, New York, 2002.

Mattei, Ugo, and Laura, Nader, *Plunder: When the Rule of Law Is Illegal*, Blackwell Publishing, Oxford, 2008.

Mehta, Pratap Bhanu, 'Quicksand of Caste', *Indian Express*, 28 August, 2012.

Menon, Nivedita, *Recovering Subversion: Feminist Politics Beyond the Law*, Permanent Black, Delhi, 2004.

MHA (Ministry of Home Affairs), 'Status Paper on the Naxal Problem', Internal Security Division, Delhi, 2006.

Michael, S.M., *Untouchables: Dalits in Modern India*, SAGE Publications, New Delhi, 1999.

Michelutti, Lucia, 'The Vernacularization of Democracy: Political Participation and Popular Politics in North India', *Journal of the Royal Anthropological Institute*, 13: 639–656, 2007.

Misra, B.B., *The Indian Middle Classes: Their Growth in Modern Times*, Oxford University Press, Delhi, 1961.

Misra, Rajesh, 'Control from the Middle: A Perspective on Indian New Middle Class', in T.K. Oommen (Ed.), *Classes, Citizenship and Inequality: Emerging Perspectives*, Longman, Delhi, pp. 141–164, 2010.

Mistry, Percy S., 'Africa's Record of Regional Cooperation and Integration', *African Affairs*, 99: 553–573, 2000.

Moyn, Samuel, *The Last Utopia: Human Rights in History*, Harvard University Press, Cambridge, 2010.

Myrdal, Jan, *Red Star over India*, Setu Prakashan, Delhi, 2012.

Narasimhan, C.R.L., 'Reinventing the G20', *The Hindu*, 29 April 2013.

Nash, Kate, *The Cultural Politics of Human Rights*, Cambridge University Press, Cambridge, 2009.

National Council of Applied Economic Research (NCAER), *Indian Market Demographics: The Consumer Classes*, Delhi, 1996.

Nayyar, Deepak, 'Globalization: What Does It Mean for Development?', in K.S. Jomo and Shyamala Nagaraj (Eds), *Globalization versus Development*, Palgrave, Houndmills, Basingstoke, Hampshire and New York, pp. 1–25, 2001.

Negri, Antonio, and Hardt, Michael, *Empire*, Harvard University Press, Cambridge, 2000.

Noorani, A.G., 'Armed Forces (Special Powers) Act: Urgency of Review', *Economic and Political Weekly*, XLIV(34): 8–11, 22 August 2009.

Nussbaum, Martha, and Glover, J. (Eds), *Women, Culture and Development*, Oxford University Press, New York, 1995.

Okin, Susan Muller, *Is Multiculturalism Bad for Women?* Princeton University Press, Princeton, 1999.

Outlook, 'NDA, UPA? Neither. A Third Front Will Emerge', Interview with Chandrababu Naidu, 13 May 2013.

Pai, Sudha, 'Understanding "Backwardness" for Affirmative Action: The Most Backward Castes/Classes in Uttar Pradesh' (unpublished paper).

Pandian, M.S.S., *Brahmin and Non-Brahmin*, Permanent Black, New Delhi, 2007.

Pandita, Rahul, *Hello Bastar*, Tranquebar, New Delhi, 2011.

Pantham, Thomas, 'Against Untouchability: The Discourses of Gandhi and Ambedkar', in Gopal Guru (Ed.), *Humiliation: Claims and Context*, Oxford University Press, New Delhi, pp. 179–209, 2009.

Pateman, Carole, 'Political Obligation, Freedom and Feminism', *American Political Science Review*, 86(1): 179–190, 1992.

Parekh, Bhikhu, 'Cultural Particularity of Liberal Democracy', in David Held (Ed.), *Prospects for Democracy*, Polity Press, Cambridge, 1993.

———, 'Dilemmas of a Multicultural Theory of Citizenship', *Constellations*, 4(1): 54–62, 1997.

———, *A New Politics of Identity*, Palgrave Macmillan, New York, 2008.

———, 'Logic of Humiliation', in Gopal Guru (Ed.), *Humiliation: Claims and Context*, Oxford University Press, New Delhi, pp. 23–41, 2009.

Patnaik, Utsa, 'It Is Time for Kumbakaran to Wake Up', *The Hindu*, 5 August 2005.

Petras, James, 'Introduction', *Latin American Perspectives*, 27(5): 3–10, 2000.

Pieterse, Jan Nederveen (Ed.), *Globalization or Empire*, Routledge, New York, 2010.

Prasad, Chandrabhan, 'OBCs Emancipator', *The Pioneer*, 13 April 2008.

Prashad, Vijay, 'Hugo Chavez: A Tribute', *Economic and Political Weekly*, 48(12), 23 March 2013a.

———, 'At WTO: A Defender of the South', *The Hindu*, 9 May 2013b.

Singh, Mahim Pratap, 'No Oustee Will be Deprived of Rights', *The Hindu*, 1 September 2012.

PUDR, *Press, Para Military and People*, Delhi, 1992, www.unipune.ac.in/snc/cssh/.../A-%20Andhra%20pradesh/20.pdf (accessed 12 January 2013)

———, *Through the Lens of National Security*, PUDR, Delhi, January 2008.

PUDR, Delhi; APDR, West Bengal; PUCL, Jharkhand; Indian Association of Peoples Lawyers; PUCL, Chhattisgarh, When the State Makes War On Its Own People: A Report on Violation of People's Rights during the Salwa Judum Campaign in Dantewada, Chattisgarh, Delhi, April 2006.

Raghavan, S., 'With a Self-Appointed Trustee Like This', *The Hindu*, 8 September 2012.

Ram, Ronki, 'Ravidass Deras and Social Protest: Making Sense of Dalit Consciousness in Punjab (India)', *Journal of Asian Studies*, 67(4): 1341–1364, 2008.

Rao, Chinna, *Dividing Dalits: Writings on Sub-categorisation of Scheduled Castes*, Rawat publications, Jaipur, 2009.

Rao, R.S., *Towards Understanding Semi-Feudal Semi-Colonial Society: Studies in Political Economy*, Perspectives, Hyderabad, 1995.

Reddy, Narsimha, and Patnaik, Arun, 'Anti-Arrack Agitation of Women in Andhra Pradesh', *Economic and Political Weekly*, 22 May 1993.

Reddy, Srinivas, 'Is the Centre Correctly Assessing Maoist Situation?', *The Hindu*, 12 September 2012.

Rodrigues, Valerian (Ed.), *The Essential Writings of B. R. Ambedkar*, Oxford University Press, Delhi, 1990.

R.N. Committee (Expert Committee of Creamy Layer Government of India), 1993, set up by National Commission for Backward Classes.

Roy, Arundhati, 'I'd Rather Not Be Anna', *The Hindu*, 21 August 2011.

Royal Danish Ministry of Foreign Affairs, 'Conditions for Social Progress', *Copenhagen Seminar*, Ministry of Foreign Affairs, 1996.

Rudolph, Lloyd I, and Rudolph, Susanne Hoeber. *Explaining Indian Democracy: A Fifty Year Perspective, 1956–2006, Volume III: The Realm of the Public Sphere: Identity and Policy*, Oxford: Oxford University Press, 2008.

Ruitters, Greg, and McDonald, David (Eds), *Alternatives to Privatization*, LeftWord Books, Delhi, 2013.

Sahoo, Niranjan, *Reservation Policy and Its Implementation across Domains in India*, Academic Foundation, New Delhi, 2009.

Sainath, P., 'The Narcissism of the Neurotic', *The Hindu*, 18 October 2010.

Sarkar Swagato, 'Political Society in a Capitalist World', in *Reframing Democracy and Agency in India: Interrogating Political Society*, Anthem Press, London, 2012.

Sassen, Saskia, 'The Global Street', 2011, www.huffingtonpost.com/saskia.../ (accessed 13 January 2013).

———, 'Why the Middle Class Is Revolting', *The Hindu*, 12 January 2013.

Sayers, Andrew, *The Moral Significance of Class*, Cambridge University Press, Cambridge, 2005.

Schmalz, Stefan, and Ebenau, Mattias, 'After Neoliberalism? Brazil, India and China in the Global Economic Crisis', *Globalizations*, 9(4): 487–501, 2012.

Scott, David, 'Culture in Political Theory', *Political Theory*, 31(1): 92–115, February 2003.

Scott, James, *Seeing Like a State*, Yale University Press, London, 1998.

———, *The Art of Not Being Governed*, Yale University Press, New Haven, 2009.

Scott, Joan, 'Theorising Experience', in Joan Scott and Judith Butler (Eds), *Feminists Theorizing the Political*, Routledge, New York, 1992.

Seligson, Mitchell, 'Popular Support for Regional Economic Integration in Latin America', *Journal of Latin American Studies*, 31 (1): 129–150, February 1999.

Sengupta, Arjun, 'The Human Right to Development', in B. A. Andreassen and S. P. Marks (Eds), *Development as a Human Right: Legal, Political, and Economic Dimensions*, Harvard University Press, Cambridge, MA, 2006.

Sen, Amartya, Development as Freedom, Oxford University Press, Delhi 1998.

———, 'Human Rights and Development', in B.A. Andreassen and S.P. Marks (Eds), *Development as a Human Right*, Harvard University Press, Harvard, 2006.

Seth, D.L. 'Caste in the Mirror of Race', in Sukhdeo Thorat and Umakant (Eds), *Caste, Race and Discrimination*, Rawat Publishers, Delhi, pp. 85–96, 2004.

———, 'Caste and the Secularisation Process in India' in Peter Ronald deSouza (Ed.), *Contemporary India: Transitions*, SAGE Publications, New Delhi, pp. 237–263, 2000.

Shah, Ghanshyam, 'Caste, Hindutva and Hideousness', *Economic and Political Weekly*, XXXVII (15): 1393, 2002.

Shani, Ornit, *Communalism, Caste and Hindu Nationalism: The Violence in Gujarat*, Cambridge University Press, Cambridge, 2007.

Shatrugna, M., 'A Pampered Lot', *Economic and Political Weekly*, XXIII(38): 1938–1940, 17 September 1988.

———, 'All Kapus as BCs: Reducing Reservation to a Farce', *Economic and Political Weekly*, 29(37): 2397–2400, 10 Sept. 1994.

Shetty, S.L., 'External Account', *Economic and Political Weekly*, 47(40): 84–85, 6 October 2012.

Shutt, Harry, *A New Democracy*, Zed Books, London, 2001.

Singh, Ajay, 'Role of Judiciary in the Protection and Promotion of Human Rights', in Abdulrahim et al. (Ed.), *Perspectives on Human Rights*, Manak, Delhi, 1999.

Singh, Ujjwal Kumar, 'Democratising State and Society: Role of Civil Liberties and Democratic Rights Movements in India', *Contemporary India*, January–June 2005.

———. *The State, Democracy and Anti-Terror Laws in India*, SAGE Publications, New Delhi, 2007.

Skaria, Ajay, 'The Project of Provincialising Europe', *Economic and Political Weekly*, 44(14), 4–10 April 2009.

Srinivas, M.N., *Caste in Modern India*, MPP, Bombay, 1992.

Srivastava, J.C., 'Economic Integration in South Asia—Not an Option but an Urgent Necessity', in Srivastava (Ed.), *Towards South Asian Integration and Unity*, Foundation for Peace and Sustainable Development, Delhi, 2004.

Stiglitz, Joseph, *Globalization and Its Discontents*, Penguin, Delhi, 2000.

Stubbs, Richard, 'ASEAN Plus Three', *Asian Survey*, 42, 2002.

Subramanium, K., 'Happy with Reasonable Success', *The Hindu*, 20 August 2013.

Suneetha, A., 'Adjudicating (UN) Domestic Battles', *Economic and Political Weekly*, 40(38): 4101–4103, 2005.

Supreme Court Case (SCC 608), Francis Coralie Mullin v. Administrator, Union Territory of Delhi and Others (1981) 1.

Surendranath, Arup, 'Succumbing to the Bogey of Fear', *The Hindu*, 26 April 2013.

Taylor, Charles, 'The Politics of Recognition', in Gutman, Amy (Ed.), *Multiculturalism: Examining the Politics of Recognition*. Princeton, New Jersey: Princeton University Press, 1994.

Teltumbde, Anand (Ed.), *Dalits and Hindutva*, Samya, Calcutta, 2002.

———, 'Race or Caste, Discrimination Is a Universal Concern', *Economic and Political Weekly*, XLIV(34): 17–20, 22 August 2009.

———, 'Criminalising People's Protests', *Economic and Political Weekly*, 48(14), 6 April 2013.

The Hindu, 'Khairlanji's shame', 20 November 2006.

———, 'Voice of the Underdog', 17 April 2010.

———, 'Joint Rally by Manmohan and Rahul in Bundelkhand Today', 30 April, 2011.

———, 'Historians Protest as Delhi University Purges Ramayana Essay from Syllabus', 15 October 2011.

———, 'Demographic Advantage for India by 2030, Says Minister', 26 August 2012.

———, 'Civil Rights Groups Worried Over Executions in India', 15 April 2013.

———, 'Unemployment Numbers Soar in Spain', France, 28 April 2013.

———, 'Guantánamo Bay Prosecutors Accuse Detainee of Conspiracy', 7 May 2013.

———, 'Environment Ministry to Decide Soon on Vedanta Project', 16 August 2013.

———, 'Allies Will Be Important for NDA in 2014', 24 August 2013.

———, "Sedition Seriously?', Editorial, 11 September 2012.

———, 'ASEAN to Reach Out to China', 26 April 2013.

The Times of India, Landmark Win for Dalits as UK Bans Caste Bias, 26 April, 2013.

———, 'India Frets as UK House Says Caste Discriminatory', 30 April 2013.

Thompson, E.P., *Whigs and Hunters*, Allen Lane, London, 1975.

———, *The Poverty of Theory*, Merlin, London, 1978.

Thorat, Sukhadeo, and Umakant (Eds), *Caste, Race and Discrimination: Discourses in International Context*, Rawat, Jaipur, 2004.

Tudoroiu, Theodor, 'Conceptualizing BRICS: OPEC as a Mirror', *Asian Journal of Political Science*, 20(1): 23–45, 2012.

Vanaik, Achin, *India in a Changing World*, Orient Longman, Hyderabad, 1995.

———, 'Africa: Future Trajectories of BRICS', 21 March 2013, http://www.tni.org/article/africa-future-trajectories-brics (accessed 6 April 2013).

Venugopal, N., *Understanding Maoists: Notes of a Participant Observer*, Setu Prakashan, Kolkata, 2012.

———. *Understanding Maoists: Notes of a Participant Observer from Andhra Pradesh*, Setu Prakashani, Kolkata, 2013.

Verma, A.K., 'Subalterns in Uttar Pradesh', *Economic and Political Weekly*, 15(48): 11–14, 27 Nov.–3 Dec. 2010a.

Verma, Vidhu, 'Reinterpetating Buddhism: Ambedkar on the Politics of Social Action', *Economic and Political Weekly*, 15(49): 56–66, 4 December 2010b.

Vincent, R.J., *Human Rights and International Relations*, Cambridge University Press, Cambridge, 1986.

Wee, Vivienne, 'Interrogating Regionalism in Relation to Ethnicity and Capital', *Journal of Contemporary Asia*, 36, 2006.

White, Lyal, 'IBSA: A State of the Art' unpublished (forthcoming in South African Year Book of International Affairs).

Wood Jolie, 'Contentious Politics and Civil Society in Varnasi', in *Reframing Democracy and Agency in India: Interrogating Political Society*, Anthem Press, London, pp. 93–124, 2012.

Yadav, Nomita, 'Other Backward Classes: Then and Now', *Economic and Political Weekly*, 37(44–45): 4495–4500, 2 November 2002.

Yadav, Yogendra, 'India's Third Electoral System', *Economic and Political Weekly*, 34(34–35): 2393–2399, 1999.

Yuk Wah, Chan, 'Ethnicity and Capital: Changing Relations between China and Southeast Asia', *Journal of Southeast Asia*, (36), 2006.

Zerzan, J. 'Enemy of the State', *Alternative Press Review*, 5(1), 2000 available online at http://www.cdfe.org/zerzan_enemy_of_the_state.htm.

Index

About the Author

Ajay Gudavarthy taught earlier as Assistant Professor at the National Law School of India University, Bangalore. He had been Visiting Fellow, Centre for Citizenship, Civil society and Rule of Law, University of Aberdeen in 2012. He was Visiting Faculty at Centre for Human Rights, University of Hyderabad in 2011 and Visiting Fellow, Goldsmith College, University of London in 2010. In 2008, he was Charles Wallace Visiting Fellow, the School of Oriental and African Studies (SOAS), London.

His published works include *Re-framing Democracy and Agency in India: Interrogating Political Society* (edited, 2012) and *Politics of Post-civil Society: Contemporary History of Political Movements in India* (SAGE Publications, New Delhi, 2013).